Xiaobai Shen

The Imitation Paradox

De Gruyter Contemporary Social Sciences

Volume 15

Xiaobai Shen

The Imitation Paradox

Two Moral Universes and China's Path to Digital Modernity

DE GRUYTER

ISBN 978-3-11-075747-7
e-ISBN (PDF) 978-3-11-075757-6
e-ISBN (EPUB) 978-3-11-075759-0
ISSN 2747-5689
e-ISSN 2747-5697

Library of Congress Control Number: 2026932241

Bibliographic information published by the Deutsche Nationalbibliothek
The Deutsche Nationalbibliothek lists this publication in the Deutsche Nationalbibliografie; detailed bibliographic data are available on the internet at http://dnb.dnb.de.

Cover image: StudioM1 / iStock / Getty Images Plus
Printing and binding: CPI books GmbH, Leck

www.degruyterbrill.com
Questions about General Product Safety Regulation:
productsafety@degruyterbrill.com

FSC www.fsc.org MIX Papier | Fördert gute Waldnutzung FSC® C083411

To the memory of my mother
Zheng Huaixiu (郑怀秀)

Preface

This book explores how China, in half a century, transformed from a poor, developing country dependent on Western technology to becoming a key player in many high-technology markets, now contesting leadership with the USA. China's unprecedented technological development has frequently been explained by Western commentators as a result of copying or even stealing ideas from the West. This book indeed highlights the crucial role that imitation has played in this process, but not as an underhanded practice. Instead, I argue that imitation has been an essential feature of successful innovation, and of social and economic life more generally. In understanding this, I draw on the hugely influential writings of the French sociologist Gabriel Tarde, whose *Laws of Imitation* (Tarde, 1903) argued that imitation was universal, a central force in social life, and a foundation for innovation.

Tarde's monadological lens (Tarde, 1893/1999) offered not only an explanation for how technologies are adopted and adapted, but also a new way of thinking about governance itself. What began as a study of imitation evolved into a broader reflection on how a multiplicity of diverse actors, monads, might be coordinated without reducing difference to uniformity. As digital infrastructures introduced new forms of traceability and feedback, the possibility emerged for a different kind of governance: one based not on universal rules or collective coercion, but on the ethical orchestration of imitative practices. The later chapters of this book return to this insight, exploring how a redefined monadology might help us rethink power, participation, and the formation of a collective self in the digital age.

Aided by these theoretical explorations, this book also captures China's iterative path of technological development through imitation. It also represents my effort to make sense of this extraordinary change, drawing on my perspective as both a Chinese-born and British-trained academic observing these developments unfold in real time. In these pages, I have revisited nearly four decades of detailed qualitative research into China's transition: its contexts, processes, and prior history. I have reworked these insights around a central theme of imitation, interweaving them with my own journey, from growing up in China to later researching its innovation both within the country and from abroad. My aim is to offer both a personal and analytical account of how China's socio-technical development has been shaped by the dynamics of imitation, improvisation, and mass participation.

https://doi.org/10.1515/9783110757576-002

Acknowledgements

This book was catalysed by an approach in 2021 from Paul Stevens, Senior Editor at Bristol University Press, who had noticed my paper in the EASST/4S conference programme and suggested the work might be relevant for his book series on *Science, Technology and Society*. This encouraged me to draft a proposal. I am grateful that De Gruyter recognised the value of this work and offered to publish it. The COVID-19 pandemic profoundly disrupted this project. For more than four years I was unable to visit China. The book was set aside until my return to China at the end of 2023, when the profound changes I observed renewed my determination to complete this reflection on China's path towards modernity.

I am especially indebted to my friend, Dr Caroline Bamford. Without her persistent encouragement this book would not exist. In our weekly Zoom calls she often reminded me, "Your cross-cultural perspective is so valuable, few people have lived in both China and Europe for over thirty years." She urged me to keep writing, even if only 100 words a day, and regularly offered comments and edits on my drafts. Her belief in this project kept it alive.

I owe much to family and friends in China who supported my remote fieldwork during the pandemic. My sister and her husband, during lockdown, put on face masks to photograph life in the Dong-shan-long district and its checkpoints. They also tested newly released apps I could not access without a Chinese ID, sharing with me how they worked in practice. My nephew's family sent photos and videos from their gated community, capturing the everyday improvisations and solidarities of lockdown life, from neighbours organising small New Year gatherings for the security guards to children helping their parents cook for the celebration.

Classmates and friends across China also became active collaborators. They shared their local Health QR codes and stories of how these systems operated, and sometimes failed, in different cities. Their accounts revealed the diversity of local arrangements and provided vivid insights into the cultural transformations of that period. Many of them offered thoughtful comments on my papers and reflections. I am especially grateful to those who took the time to provide me with detailed verbal and written exchanges and feedback.

I wish to acknowledge the assistance of colleagues and friends in academic institutions across China, particularly those in the Chinese Academy of Sciences, in particular the Institute for Policy and Management and the Institute for the History of Natural Sciences, Tsinghua University's Centre for Science and Society, Peking University's Law School, Zhejiang University's School of Management, the Shanghai Institute for Science of Science, and Shanghai Jiao Tong University. I

https://doi.org/10.1515/9783110757576-003

also thank interviewees—academic and industrial practitioners across China—many of whom became long-term collaborators and friends.

Many people shaped my intellectual journey in earlier years: my mentor and close friend Zhang Yongqian; my MPhil supervisors Feng Zhijun and Li Huiguo; and colleagues and friends in a wide range of fields with whom I met and exchanged views about the embryonic reforms in politics, natural science, Science of Science, and China's journalism.

I owe a special debt to my husband Robin and to our sons Ben (本) and Leon (亮). During the long months of lockdown, they endured my unfashionable dinner-table monologues filled with old Chinese sayings and unstructured thoughts, and were often enlisted to comment on my papers or *Medium* blogs.

I am forever indebted to my parents. My father, through his regular letters from the years of his absence from the family, and my mother, through her quiet deeds, sowed in me the deepest understanding of 做人的准则 (zuòrén de zhǔnzé)—the principles of being human. I wish I had had the chance to thank them for this whilst they were still alive.

Finally, I extend my heartfelt thanks to those around me in the West. Professor Robin Williams offered constructive critiques of my China-oriented perspectives and invaluable comments on draft chapters. Professor Donald MacKenzie provided incisive feedback on the book proposal. Dr Anne Stafford kindly read some of the early chapters and encouraged me to keep going. Friends and relatives in the UK outside academia have also been a source of support and patience. To all of them, I owe more than I can say.

Contents

Abbreviations

3GPP	3rd Generation Partnership Project
AI	Artificial Intelligence
ATIS	Alliance for Telecommunications Industry Solutions (US)
BAT	Baidu, Alibaba, Tencent
BSA	Business Software Alliance
BTM	Bell Telephone Manufacturing Company (Belgium)
CATT	Chinese Academy of Telecommunications Technology
CDMA2000	Code Division Multiple Access 2000
CIPR	Co-operative Management of Intellectual Property Rights (referenced via PRIME project)
CIT	Centre for Information Technology (People's Liberation Army, at Zhengzhou)
COCOM	Coordinating Committee for Multilateral Export Controls
CREATe	Centre for Copyright and New Business Models in the Creative Economy
DS series	Domestic switching R&D line under MPT
DSL	Dong-shan-long (Hangzhou neighbourhood)
ETSI	European Telecommunications Standards Institute
EURAS	European Academy for Standardisation
FDD	Frequency Division Duplex
FP7	EU 7th Framework Programme
GAF	Google, Amazon, Facebook
GNU	GNU's Not Unix
HCI	Human–Computer Interaction
HJD-04	Indigenous digital switch (China)
HQ	Health QR (code)
ICT	Information and Communication Technology
IFPI	International Federation of the Phonographic Industry
IP	Intellectual Property
IPR	Intellectual Property Rights
ITU	International Telecommunication Union
LSI	Large Scale Integration (semiconductor chips)
MEI	Ministry of Electronics Industry
MMEI	Ministry of Machinery and Electronics Industry
MII	Ministry of Information Industry (China)
MIIT	Ministry of Industry and Information Technology (China)
MNEs	Multinational Enterprises
MOST	Ministry of Science and Technology (China)
MPT	Ministry of Posts and Telecommunications
NDRC	National Development and Reform Commission
OEM	Original Equipment Manufacturer
OSS	Open Source Software
PC	Personal Computer
PDSS	Public Digital Switching Systems
PRC	People's Republic of China
PTIC	Posts and Telecommunications Industrial Corporation

https://doi.org/10.1515/9783110757576-004

QR	Quick Response (code)
R&D	Research and Development
REF	Research Excellence Framework
RCUK	Research Councils UK
SESA	Sociedad Española de Sistemas de Automática (Spain)
SISS	Shanghai Institute for Science of Science
SMEs	Small and Medium-sized Enterprises
SST	Social Shaping of Technology
STS	Science and Technology Studies
TD-CDMA	Time Division Code Division Multiple Access
TDD	Time Division Duplex
TDIA	TD-SCDMA Industry Alliance
TD-SCDMA	Time Division Synchronous Code Division Multiple Access
TRIPS	Trade-Related Aspects of Intellectual Property Rights
WCDMA	Wideband Code Division Multiple Access
WTO	World Trade Organisation

Glossary of Chinese Phrases and Terms

百花齐放，百家争鸣 **(bǎihuā qífàng, bǎijiā zhēngmíng)**	let a hundred flowers bloom, a hundred schools of thought contend
吃瓜群众 **(chī guā qúnzhòng)**	onlooker mentality (Lu Xun's critique, implied in text)
崇洋媚外 **(chóng yang mèi wài)**	foreign fever
臭味相投 **(chòuwèi xiāngtóu)**	sharing the same rotten taste (finding like-minded peers)
大跃进 **(Dàyuèjìn)**	Great Leap Forward
单位 **(dānwèi)**	work unit (socialist workplace system)
凤凰周刊 **(Fènghuáng Zhōukān)**	Phoenix Weekly (magazine)
工宣队 **(gōng xuān duì)**	workers' propaganda team
和国际接轨 **(hé guójì jiēguǐ)**	connect with international tracks
户口 **(hùkǒu)**	household registration system
剑网行动 **(Jiànwǎng xíngdòng)**	Sword Net Campaign
劫富济贫 **(jié fù jì pín)**	rob the rich to help the poor
巨龙 **(Jùlóng)**	Great Dragon (national telecom entity created in 1995)
君者舟也；庶人者水也。水则载舟 水则覆舟 **(jūn zhě zhōu yě; shùrén zhě shuǐ yě. shuǐ zé zài zhōu, shuǐ zé fù zhōu)**	The ruler is like a boat, the people like water; water can carry the boat and overturn it
炕 **(kàng)**	heated brick bed
科学主义 **(Kēxué zhǔyì)**	scientism
两条腿走路 **(liǎng tiáo tuǐ zǒulù)**	walking on two legs (foreign transfer + indigenous development)
摸着石头过河 **(mō zhe shítou guò hé)**	crossing the river by feeling the stones (Deng Xiaoping's phrase)
逆风飞飏 **(Nìfēng fēiyáng)**	*Flying Against the Wind* (Wu's memoir)
枪打出头鸟 **(qiāng dǎ chūtóu niǎo)**	the gun shoots the bird that sticks its head out (warning against standing out)
群众路线 **(qúnzhòng lùxiàn)**	mass line
群众文艺 **(qúnzhòng wényì)**	mass art
人民素质的提高 **(Rénmín sùzhì de tígāo)**	improvement of civic quality
三反，五反 **(sān fǎn, wǔ fǎn)**	Three-Anti, Five-Anti campaigns
山寨 **(shānzhài)**	"mountain stronghold," used for copycat/rebel products
师傅 **(shīfu)**	master/teacher in apprenticeship
实用主义 **(shíyòng zhǔyì)**	pragmatism or utilitarianism
水乳交融 **(shuǐ rǔ jiāo róng)**	harmonious as water and milk
危机 **(wēijī)**	crisis (danger + opportunity)
文化大革命 **(Wénhuà Dàgémìng)**	Cultural Revolution
我们不能让自己在一棵树上吊死 **(wǒmen bù-néng ràng zìjǐ zài yī kē shù shàng diàosǐ)**	"We cannot hang ourselves on a single tree until death," i.e., don't rely on one option
无为 **(wúwéi)**	non-coercive responsiveness (Daoist)
西海固 **(Xīhǎigù)**	Xi-Hai-Gu region (Ningxia)

https://doi.org/10.1515/9783110757576-005

修身 **(xiūshēn)**	cultivating the self or self-discipline
玄学 **(Xuánxué)**	metaphysics
养牛致富 **(yǎng niú zhì fù)**	raising cows brings wealth
样板戏 **(yàngbǎn xì)**	model plays (Eight Model Plays)
一盘散沙 **(yī pán sǎnshā)**	a plate of loose sand (metaphor for disunity)
义 **(yì)**	righteousness, moral rightness (Confucian ethics)
右派 **(yòupài)**	rightist
正能量 **(zhèng néngliàng)**	positive energy
知识产权 **(zhīshì chǎnquán)**	intellectual property
中国科学社 **(Zhōngguó Kēxué Shè)**	Science Society of China
中南海 **(Zhōngnánhǎi)**	central government compound in Beijing
中体西用 **(Zhōng tǐ xī yòng)**	Chinese learning as essence, Western learning as utility
中庸之道 **(Zhōngyōng zhī dào)**	Doctrine of the Mean (Confucian moderation)
自主标准 **(zìzhǔ biāozhǔn)**	indigenous standards
走向未来丛书 **(Zǒuxiàng wèilái cóngshū)**	*Towards the Future* book series
《科学》 **(Kēxué)**	*Science* journal
《让科学的光芒照亮自己》	*Let the Light of Science Illuminate Itself*
《山海情》 **(Shānhǎi Qíng/*Minning Township*)**	TV series on poverty alleviation
《天注定》 **(Tiān Zhùdìng/*A Touch of Sin*)**	film by Jia Zhangke

Glossary of Conceptual Terms and Frameworks

Governance and Imitation

Experimentalist approach/experimentalist governance	Trial-and-error coordination (learning-by-doing) with local discretion and iterative feedback; protocols stabilise and scale once proved.
Governance by affordance	Steering behaviour by configuring interfaces, checkpoints and feedback so the compliant action is the easiest action.
Crisis governance	Adaptive, experimental coordination under stress (health, safety, supply) that generalises beyond pandemics.
Governance of distributed imitation	Coordinating imitative practices that arise across dispersed actors, firms and users, treating imitation itself as a governable domain.
Feedback loops	Mechanisms whereby system outputs (data, ratings, sanctions, rewards) reshape inputs (use, compliance, design), enabling ongoing adjustment.
Imitation paradox	Imitation as both dependency and creativity: constraint when it entrenches external standards; resource when recombined for local capability and inclusion.

Participation and Collective Practice

Mass participation	Large-scale, routine uptake of practices that turns "use" into a constitutive force of governance and innovation.
Critical mass	The density of users and actions at which adaptive practices tip into infrastructure or common standard.
Co-production	Outcomes (rules, norms, artefacts) made jointly by state, firms and users through situated interaction rather than top-down design.
Collective-self (self-discipline)	An emergent civic capacity for mutual restraint and cooperation scaffolded by visible, traceable infrastructures.

Visibility, Traceability and Surveillance

Dataveillance	Data-intensive visibility systems that coordinate behaviour and services at scale, between diverse players, beyond a one-way sovereign gaze.
Digital panopticon	Recast from simple surveillance to relational visibility and traceability that enables coordination and redress among actors.
Visibility and traceability	Socio-technical conditions that render actions legible for coordination, accountability and learning.
Interessement devices	Interfaces (e. g., checkpoints, code scanners) that enrol heterogeneous actors into shared programmes of action.

https://doi.org/10.1515/9783110757576-006

Infrastructures, Platforms and Devices

Infrastructural technology	Large-system, backbone technologies (transport, telecoms, data) whose socio-technical integration shapes downstream possibilities.
Platform ecosystem	Multi-sided digital environments where services, complementary providers and users co-evolve under data-driven coordination.
Affordable engineering	Pragmatic, cost-conscious design that widens access while remaining compatible with existing frames and practices.

Theoretical Frameworks (STS)

Monads (traceable units)	Following Tarde: relational actors whose multiple histories and ties can be empirically followed through infrastructures of data.
Multiplicity as resource	Treating diversity and difference as productive inputs for coordination and innovation, not obstacles to be removed.
Socio-technical entanglement	The inseparability of technical forms and social orders in design, uptake and governance.
Socio-technical specificity	The situated fit of technologies within local infrastructures, norms and constraints.
Socio-technical becoming	Provisional: modernisation as an open-ended process of co-evolution rather than linear planful "catch-up."
Digital enlightenment	Provocative concept cultivating plural, situated ethics through traceable coordination, rather than replicating a singular European model.

1 Introduction

> Society, Gabriel Tarde[1] argued, is rooted in imitation, both conscious and unconscious. All inventions and discoveries spread not by rote copying but through repeated imitation and adaptation. (The Laws of Imitation, 1903).

1.1 Between Two Moral Universes

"We are all biased one way or another." This is a point I make to my students in the first lecture of the course *Innovation in China, from an emerging economy to global power.* Studying and working in the UK and Europe for over 30 years, I developed the course in 2021 to explore research I had conducted on China's imitation of the West. How did China, long labelled as a copycat and even a technological thief, reach the world stage? I started from my own lens, my lived experience in China and abroad, and I framed and developed my approach through academic study. Gabriel Tarde's imitation theory (1903), along with frameworks from Science and Technology Studies (STS) and especially the Social Shaping of Technology (SST) perspective (MacKenzie & Wajcman, 1985; Williams & Edge, 1996), have been key influences on my academic approach.

Standing at the front of the lecture hall, I can feel the room evaluating me, waiting to hear what I will say. About twenty per cent of the class have Chinese surnames, some from mainland China, others from Hong Kong or Taiwan, and others are children of the diaspora raised in the West. Many arrive sceptical, framing China as an "authoritarian state" where collectivism suffocates freedom and imitation substitutes for originality. In these moments, the classroom becomes a microcosm of global perception gaps: students project their assumptions, test their boundaries, and struggle with what counts as truth.

Perception is selective, shaped by our value systems, backgrounds, and lived experiences. As Karen Barad (2007, p. 185) argues through her concept of the onto-ethical-epistemic, knowledge is performative, simultaneously shaping and being shaped by our contexts and experiences. My task is not to declare a single version of reality, but to help them see why their perceptions diverge, and how knowledge

---

1 Gabriel Tarde (1843–1904), a French magistrate, philosopher, and sociologist, is regarded as a classic figure in social theory. His *Les Lois de l'Imitation* (1890; English translation, *The Laws of Imitation*, 1903) emphasised imitation as the fundamental process of social life, in contrast to Durkheim's focus on social structures. Though long overshadowed by Durkheim, Tarde has regained attention in contemporary sociology, philosophy, and science and technology studies, in particular through the hugely influential writings of Bruno Latour (Latour 2005).

https://doi.org/10.1515/9783110757576-007

itself is always situated (Haraway, 1988). This is also the stance I take in this book. My philosophical anchor is Barad's agential realism: technologies are not separate objects to be adopted or rejected by society, but entangled *intra-actions* of matter and meaning (Barad, 2007).

China's technological rise, as I will argue, can only be understood as such an entangled process, never a linear trajectory, but a socio-technical becoming shaped by improvisation, imitation, and collective struggle.

Early Journeys in China

The tie between me and technology began during the Cultural Revolution when I worked as a mechanical worker in a silk weaving factory. I still remember asking my *shifu* (师傅, master craftsman) whether we could automate the machines. He responded seriously: "Why should we do that? Think! They all (pointing to the women workers at their looms) need that job." This conversation, for some reason, stayed with me for many years.

After the Cultural Revolution ended, I entered university to study electronic engineering, convinced, like many of my generation, that our future was bound to science and technology. The 1980s became an era of intellectual awakening. A wave of translations and publications sought to reintroduce scientific thought into China's re-opening society. Among them, the book series *Towards the Future* (走向未来丛书) published by Sichuan Publishing House had a profound impact on me. I was particularly struck by Liu Qingfeng's *Let the Light of Science Illuminate Itself* (《让科学的光芒照亮自己》), which asked: Why had modern science not developed in China's history? (Liu, 1984). For me and many young academics, this was not just a historical question but a provocation: could we imagine a different future for China?

Under the supervision of Feng Zhijun and Li Huiguo, pioneers in the field of Science of Science in China, I undertook research into the history of Chinese overseas students in the U.S. and their efforts to bring Western science and technology home. They had founded the Science Society of China (中国科学社) and launched the first Chinese journal of science, *Science* (《科学》), which notably adopted left-to-right writing, a small but symbolically significant act of modernisation. Their struggles display the difficulties of translating not only technical knowledge but also the social and cultural environments that sustained it.

I buried myself in various libraries' archives and read every issue of *Science* 《科学》 that I could find. *The Science Society of China in the Process of Modernising China's Scientific Development* (近代中国科学化进程中的"中国科学社", 科学团体个案分析) (Shen, 1988) has informed my work ever since. The struggles of these students were a strong outcry: the main obstacles for China were not science and technology, but rather the "land and soil" which nurture them, and especially Chinese society, from the governing bodies to the masses.

Writing the thesis gave me a window into the aspirations and frustrations of scholars who sought to integrate Western science into China's modernisation process. Their challenges echoed in my own intellectual journey. This was the foundation for my next and longest journey: leaving China for a PhD at the University of Edinburgh. What began then has become more than three decades of research into China's path of science and technology development, continually informed by the frameworks of the Social Shaping of Technology (SST) perspective. It emerged from the field of Science and Technology Studies (STS), and the critiques of technological determinism, and these, together with my own lived experiences of crossing cultural, institutional, and epistemic worlds, have deepened my analytical framework. In this book, I bring these strands together: a personal trajectory intertwined with China's evolving place in global science and technology.

The Force of Globalisation

The thirty years that followed my first arrival in Britain revealed the transformative power of globalisation. What once seemed like clear contrasts between East and West gradually dissolved into a set of uncanny similarities. In workplaces, universities, and everyday life, I witnessed how systems of evaluation, competition, and standardisation proliferated globally, erasing distinctions that had seemed fundamental in the early 1990s.

In academia, the shift was particularly striking. British universities that I had once admired as sanctuaries of free thought became increasingly commercialised, entangled in global ranking systems and managerial metrics (Biagioli & Lippman, 2020). The Research Excellence Framework (REF) exerted pressure on scholars to prioritise journal publications over teaching or public service (Watermeyer, 2016). Soon journals themselves were ranked, universities were benchmarked, and degree programmes standardised. I recognised this as a form of global imitation: practices that began in Britain spread across Europe, North America, and eventually to China. Chinese academics, too, became enmeshed in this system, competing for space in Western journals and reproducing the same structures of gatekeeping and prestige (Yang, 2003).

Globalisation also reshaped the field of Science and Technology. Corporate expansion and outsourcing spread Western consumer logics into developing countries, with China both a major site of outsourced labour and, increasingly, a key player in shaping global markets (Harvey, 2005). Intellectual property protection, once a national matter in the West, became a cornerstone of international governance, promoted most strongly by the very countries whose technologies dominated global markets (Drahos & Braithwaite, 2002). The cycle was self-reinforcing: technologies circulated with capital, and capital demanded ever tighter controls on knowledge.

Globalisation thus produced a paradoxical symmetry. China grew more like the West in its embrace of markets, metrics, and competition. China, a socialist country, in many aspects, became more capitalist than a capitalist society, whilst the West adopted practices of improvisation and suspicion that I had once thought uniquely Chinese. When I first arrived in the UK in the early 1990s to begin my doctoral studies, I can still recall the feeling of stepping into the University of Edinburgh library, the quiet hum of study, the smell of old books, and the astonishing sense that I had entered a space of openness and trust, free to borrow books with the expectation of responsibility. In those moments, I felt a new "Me" emerging, one shaped by accountability, dignity, and freedom. "The moon is rounder in the West", I wrote to my family, a Chinese saying meaning things seem better elsewhere. Compared to then, I came to see that the moon's shape was refracted differently depending on where one stood, and that imitation was the unseen force reshaping societies on both sides.

The Moral Shock

The shock that crystallised these observations came during the COVID-19 pandemic. Living in the UK during the COVID-19 crisis, I found myself straddling two epistemological universes. On one side, through my family in Hangzhou, I closely followed the operation of lockdowns: how a QR code[2] could secure food deliveries, coordinate neighbourhood safety, and protect the elderly. On the other side, in Europe and North America, any mention of such systems evoked George Orwell's *Big Brother*, the black mirrors of digital dystopia, or Edward Snowden's warnings of state overreach. The same artefact, a QR code, was framed either as protection or as coercion, coordination or domination.

In Hangzhou, my relatives experienced the Health QR Code as a reassuring, almost mundane tool of coordination. A scan at a checkpoint determined whether

2 A QR Code (Quick Response Code) is a type of two-dimensional barcode that can store information in a grid of black squares on a white background. Unlike the traditional one-dimensional barcodes, you see on products, which hold about 20 characters, a QR code can hold thousands of alphanumeric characters.

one could enter a shop or board a bus; status updates kept families attentive to one another's risks. The system was not perfect, but it reduced uncertainty, offering reassurance in a moment of collective anxiety. By early 2021, China's official fatality rate remained astonishingly low, fewer than 5,000 deaths in a population of 1.4 billion.

In the UK, by contrast, I lived through waves of preventable loss. Daily death tolls were reported in the thousands. Care homes struggled, hospitals overflowed, and lockdowns faltered. Yet in the major newspapers, China's achievement in minimising mortality was scarcely mentioned. Instead, China was placed on the government's "red list" for international travel, framed as a source of danger rather than as a site of potential lessons.

The divergence was strikingly illustrated by Bloomberg's "COVID Resilience Ranking" in June 2021. At that time, the United States, with more than 600,000 deaths, roughly 1,800 per million, was rated near the top. China, with a rate of about three deaths per million, was near the bottom. By Bloomberg's criteria, "resilience" was not measured by lives saved, but by a composite index privileging openness, freedom of travel, and stock market stability.

For me, this was disorienting. How could "freedom" and "openness" be privileged so absolutely over survival, over the basic capacity to protect human life? To judge China's response as failure, despite its extraordinarily low mortality, was to reveal an ethical framework profoundly at odds with the one I had inherited.

This Book, This Perspective

The reflections I have offered so far, on perception, positionality, and my own classroom encounters, are not merely personal anecdotes. They reveal the entangled nature of how knowledge is formed, situated, and transformed. This book, like the technologies and policies it explores, is the product of a specific perspective: one that has been shaped over decades of research, lived experience, and continuous re-evaluation. It is neither a fixed viewpoint nor a grand theory. Rather, it is a perspectival realism, informed by encounters across epistemic cultures, institutional regimes, and moral worlds.

My analytical stance is grounded in three interwoven traditions. First is Karen Barad's agential realism, which demonstrates that knowledge is not simply representational but performative, always already entangled with the apparatuses, relations, and values that produce it. Second is the imitation theory of Gabriel Tarde (1903), whose view of social transformation as emergent from monadic interactions, repetitions, and variations provides a generative lens for viewing China's iterative developmental experiments. Third is the tradition of Science and Technology Studies (STS), especially the perspective of the Social Shaping of Technology (SST), which posits that technologies are not neutral tools or inevitable trajectories, but socio-technical assemblages shaped by human choices, institutional arrangements, and cultural meanings.

These frameworks allow me to explore China not as a deviant case or exceptional other, but as a complex actor engaged in a dynamic process of socio-technical becoming. They also caution me against linear explanations, against the temptation to attribute China's rise to any single cause, whether Confucian ethics, authoritarian governance, or Western mimicry. Instead, I approach China's transformation as the outcome of multiple, layered, and often contradictory practices of imitation, improvisation, and negotiation.

Throughout the chapters that follow, one set of tensions recurs in different forms, what I call the imitation paradoxes. These are not merely analytical categories, but reflections of patterns I have witnessed across different historical junctures and technological domains:

- State-led imitation of the West, intended to secure strength and modernity, yet often reproducing dependency and internal dissonance.
- Bottom-up imitation among individuals and enterprises, which spurs improvisation and responsiveness, but can generate moral hazards and fragmentation.
- The paradox of control and empowerment, in which centralised governance models, designed for control, paradoxically create conditions for distributed agency and civic participation through digital infrastructures.

These paradoxes do not appear uniformly but sometimes overlap and sometimes collide. But taken together, they illuminate how China's socio-technical systems evolve, not through pure planning or pure chaos, but through selective imitation, contested appropriation, and situated experimentation. At the heart of these dynamics lies a utilitarian approach (Shen, 2005).

In writing this book, I am also aware that my own understanding has changed. It has been shaped not only by empirical evidence or theoretical refinement, but also by lived contradictions: being raised in a politically stigmatised family in Mao-era China; conducting fieldwork in poor villages and smart cities; publishing in Western journals whilst resisting their epistemic gatekeeping. I do not claim a neutral view from nowhere. What I offer is a view from manywheres, formed through crossings, negotiations, and ethical reckonings.

This is not the perspective I held at the beginning of my academic journey. It is the one I have come to hold now, at the point of completing this book. And like China's own trajectory, it remains open-ended, shaped by new encounters, new dilemmas, and new questions.

1.2 Why The Mass Line?

The Memories of My Early Years

I belong to the generation that grew up under Mao's *mass line* (*qunzhong luxian* 群众路线). In that era, intellectuals and professionals who had served in the pre-revolutionary government of China were often made targets of political campaigns under the leadership of those with backgrounds as workers, peasants, or soldiers. My father, a member of Sun Yat-sen's Kuomintang party, worked for the Kuomintang government as an economist before the liberation. His experience led him to detest that government for its decadence and corruption. Even his enthusiastic response to the Maoist's government's call to "Let a hundred flowers bloom and a hundred schools of thought contend" (bǎihuā qífàng, bǎijiā zhēngmíng百花齐放，百家争鸣) did not protect him from being categorised as a "rightist" (yòupài右派). He was sent away from the family for 22 years and only experienced redress after the Cultural Revolution. But he never expressed resentment towards those who had mistreated him. His life-long and unwavering support for Mao's mass line bewildered me. As children raised in such a family, my sister and I could only feel that the world was incomprehensible.

During the ten-year Great Cultural Revolution, we saw workers (*gongxuandui* 工宣队) entering schools, colleges, universities and neighbourhood people's bureaus, establishing and leading every "revolutionary committee". My mother was suspended from her teaching job and ordered to write self-criticism daily. My father lost his entitled 12 days annual home visit, and he could not come back, even when my mother was taken to hospital in a critical condition. In his late years, he still believed the mass line was the right principle. I had a serious argument with him, something I came to regret many years later. It was perhaps this contradiction, between personal suffering and political faith, that first seeded in me a deeper ethical inquiry: how could one remain committed to a principle that caused so much harm? This ambivalence, I now realise, was a crucial moment in my own epistemic becoming, a formative rupture that would shape my research sensibilities for decades to come.

Those years left me with ambivalent memories. On the one hand, I remember the kindness of teachers, nursery carers, and factory co-workers; on the other, I recall the humiliation of families like mine caught in cycles of suspicion. The experience taught me early in life that the "masses" were not a homogeneous entity but a force that could be mobilised in very different directions, sometimes for dignity and solidarity, sometimes for repression or in search of personal vested interests (Perry, 2008). The reality I saw was confusion and suffering, as ordinary people copied each other's gestures of power, often blindly, sometimes cruelly, under the name of *mass line* (*qunzhong luxian* 群众路线).

Lessons of Poverty and Recognition

One of the most formative experiences of my youth came in 1987, when I joined Professor Fei Xiaotong's research project on the "Exploitation of the Multi-Ethnic Economic Zone in the Upper Yellow River Basin." Fei was not only China's most eminent sociologist but also a public intellectual and political leader. Under his guidance, we travelled to Xi-Hai-Gu (西海固), a cluster of counties in southern Ningxia Hui Autonomous Region officially designated as one of the country's poorest and most ecologically degraded areas.

What I encountered there remains etched in my memory. Families lived in cave dwellings dug into the brittle hillsides. The only furniture was the *kang* (炕, raised brick bed), filling the entire space of the cave. At the end of the *kang* stood a small stove with an iron pot, in which I saw a thin grey-green soup meant to feed five people. The land was barren, the soil saline and lifeless. Water was scarce, often polluted. For many young people, there was no work, no prospect of change.

The shock of that field trip never left me. It altered not only my intellectual orientation but my ethical framework. Do people like me, city dwellers and scholars, truly understand what life means in such conditions? At that time, I had no camera, no way to capture the images. My report of the fieldwork was perhaps only internally circulated and never published. I wish now that I had had a mobile phone with a camera and an internet information infrastructure like today.

In Britain, I recall a video report by the BBC on the Chinese government campaign to relocate people like those in this village. One clip showed villagers reluctant to leave their homes. The video footage was used to demonstrate the violation of human rights by the Chinese government. I wished the reporter had watched the Chinese TV series *Minning Township* (《山海情》), which reminded me of the field trip I had done. The eventual relocation brought measurable improvements: people moved out of the desolate land, participated in a poverty alleviation project and built a new home with a prosperous future. These villagers might well have felt scared to move to a strange place, but they would never want to go back to poverty.

This contrasts sharply with the Western liberal imaginary, where privacy, "the right to be left alone", is seen as an essential human right. My experience demonstrates that these are not simply philosophical abstractions. Context is the only clue to ethical matters.

When Deng Xiaoping's reforms opened up the economy, many of the intellectuals who had endured hardship joined the ranks of administrators, entrepreneurs, and academics. They carried with them both scars and aspirations. Like many in my generation, I saw that after the 1990s, when Deng Xiaoping opened up China, people no longer worried about food and clothing; instead, they began to worry about food safety, polluted water, contaminated milk powder, and pesticide-sprayed fruits and vegetables. The whole population was encouraged to act and look for new ways of life, for opportunities to contribute to national rejuvenation. Yet, as the market reforms deepened, the gap between rich and poor grew wider, and corruption seemed to permeate the very fabric of society.

The erosion of trust became systemic. Counterfeit goods, pyramid schemes, food fraud, and scams proliferated. The 2008 melamine milk scandal crystallised these dynamics. Once, milk had been a relational good, produced and distributed through cooperative channels where producers and consumers often knew one another. With reforms, milk became abstracted into metrics: protein levels, nitrogen counts, fat percentages. This shift from relational accountability to technical indicators opened space for manipulation. Farmers blindly imitated each other to buy cheap milk powder and supply diluted milk. Traders adulterated it and intermediaries turned blind eyes. When melamine was added to inflate protein readings, the result was catastrophic: nearly 300,000 infants were affected; six died.

A few years before the pandemic, I watched Jia Zhangke's film *A Touch of Sin* (《天注定》) at the Edinburgh Film Festival. It affected me like no theoretical treatise ever had. One story, of Dahai, a coal miner turned whistleblower, struck a deep chord. Discovering that his village's collectively owned coal mine had been sold off by local officials for private gain, Dahai tried to file a formal complaint. In his modest room, Dahai carefully wrote a letter of complaint and, filled with hope, he walked to the post office. He told the young woman at the service counter that he wanted to send a registered letter, to Beijing, Zhongnanhai, the Central Commission for Discipline Inspection Zhongnanhai (中南海) was the seat of China's highest political authority. But at the post office, his hope was crushed: he was told that without a detailed address, the letter could not be accepted and was undeliverable. He declared he was going to Beijing to report the wrongdoing to higher authorities. But he was beaten up and his hope was totally shattered. Dahai turned to violence, ending in tragedy.

A New Light of Hope

It was digital data-driven technology, and in particular its application during the COVID-19 pandemic, which showed how things could be done differently: how the platform information infrastructure and contact tracing technology could engage the whole population to act collectively and successfully to contain the pandemic. During 2020, I did a remote ethnographic study of Health QR code development in a small residential district in Hangzhou. I wrote an academic paper about the entanglement of technology and people's lives and the context in which they were embedded (see Chapter 8). However, I discovered that it could not be published in a Western academic journal without first inserting the requisite liberal critiques of privacy and authoritarianism. Nevertheless, the study made me hopeful and excited. Unlike many countries in the West, which abandoned the contact tracing apps after COVID, China built on their success. It applied these technologies to establishing infrastructures for governing and transforming society through the cooperation between the state and platform companies.

At the turn of the year 2020–2021, colleagues at the Shanghai Institute for Science of Science (SISS) invited me to propose a "keyword" that might capture the year ahead. I responded without hesitation: dataveillance (Shen, 2021). The term seemed both timely and inescapable. The pandemic had made visible how data infrastructures, health QR codes, algorithmic triage, community-level monitoring, were not peripheral, but central to the ordering of everyday life. I envisioned a bright future for China: a people-centred socio-technical[3] infrastructure, marked by increasing visibility and traceability, that would chart a new path towards national rejuvenation. Yet at the same time, these very infrastructures provoked heated debate: were they instruments of authoritarian control, or vital scaffolds of public health?

To me, and to those who share similar ontological and epistemological worldviews, the film *A Touch of Sin* is a critique of failed information infrastructures, a meditation on the emotional and political costs of being unheard and unseen. For those of us working within STS, I came to see in the new socio-technical form of dataveillance not only the risks of surveillance, but also a source of hope for a developing country like China and its 1.4 billion people. We should be asking not only how surveillance operates, but where it is absent. Every person has the right to speak, record, and respond. At the same time, those whose actions involve unruly behaviours, whether driven by selfish motives or by a lack of scientific

3 Socio-technical and Social-technical are used in this book interchangeably.

knowledge, must also be monitored and recognised, for their choices can inflict serious harm on society.

My studies over four decades have followed China's shifting technological landscape, from the building of telecommunications infrastructure to the rise of software, mobile, and online creative technologies, and, most recently, artificial intelligence (AI). This journey has continually brought me back to the promise of technology: that scaffolding technologies, for all their risks, might engage the whole population. I have witnessed this in a country of 1.4 billion people, and I can imagine how the energy of its people, its monads (for monadology, see Chapter 8), capacitated from the highest levels of governance to the grassroots, could be directed towards cultivating competence, understanding, and civic quality, and could drive selective imitations that contribute to a self-constructed collective good, in Chinese *renmin suzhi de tigao* (人民素质的提高, raising the quality of the people).

My integration into Western societies has also made me conscious of the frustrations that accompany their cultural and social manifestations. Societies have become increasingly divided, views contradictory, and governance often ineffective. Digital and data-driven technologies, for all their risks, have begun to reshape China's socio-technical infrastructures. They open new ways to monitor ordinary people's daily lives whilst also enabling them to voice concerns, to be seen, and to influence outcomes (Zeng, 2016). In the past, among 1.4 billion people, how many voices could ever be heard? Even social elites, seeking attention, resorted to gestures such as sending flowers or calcium tablets to the Ministry of Foreign Affairs, whether in silent protest or support. Digital platforms have now allowed for far broader and faster communication of public sentiment. The state, once distant, must respond to the digital traces and collective voices of millions. It reminded me of an old Chinese saying: *The ruler is like a boat and the people the water; the water can carry the boat and can also overturn it* (*junzhe zhouye; shuren zhe shuiye. Shui ze zai zhou, shui ze fu zhou* 君者舟也；庶人者水也。水则载舟，水则覆舟).

Looking back, I sometimes think this was also the unfulfilled dream of Confucius, Laozi, the dedicated yet frustrated overseas Chinese students, and later leaders such as Mao. Today, it has been reframed as a governance infrastructure through which current leaders must envisage their populations as capable of generating collective momentum (see Chapter 5), a distinctive asset on which China's future may ultimately depend.

Digital technologies now extend this logic into new terrains, amplifying both surveillance and participation. They carry risks of control, yet they also open new channels for accountability and renewal. It is this paradox, and this hope, that guides the reflections in the chapters that follow. China's long tradition of governance through family, school, and society has shaped mental structures: in the absence of any overarching moral framework, everyday life continued to be governed by hidden rules and by the belief in the virtue of following those who were seen to know better.

1.3 A Roadmap of the Book

This book traces China's technological experimentalism through concrete case studies and historical trajectories as China has evolved from technological backwater to global power, and each reflects my own evolving understanding.

- Chapters 2–5 explore China's telecommunications leap. They trace the importation of Western technologies such as System-12 and the indigenous HJD-04 development, the dilemmas of intellectual property, and the effort to create an indigenous 3G standard, TD-SCDMA. These chapters reveal how imitation, adaptation, and state intervention produced both breakthroughs and failures, showing that "indigenous innovation" was never a straightforward path.
- Chapters 6–7 turn to the broader culture of imitative innovation and innovative imitation. Here we examine the *shanzhai*[4] spirit, the rise of Alibaba, and the laboratory as a site of improvisation. These case materials reveal how imitation became not a barrier but a resource, enabling responsiveness to local needs and producing unexpected modes of creativity.
- Chapters 8–9 bring the narrative into the digital era. They investigate how data-driven technologies, from health QR codes to AI governance, have transformed the relationship between state and society. Concepts such as governance by affordance and performative surveillance highlight how China's governance has become experimental, participatory, and fraught with ethical tensions. The conclusion reflects on what these transformations mean for China's place in the world and for the future of socio-technical governance more broadly.

These chapters also present my interpretation of Tarde's theoretical framework of monadology. Building on Latour's nuanced work on monads in the digital age, I treat them as 'traceable units' (*kezhuizong danyuan* 可追踪单元): an individual, a firm, or even a country, not defined by fixed categories but recognised through the traces of its actions, histories, and relations.

4 The informal economy of *shanzhai* (copycat) phones. See Chapter 6 for details.

Unlike the Western tendency towards horizontal generalisation, for example, labelling China simply as "communist" and therefore "authoritarian," and thus a potential enemy, a trace-based perspective emphasises longitudinal trajectories. It highlights China's long record of avoiding wars and invasions; the way a firm builds trust and loyalty with users over years; or how a migrant, even if arriving under irregular circumstances, can become a bridge between cultures and contribute uniquely to society. Monads become visible once we treat them as traceable units rather than abstract instances of a type. Each has specific characteristics that evolve through its own distinctive trajectory.

Taken together, these arcs illustrate the central argument of this book: China's technological rise was not preordained, nor simply imposed from above. It was co-produced through imitation, improvisation, and the force of the masses, sometimes empowering, sometimes constraining, always shaping. This learning curve, both China's and my own, is the thread that binds the chapters together.

At the same time, China now stands at a profound crossroads. One path is to follow the rules set largely by the West: to reinforce intellectual property protection systems and to project military might as a way of claiming global power. This would mean following Western patterns not only in protecting knowledge but also in military projection, as seen in interventions from Iraq to Ukraine. The other path is to turn more decisively towards building new modes of social governance and contributing to the development of humanity (*ren de suzhi* 人的素质) through data-driven and participatory approaches. Which path China chooses will not only shape its own future, but also influence the trajectory of global science, technology, and governance.

At the heart of this dilemma lies the same truth that has guided my reflections: the people remain central. Whether through protests in London's streets or small gestures in Beijing, a bouquet of flowers, a bottle of calcium tablets, acts of protest or defiance may not achieve their intended effect yet still carry weight. In the West, people tend to see only the actions and policies of the state. I include them here to give readers vivid images of the complex relations between people and the state, of how digital voices amplified across platforms enable the masses to continue to shape history in ways that states cannot fully manage and control. The chapters that follow explore how China's past of imitation and improvisation has prepared the ground for this crossroads, and why the outcome will matter far beyond China's borders.

This book reflects not only on China's historical crossroads, but also on my own. Over the decades, moving between China and the West, fieldwork and theory, personal grief and civic hope, I have come to see that my understanding, like China's governance, has never been fixed. It has been iterative, fragile, and often formed through ethical struggle. This, I have come to realise, is the nature of epistemic becoming.

1.4 Imitation Paradoxes: Learning Without Mastery, Reproducing Without Becoming

At the heart of China's developmental trajectory lies a fundamental tension: the desire to imitate, the capacity to innovate, and the struggle to govern the outcomes of both. In the Chinese context, imitation has never been straightforward, nor simply a technical exercise in catch-up. It is layered, socially situated, and often morally ambiguous. As I reflect on China's transformation over the past four decades, from science-starved isolation to digital innovation powerhouse, I have come to see that imitation in China operates through paradoxes, each revealing entangled relations between the state, society, and technology.

These paradoxes are not theoretical abstractions; they are empirical patterns I have observed across multiple cases, from historical science societies to telecommunications infrastructure, from *shanzhai* creativity to the politics of QR codes. They emerge from lived experiences and socio-technical specificities, and they continue to structure China's engagement with global knowledge, institutions, and values. Each paradox illuminates how China's efforts to learn from the West have produced unexpected outcomes, including contradictions within its own tradition and governance model.

Imitating the West to Strengthen the East

The first paradox emerges from China's long-standing effort to imitate Western institutional and technological forms, often with the ambition not to converge, but to compete. From intellectual property law to economic liberalisation, from global trade norms to academic metrics, the Chinese state has embraced a top-down imitation strategy. This began as a rational calculus: to survive and prosper in a global order designed by others, one must learn its rules. Yet this very process of learning often reinforces dependency and diminishes indigenous creativity.

Moreover, the paradox deepens when imitation of external forms comes at the cost of internal dissonance. The emphasis on market competition and proprietary knowledge, for example, diverges from traditional Chinese governance logics, which prioritise harmony, relationality, and collective well-being. China's attempt to secure legitimacy in global regimes by adopting Western norms has brought material success, but also moral uncertainty. The more China excels at intellectual property protection or technological militarisation, the more it risks becoming what it originally sought to resist.

Bottom-Up Imitation as Improvisation and Deformation

The second paradox arises not from the state, but from society. China's reforms opened space for spontaneous, decentralised, and often chaotic imitations by individuals, firms, and local governments. This bottom-up imitation takes multiple forms: from blind replication of business models to tactical adaptation of Western norms, from counterfeit consumer goods to entrepreneurial leapfrogging. Some of these imitations are conscious and strategic; others are unconscious and mimetic, driven by short-term incentives and peer comparison.

Here lies the paradox: whilst often derided as low-quality or ethically problematic, these imitative practices have seeded a culture of improvisational innovation, a kind of socio-technical bricolage. The *shanzhai* movement, for instance, emerged as a response to both scarcity and aspiration. At times, it enabled responsiveness to local needs better than top-down systems. Yet it also reproduced the very asymmetries it claimed to overcome, such as quality risks, information fraud, and systemic distrust. When the melamine milk scandal unfolded, what appeared to be entrepreneurial adaptation revealed itself as moral erosion: the blind following of indicators, detached from relational accountability.

This paradox forces us to ask: can society innovate without trust? Can improvisation yield durable institutions? What governs the ethics of imitation when markets move faster than regulation, and incentives override responsibilities?

Centralised Governance Enabling Distributed Co-Responsibility

The third paradox is perhaps the most difficult to reconcile. It is the paradox of control and empowerment. The state initially incentivised wealth creation, then combated corruption and crime, and lately has managed society through surveillance and intervention. Yet this process has enabled new forms of collective agency with self-discipline. The most vivid example emerged during the COVID-19 pandemic. Through digital platforms, health QR codes, and data infrastructures, the Chinese state mobilised the entire population with remarkable speed. What appeared externally as coercive and opaque was internally experienced, by many, as protective, coordinated, and morally grounded.

This governance model, which I describe as data-driven scaffolding, does not fit neatly into Western liberal dichotomies of freedom versus control. Rather, it reflects a Confucian-inflected logic of relational governance: cultivating the self (*xiushen* 修身) or self-discipline anchored in collective responsibility. The infrastructures were state-initiated, their success hinged on mass participation, such as self-tracking, digital volunteering, neighbourhood coordination, and platform collaboration. It was an entangled system where the people were not only subjects of governance but also co-producers of it.

The paradox is that a top-down system premised on control has enabled the emergence of bottom-up agency through digital traceability. Visibility, once feared as surveillance, also enabled responsiveness, inclusion, and civic recognition. Of course, the risks are real: algorithmic opacity, data misuse, and loss of privacy. But equally real is the possibility that China may be forging a distinctive model of performative governance, where participation and visibility are not mutually exclusive.

These paradoxes are not isolated episodes. They interweave throughout the chapters that follow. They structure the trajectory of Chinese science and technology development not as a linear ascent, but as an experimental entanglement of imitation, improvisation, and institutional recalibration.

1.5 Framing the Contribution

This book does not tell a trajectory of linear progress, nor of a grand plan executed from above. Rather, it demonstrates that China's path of technological development has been improvisational, contingent, and deeply entangled with its social, political, and cultural conditions. Imitation emerges here not as a sign of weakness, but as the fundamental condition of modernity, an unavoidable practice through which societies learn, adapt, and innovate (Tarde, 1903). In China, imitation has operated not only as a way of catching up, but also as a means of improvising new modes of creativity and governance.

One of the key arguments running through the chapters is that the technical and the social are inseparable. Telecommunications infrastructure, laboratories, entrepreneurial practices, and digital platforms cannot be understood as mere technical systems. They are socio-technical formations in which values, norms, and political structures are embedded (Hughes, 1987; Bijker et al., 2012). Each case in this book, from System-12 to *shanzhai*, from Alibaba to health QR codes, demonstrates how technology becomes a site of negotiation between global models and local practices.

Another theme is the paradox of imitation. Imitation can reproduce hierarchies of dependence, but it can also generate unexpected creativity and resilience. China's "imitative innovation" shows how replication, modification, and improvisation can create new opportunities, even whilst reproducing old asymmetries (Keane, 2007). This paradox is not unique to China; it is a condition of modernity itself, but China's scale and speed make it especially visible.

A further thread running through this book is utilitarianism as an enduring core of Chineseness. This orientation has been a double-edged sword: enabling rapid technological catch-up and innovation whilst also intensifying state control, fuelling cut-throat competition, and polarising society, as captured Deng Xiaoping's economic reform slogan, "to become rich is glorious." Understanding China therefore requires more than horizontal categories and static labels. Western analytical traditions, thorough though they are, often risk overgeneralisation, for example, classifying China simply as "communist" and therefore "authoritarian." By contrast, this book highlights the need for vertical tracing of historical trajectories and relational practices, as argued by authors such as Martin Jacques (2012) and Kishore Mahbubani (2020). This vertical perspective serves here as a conceptual thread, through which my understanding of China is unfolded.

This book also argues that contemporary digital governance in China extends these historical patterns into new domains. Data-driven and AI-based systems are not ruptures from the past but continuations of older struggles over how to mobilise the masses, how to balance control with responsiveness, and how to turn imitation into governance (Creemers, 2018). What emerges is a hybrid governance ecosystem, part state-driven, part market-driven, and part mass-driven, where digital traces become both instruments of surveillance and channels for participation.

Finally, this book positions China at a crossroads. Will it continue to imitate Western logics of intellectual property enforcement and military might, or will it begin to innovate in the sphere of governance by developing new models of participation and humanity-centred development? This choice, I argue, will shape not only China's future but also the trajectory of global science and technology governance.

The chapters that follow, then, are not simply case studies of telecommunications, entrepreneurship, or digital governance. They are windows into a broader argument: that China's technological rise is best understood as a socio-technical becoming, shaped by imitation, improvisation, and the force of the people. This is the contribution I hope to make, not only to the study of China, but to global conversations about science, technology, and the possibilities of governance in our time.

Epistemic BecomingA Self-Reflective Note

Living and working in Western societies has also made me conscious of the frustrations that come with their own traditions of analysis and governance. Too often, isolated incidents are taken as grounds for generalised rules or blanket judgements. Because of the criminal behaviour of a few migrants, immigration as a whole is condemned. Because some black individuals have been convicted of crimes, police check disproportionately target black people. After a single attempted use of liquid explosives, airports worldwide imposed rigid restrictions on carrying liquids of more than 100 ml. These examples reveal the strength and the weakness of Western analytical traditions: their capacity to establish general rules is also their tendency to overgeneralise, producing uniform categories that obscure nuance and create unfairness.

By contrast, the monadological approach that I came to appreciate later in my work, along with Chinese traditions of relational governance, emphasises multiplicity and situatedness. Rather than extrapolating from single cases to govern whole populations, they call for recognising diversity in practice and relation. This perspective points to infrastructures that make these differences visible and traceable, so that governance can proceed through relational accountability rather than through blanket generalisation (Tarde, 1903; Latour, 2010).

My thinking about China has not remained stable over time. As this book reveals, I have moved across institutions, disciplines, and moral terrains. From the trauma of political violence in my youth to the trust I encountered in a Scottish university library, from despair over food scandals to hope through data infrastructures, each moment has transformed how I understand imitation, governance, and participation.

I do not write this book as an external observer. I write as someone entangled, as someone whose own becoming has unfolded alongside China's. If the chapters seem layered and contradictory at times, that is because the process has been so. My aim is not to resolve these tensions, but to share them as a method of learning.

The paradox of imitation, at once generative and corrosive, runs throughout China's technological trajectory. From grassroots improvisations to state-led experiments, the decisive question has never been whether China could innovate, but how collective participation could be mobilised, sustained, and transformed into civic capacity. The following chapters trace this thread across scandals, experiments, and infrastructures, showing that China's "miracle" is not simply a story of technology or policy, but of how the masses were enrolled into building and remaking the very systems on which they depended.

These frustrations, drawn from my years of living between two worlds, reminded me that neither Chinese nor Western traditions hold all the answers on their own. The challenge, and the opportunity, lies in finding ways of thinking that can hold together the Western drive for analytical clarity with the Chinese emphasis on relational multiplicity. This conviction has gradually led me towards an appreciation of Tarde's monadology and of the potential of infrastructures that make social life visible and traceable, themes that will surface again in the later chapters of this book.

2 Globalisation Paradox

My engagement with globalisation debates coincided with China's own dilemmas of imitation and adaptation, and I found myself tracing in my research the same oscillation between convergence and divergence that China was experiencing on the ground.

2.1 Introduction: Globalisation as Imitation

Imitation has long carried an uneasy connotation in global politics and economic discourse. In the Western imagination, to imitate is often to betray a lack of originality, to be a copycat, or worse, a thief. This perception has been particularly persistent in assessments of China's rise. From accusations of "intellectual property theft" to dismissals of Chinese firms as "mere imitators" of their Silicon Valley counterparts, the global conversation too often frames imitation as derivative and morally suspect (Alford, 1995).

This suspicion reveals a profound cultural asymmetry. In Chinese intellectual and artistic traditions, learning has always been inseparable from imitation. Classical Confucian education valorised the close study and repetition of canonical texts as the foundation of self-cultivation. The literati who mastered calligraphy began by copying the brushstrokes of the ancients; apprentice painters traced classical scrolls before attempting original compositions; craftsmen and engineers refined their skills through emulative practice, understanding and absorbing the wisdom of predecessors before developing it further (Elman, 2005). In this worldview, copying is not theft but apprenticeship, a necessary path to mastery and ultimately to transformation. Imitation is thus an active engagement with knowledge and skill, a creative process that carries within it the seeds of renewal.

Recognising the interplay between imitation and creativity allows us to see globalisation in a new light. Rather than a flattening worldwide convergence of increasingly identical institutions and technologies, globalisation emerges as a field of imitative relations where power and creativity intermingle. Every act of imitation involves choice: what to adopt, what to adapt, and what to resist. In this sense, imitation is both a mechanism of global connectivity and a driver of local differentiation, producing a world patterned by surface similarity and underlying divergence.

The Chinese experience in the last two centuries crystallises this dynamic. Following the defeats of the Opium Wars, China confronted the unsettling truth that its own technological and institutional traditions were insufficient to shield it

https://doi.org/10.1515/9783110757576-008

from the asymmetries of modern power (Fairbank & Goldman, 2006). What followed was a persistent desire, sometimes voluntary, often coerced, to imitate the West. From the self-strengthening movements of the late Qing dynasty to the Republican-era fascination with Western science, from Soviet-inspired industrialisation to the post-1978 economic reforms, imitation became a recurrent mode of survival and transformation. Yet each wave bore a distinct utilitarian character: Western science and technology were embraced as instruments for national salvation and economic modernisation, whilst deeper questions about their social and ethical implications lingered.

Imitation is never passive submission. To imitate is to interpret. Every act of adoption embeds a cultural and strategic choice: what to retain, what to discard, and what to reshape based on local needs, historical memory, and socio-technical conditions, including contemporary geopolitical pressures such as the semiconductor export restrictions that spur China's urgency in advancing indigenous capabilities. Thus, globalisation has produced not a flat, uniform world but a patterned heterogeneity. Western observers often misread China's pathways. When Alibaba or Tencent are dismissed as mere copies of Amazon or Facebook (Zenglein & Holzmann, 2019), this overlooks how these imitative beginnings evolved into novel socio-technical formations deeply embedded in China's digital economy, governance, and cultural ecosystem.

In reflecting on China's trajectory, a Western academic once remarked that the country had, in crucial respects, "become one of us." This was not meant in the simplistic sense of cultural assimilation or wholesale adoption of Western practices, but rather as a recognition that China had successfully embedded itself into the institutional logics, standards, and infrastructures of the global science and technology system. From this perspective, China's rise is not merely a story of external imitation, but of active participation in, and partial reshaping of, the very rules of the game. Similar arguments have been advanced by Steinfeld (2010), who suggests that China's ascent has occurred through "playing our game," by internalising the global frameworks of capitalism and technological innovation whilst adapting them to its own developmental context.

Yet beneath that surface recognition lies a profoundly different developmental logic. Imitation, in this view, is the seed of differentiation, not its negation.

The paradox of globalisation lies in the tension between surface similarity and underlying difference. Imitation generates recognition, sometimes celebrated, often resented, whilst simultaneously producing divergence through local adaptation, socio-technical entanglement, and historical contingency. This tension shapes our contemporary world: a world in which power flows along the channels of imitation, but outcomes are never fully controlled by the original donor.

This chapter takes that paradox as its point of departure. In the sections that follow, I explore the theoretical foundations of imitation, drawing on Gabriel Tarde's sociology of imitation (Tarde, 1903), Deleuze's philosophy of difference (Deleuze, 1994), and Science and Technology Studies (STS), especially the social shaping of technology perspective (Monteiro & Hanseth, 1996; Williams & Edge, 1996; MacKenzie & Wajcman, 1985). I then turn to the historical and socio-technical trajectories of China, showing how imitation, far from passive replication, functions as a driver of global variation, carrying with it the seeds of cooperation and conflict, convergence and difference. Through this lens, globalisation appears not as a march towards homogeneity but as a living process of translation and transformation, in which each act of imitation reshapes the world anew. In the contemporary digital era, these acts of selective imitation represent a mode of governance through crisis, where imitation reorganises social and moral orders.

In what follows, this chapter provides an integrated conceptual framework to understand China's innovation trajectory through imitation. Section 2.2 surveys classical and contemporary theories of imitation, situating China's case within, and sometimes against, dominant paradigms of modernisation, diffusion, and dependency. Section 2.3 reconstructs the historical layers of China's adaptive strategy, tracing how successive waves of imitation have responded to shifting geopolitical, ideological, and technological conditions. Section 2.4 advances the argument that imitation in China has been shaped by socio-technical specificity, the emergent interplay between infrastructures, moral reasoning, and data-mediated governance. Section 2.5 turns to the paradox of intellectual property rights, showing how China's embrace of Intellectual Property (IP) regimes, whilst globally compliant, has produced internal tensions and opened space for reimagining innovation through traceability and co-production. Together, these sections set the stage for a broader argument that China's long arc of imitation may not culminate in convergence with Western norms, but in the proposition of alternative infrastructures for global governance. In this view, the very mechanisms once used to catch up may become the foundations of a new socio-technical modernity, explored further in Chapter 9.

2.2 Theoretical Foundations of Imitation

To understand the paradoxical nature of globalisation as an imitative process, we must begin with a firm theoretical grounding. Imitation is not merely a practical action; it is a social, cognitive, and ontological act. It has been addressed by classical sociology, philosophy, institutional theory, and, in recent decades, Science and Technology Studies (STS). This section outlines the conceptual architecture guiding this chapter, weaving together Gabriel Tarde's sociology of imitation, Deleuze's philosophy of difference, STS's emphasis on socio-technical specificity, and the concept of isomorphic difference developed by Irwin et al (2021). These lenses illuminate how imitation in globalisation is adaptive, relational, and generative.

Gabriel Tarde and the Social Logic of Imitation

Tarde's contribution to the sociology of imitation can be organised around three key elements, each illuminating a distinct dimension of how imitation operates as the basis of social life.

Monadology: Tarde's sociology places imitation at the heart of social life, but his later work on *Monadology and Sociology* (1893/1999) pushes this claim further. Here Tarde insists that the foundations of society lie not in abstract institutions but in the countless actions of individuals, monads, whose repetitions, inventions, and variations generate social order. Unlike Durkheim's emphasis on external social facts, Tarde depicts the social as a constellation of micro-actions continually composing and recomposing collective life. Each monad is at once an atom of action and a window onto larger aggregates: society is the sum of these acts, not an entity above them. Latour (2010), in his chapter *Tarde's Idea of Quantification* in *The Social After Gabriel Tarde*, revitalises this monadological perspective by connecting it to contemporary practices of digital trace-making. For Latour, monads become visible today through the proliferation of data traces—searches, clicks, payments, and movements—that render individual actions legible and aggregable. Quantification does not erase individuality but multiplies it, producing a fabric of relations through which collective selves can be constructed. In this sense, Tarde's emphasis on the primacy of individual action finds new relevance in the digital era: mass participation through innumerable micro-traces forms the basis for novel socio-technical collectivities, a theme that underpins this book's analysis of imitation and the emergent collective-self.

Forms of Imitation: Tarde also distinguished among different forms of imitation—custom and fashion, sympathy and obedience, voluntary and involuntary—all context-dependent and relational. Central to his theory is the law of imitation of the superior by the inferior (Borch & Stäheli, 2009). Superiority and inferiority are not intrinsic but relational, shaped by prestige, belief, and desire. This extends to global power dynamics: nations and institutions copy others based on relative prestige, yet the result is never identical; it is always mediated by distance, perception, and local aspiration.

The Optical Point: Tarde highlights a key challenge facing both decision-makers seeking to emulate and analysts trying to understand imitation. He argues that imitation occurs at what he calls the "optical point", a distance that permits observers to see surface forms whilst obscuring underlying mechanisms (Tarde, 1903, p. 392). This perceptual gap enables divergence. When China adopts Western corporate or technological forms, it may absorb the visible arrangements whilst reconfiguring them according to its own socio-technical logic.

Deleuze: Difference, Repetition, and the Creativity of Imitation

Whilst Tarde maps the social mechanics, Gilles Deleuze (1994) reveals how imitation is ontologically generative. In *Difference and Repetition*, he argues that each repetition transforms, producing difference rather than sameness (Deleuze, 1994). Every repetition transforms; nothing is ever the same. There is only difference—copies are something new, reality is a becoming, not a being.[5]

In globalisation, imitation thus becomes a form of creative divergence, not a slavish copy. The adoption of Western digital business models by Chinese firms gave rise to distinct socio-technical worlds, like Alibaba's ecosystem or Tencent's WeChat super-app, phenomena unanticipated in Silicon Valley. Here, imitation incubates innovation, giving rise to forms that are at once familiar and radically new.

STS and Socio-Technical Specificity

Science and Technology Studies (STS) offers a methodological bridge between Tarde's micro-sociology and Deleuze's ontology. STS emphasises that technologies and institutions are embedded in material infrastructures, social practices, and cultural norms (Bijker et al., 2012; Law, 2004).

This becomes evident in the quantification of the social, where interactions, transactions, and moral behaviours are captured as data points. Such quantification not only mediates imitation but also enables new forms of governance and self-regulation, foreshadowing the digital panoptic effects discussed in later chapters.

In earlier research on agricultural biotechnology, I proposed the term "socio-technical specificities," suggesting that different technologies carry distinct pat-

5 See Internet Encyclopaedia of Philosophy: Giles Deleuze (1925–1995). https://iep.utm.edu/gilles-deleuze/?utm_source=chatgpt.com (accessed 05/09/2025)

terns of social engagement, interface intensity, and uncontrollable risks[6] (Shen, 2010). This concept is applicable to digital and data-driven technologies, which involve deep entanglements with individual, social, and state life.

Major Chinese projects like System-12 telephony, TD-SCDMA mobile networks, and social credit systems all began with external models but, due to internal and external socio-technical conditions ranging from rural infrastructure gaps to geopolitical constraints, unfolded along unique, path-dependent trajectories. These illustrate how global imitation is a negotiation in which adaptation is as crucial as adoption.

Isomorphic Difference: The Coexistence of Convergence and Divergence

To capture the paradox of surface similarity and deep divergence, I draw on the concept of *isomorphic difference* (Irwin et al., 2021). Whilst DiMaggio and Powell's (1983) classic account of institutional isomorphism emphasises convergence under coercive, mimetic, or normative pressures, isomorphic difference allows us to see how institutions that look similar externally can function very differently internally.

Irwin, Vedel, and Vikkelsø use this concept to show how national research and innovation policies can display global familiarity whilst retaining local distinctiveness. The same logic applies to China's techno-policy pathway: a Western-style patent law or credit system might appear homologous, but its embeddedness within China's political economy transforms both its meaning and function.

In sum, this theoretical frame positions imitation as a dynamic, relational, and productive process. Tarde reveals its social architecture; Deleuze its ontological possibility; STS its material embeddedness; and isomorphic difference its capacity for variation within similarity. With this toolkit, we can interpret China's imitative globalisation not as imitation alone but as an evolving translation, one that shapes new socio-technical and political worlds.

This theoretical foundation leads directly into the historical analysis of Section 2.3, which reconstructs the layered trajectories of Chinese imitation across time and shifting geopolitical contexts.

6 This working paper was circulated as Shen, X. (2007). Socio-technical specificities of GM technologies: Social-technical interfaces, risk and uncertainty, later published in the Journal of Development Studies in 2010.

2.3 Historical Paradoxes of Chinese Imitation

Understanding the paradoxes of Chinese imitation requires tracing its deep historical and cultural roots. China's engagement with the world has never followed a linear march towards Westernisation, nor has it simply resisted or closed itself off. Rather, it is a history marked by oscillation between admiration and suspicion, selective borrowing and cultural self-assertion. From the late Qing dynasty to the post-reform era, imitation has served as a recurring strategy, often utilitarian in spirit, producing hybrid, adaptive, and sometimes unintentionally transformative outcomes.

The Late Qing Awakening: Humiliation and Desire

The first significant wave of Chinese imitation emerged under the shadow of national humiliation. The defeats in the Opium Wars (1839–1842, 1856–1860) revealed a stark asymmetry between the Qing Empire's institutions and the industrial and military power of the West. This crisis catalysed a profound recognition: survival in the modern world would require learning from, and imitating, the West.

The Self-Strengthening Movement (1861–1895) exemplified this pragmatic imitation. Reformist officials such as Zeng Guofan, Li Hongzhang, and Zuo Zongtang sought to import Western military and industrial technologies whilst preserving the Confucian moral core of the state. Zhang Zhidong's famous principle, *zhongti xiyong* (中体西用, Chinese learning as essence, Western learning as utility) (Zhang, 1898), reflected an instrumentalist approach: adopt Western tools for national survival, whilst retaining Chinese cultural and political essence.

My early historical research explored how Chinese intellectuals and scientific associations, like the China Science Society (中国科学社), navigated this tension (Shen, 1988). This case study foreshadowed the utilitarian orientation that would persist in China's approach to contemporary science and technology: learning for survival and national strength rather than for universalist or disinterested knowledge (Shen & Williams, 2005).

This created the first paradox of imitation: it was both necessary for survival and potentially threatening to cultural identity.

The Epic Debate: Scientism vs. Metaphysics

In the early 20th century, imitation extended into science, philosophy, and epistemology. The May Fourth (1919) and New Culture Movements launched a national debate over knowledge foundations, an "epic debate" (Kwok, 1965; Wang, 1991).

Two currents collided. *Scientism* (*kexue zhuyi* 科学主义), championed by figures like Hu Shi and Chen Duxiu, demanded wholesale adoption of Western scientific rationality. *Metaphysical* or cultural-essentialist thinkers such as Liang Shuming, Zhang Junmai, and Xiong Shili warned that this would erode China's moral traditions rooted in Confucian and Buddhist thought.

This debate echoed a global concern: Can imitation foster authentic renewal, or does it risk self-effacement? In practice, a pragmatic synthesis prevailed: Western science was embraced as a developmental tool, whilst deeper philosophical tensions remained unresolved. I have critiqued this instrumental framing of science as a hallmark of China's modernisation path (Shen & Williams, 2005).

Republican and Early PRC Pragmatism: Utilitarian Imitation

During the Republican era (1912–1949), imitation became institutionalised. Western-style universities, professional associations, and legal codes proliferated, often with foreign models. Yet adoption remained uneven: elites embraced Westernisation in urban centres like Shanghai, whilst rural life remained steeped in traditional socio-technical rhythms.

Under the early People's Republic of China, a new form of imitation took hold: the Soviet model. From the First Five-Year Plan (1953–1957) onwards, entire institutional and technological systems were imported from the USSR. This was a coercive and comprehensive mode of imitation, extending to education, industrial design, and bureaucracy.

Yet even this wave yielded divergence. Programmes such as the 156 Projects resulted in hybrid configurations shaped by local conditions, materials, labour, and political campaigns (Naughton, 2007). Thus, even top-down imitation became an adaptive process.

Reform Era Imitation: State Ambition and Grassroots Fever

The post-1978 reform era marked the most complex phase of imitation. On one side, the state engaged in deliberate, large-scale imitation to construct modern infrastructures: telecommunications, energy grids, stock exchanges, IP regimes, and corporate governance.

On the other side, grassroots society pursued spontaneous, often informal imitation, a phenomenon referred to as "foreign fever" (*chongyang meiwai* 崇洋媚外). Rural entrepreneurs and urban traders engaged in reverse engineering, adaptive creativity, and informal innovation (Keane, 2007).

This produced another paradox: whilst the state pursued systemic transformation, individuals pursued commercial gain. Society often appeared "more capitalist than capitalist," with unintended consequences, especially the erosion of collectivist ethics and the rise of individual ambition.

These entanglements between socio-technical systems and moral governance would later define China's digital transformation in the 21st century.

This historical discussion, in turn, opens onto the digital era, where imitation, adaptation, and innovation become most visible in socio-technical transformations, as discussed in Section 2.4.

2.4 Socio-Technical Specificities of Digital Transformation

If earlier phases of China's imitation unfolded in shipyards, steel mills, and Soviet-style ministries, the 21st century has shifted the arena of imitation to digital and data-driven technologies. These technologies do not merely replicate machines or institutions; they penetrate social life directly. They engage individuals at all levels, reshape information infrastructures, prompt new forms of governance, and generate novel global asymmetries.

It is here that imitation, adaptation, and innovation intertwine most vividly, producing the socio-technical divergence that defines China's digital transformation. In this shift, traceability and the quantification of the social emerge as foundational mechanisms. They do not simply manage risk; they construct the infrastructures through which future governance, morality, and collective life are enacted.

The concept of *socio-technical specificities* first emerged in my research on genetically modified (GM) crops, which became focal points of controversy in Europe under the precautionary principle. These debates often centred on imagined risks—some unknown, others "unknown unknowns", that science alone could not fully resolve. I argued that long-accumulated agricultural knowledge and socio-cultural experience were essential for understanding how technologies interact with social environments (Shen, 2010).

Extending this to digital technologies, each carries its own socio-technical fingerprint, shaping how imitation and adaptation unfold. Unlike traditional industrial technologies, digital platforms like mobile apps and e-commerce systems interact directly with daily life. They depend on continuous user participation, from payments to social media, and require cultural trust, behavioural alignment, and policy integration. Simultaneously, they introduce new, often invisible risks: data breaches, algorithmic bias, systemic vulnerabilities. These risks echo the epistemic uncertainties I explored in biotechnology governance (Beck, 1992; Wynne, 1992).

Thus, imitating a digital platform is never a simple act of transplantation. It must resonate with local social practices, regulatory frameworks, and the state-market relationship. In China, this has produced hybrid and adaptive forms of imitation, shaped by internal socio-technical conditions, such as a highly connected population and uneven development, and external ones, like U.S.-led restrictions on semiconductor and AI technology exports.

Crucially, this digital transformation makes society traceable. Every click, transaction, and movement becomes a data point within an infrastructure that can be acted upon, analysed, and fed back into governance systems (Zuboff, 2019). This quantification supports risk management and scaffolds a prospective socio-political order.

Western observers often dismiss Chinese platforms as mere copies of Silicon Valley giants. But this misperception ignores the divergence born of deep socio-technical entanglements. China's internet giants—Baidu, Alibaba, Tencent (BAT)—began by imitating their Western counterparts Google, Amazon, Facebook (GAF), yet evolved into super-infrastructures embedded in China's governance and daily life (Shen, 2019). With 1.4 billion users, these platforms are not only commercial utilities; they are governance tools, deeply intertwined with both state systems and individual lives.

In Callon and Latour's terms, these platforms function as *interessement devices*, mechanisms that align the interests of state, market, and individual (Callon, 1986; Latour, 2005). They have become living socio-technical ecosystems capable of adapting to global volatility. The convergence of traceability and quantification generates a participatory digital panopticon. Unlike Bentham's coercive model, this is voluntary: users contribute data in exchange for services, enabling behavioural guidance through digital affordances (Foucault, 1977; Lyon, 2018).

Governance increasingly operates through affordances embedded in code, designing the digital environment so that the preferred behaviour is the easiest path to follow. Here, individuals are not merely surveilled; they become nodes in a relational governance network, co-producing a moral and political subject through data (Latour, 2010). Governance increasingly operates not through laws but through code: interfaces and feedback loops subtly shape behaviour, forming what I describe as a collective-self.

This evolution is most evident in China's social credit system. The system's trajectory moved through three stages: (1) imitating Western financial risk models; (2) commercial adaptation via platforms like Alibaba's Zhima (*Sesame*) Credit, which integrated behavioural data into credit assessments; and (3) state appropriation of platform infrastructures into a national trust system, enabling new forms of regulation and behavioural management (Liang et al., 2018; Creemers, 2018).

Thus, imitation becomes infrastructural world-making. Data infrastructures enable not only governance but also the moral repair of society. They quantify behaviours, create feedback loops, and offer a model of governance by affordance, a form of soft power embedded in interfaces.

The COVID-19 pandemic crystallised this logic. Tools such as QR health codes, contact tracing apps, and big data epidemiology, often developed in the West, were adapted and scaled rapidly in China. Platform ubiquity (WeChat, Alipay), collective-action norms, and pre-existing infrastructures enabled seamless engagement. Western privacy-driven backlash was largely absent. Public compliance, platform-state collaboration, and techno-governance coalesced into an agile, responsive apparatus (Shen, 2020; Cong, 2021).

The pandemic revealed that data infrastructures can serve as society's nervous system, enabling dynamic adaptation during crisis. It established a new principle: governance through crisis, not merely despite it.

In global terms, these infrastructures also interact with international regimes such as Trade-Related Aspects of Intellectual Property Rights (TRIPS) and World Trade Organisation (WTO) IP norms. China's compliance coexists with strategic divergence. Datafication enables traceable innovation that bypasses individual privacy protection models entrenched in the West. It offers a pathway towards more inclusive governance, grounded in contribution, coordination, and relational accountability.

Thus, imitation has become a tool for world-making. What began as pragmatic copying has evolved into the creation of hybrid moral landscapes, where innovation, governance, and identity are co-produced in digital infrastructures.

The socio-technical dynamics of the digital age thus intersect with questions of global governance, particularly around intellectual property rights, the focus of Section 2.5.

2.5 Global Governance, Power, and the Paradox of Intellectual Property

Among the most consequential, and paradoxical, outcomes of China's long arc of imitation is its full-scale adoption of the global intellectual property (IP) rights system. What began as a compliance strategy has matured into a comprehensive legal and administrative infrastructure. Today, China is not only a major implementer of IP regimes but also a significant contributor to their global expansion (Shen, 2005). Yet this very success reveals a deeper structural contradiction.

Internally, the institutionalisation of IP rights has not only protected innovation; it has also intensified domestic competition, sometimes to a pathological degree (see Chapter 7). In key industries, IP has become a tactical weapon in intranational rivalries, undermining collaboration and eroding the spirit of collective development that defined earlier phases of China's industrial ascent. The internalisation of Western IP norms, instead of transforming global rules, has reshaped domestic behaviour in ways that reinforce market individualism and rivalrous logic (Shen, 2005).

This tension stems from a civilisational misalignment. civilizational The Western IP regime is grounded in liberal individualism, where knowledge is treated as proprietary, belonging to individuals or corporations. In contrast, Chinese epistemologies, like many non-Western traditions, regard innovation as a product of socialisation, lineage, and civic contribution. The global IP system, particularly under WTO and TRIPS, privileges industrialised nations' epistemic norms, contributing to polarisation rather than equitable knowledge distribution (Chang, 2002; Sell, 2003).

Increasingly, the global IP system appears to obstruct inclusive innovation. It restricts access to essential technologies, entrenches monopolies, and stifles collaborative problem-solving, precisely when planetary challenges demand coordinated, cross-border responses (Heller & Eisenberg, 1998).

At this transitional moment, China stands at a crossroads. It can continue deepening its investment in an IP system that reproduces past inequalities, or it can pioneer a post-IP global order (Gürkaynak et al., 2018). In the current context, China's emerging data infrastructures offer a novel alternative. By enabling traceability, the capacity to document, monitor, and validate innovation, datafication opens the door to non-proprietary recognition systems. Such systems could acknowledge contributions without enforcing exclusion, support coordination without commodifying knowledge, and foster more just architectures for global co-production (Latour, 2005).

However, realising this vision is fraught with difficulty. Domestically, China faces the challenge of crisis governance: balancing state power, market competition, and infrastructural experimentation amid profound uncertainty. Internationally, no single country can replace the IP system alone. What is needed is a new mode of global governance by affordance, a system that scaffolds cooperation across heterogeneous actors through flexible, participatory infrastructures. China could pioneer the infrastructural basis for a post-IP global order, one premised on traceability, quantification, and co-production.

Whether such a system can be actualised depends not only on technological capacity or geopolitical will, but on the willingness to reimagine the very ontology of innovation. In this light, China's experience may not be an anomaly, but a harbinger of new forms of infrastructural governance: participatory, traceable, and globally co-produced. These themes will be further explored in Chapter 9, which examines speculative horizons for a future socio-technical order rooted in relational ethics, technological reflexivity, and collective responsibility.

Conclusion

As the global intellectual property regime strains under pressures of geopolitical fragmentation and technological convergence, China's trajectory reveals both the possibilities and the limits of imitation. The internalisation of IP norms, once a marker of alignment with the Western institutional order, has produced contradictory effects. It has facilitated industrial upgrading and enabled participation in global value chains, yet it has also intensified domestic competition and reinforced a proprietary logic at odds with China's historical ethos of collective development.

This contradiction invites a deeper question: *What if the future of global governance lies not in the expansion of IP protection, but in its transformation?* The European Union's PRIME project (2005) identified the "anti-commons" phenomenon, where excessive IP fragmentation hinders innovation, and proposed a Co-operative Management of Intellectual Property Rights (CIPR) model to prioritise collective advancement over competitive exclusion.

China's experiments with datafication and traceability now provide an alternative epistemic and infrastructural foundation for such a vision. By embedding innovation and imitation within traceable, participatory networks, China's approach creates the potential for a new governance logic, one not grounded in exclusion and ownership but in relational accountability, collective participation, and recursive co-production.

These infrastructures do not merely manage behaviour; they configure the conditions for mass participation in innovation. They allow individuals, enterprises, and even states to become collective-selves, nodes within a socio-technical ecology bound by mutual recognition and shared responsibility.

In this light, imitation is no longer the opposite of innovation. It becomes one of its modalities. Imitative innovations, when embedded in traceable infrastructures, can drive inclusive and sustainable development. But this vision cannot be realised by any one country alone. It requires a new form of global governance by affordance: a system built on shared protocols, interoperable infrastructures, and distributed epistemic legitimacy (Amoore, 2013; Hilgartner et al., 2017).

Thus, the paradox of imitation may yet yield a productive transformation. If China can move beyond proprietary replication and towards building the infrastructural grammar of global co-production, its experience may not only reflect global norms but actively refashion them. In this emerging order, traceability, participation, and collective responsibility may supplant ownership, secrecy, and competition as the foundational principles of technological governance.

Chapter 9 takes up this perspective in full, exploring how the infrastructural conditions forged under crisis, amid fragmentation and experimentation, may be converging towards a new horizon of digital modernity, in which the future of global governance is not imposed, but co-produced.

3 Catch-up, Lessons from Two Paths

Preamble

My fieldwork in the early 1990s, carried out just as China's telecommunications sector was wrestling with both foreign technology transfer and indigenous innovation, became a microcosm of the country's broader trajectory of "*liǎng tiáo tuǐ zǒulù* (两条腿走路, walking on two legs)".

In late 1992 and early 1993, I embarked on my PhD fieldwork in China. This experience profoundly shaped both my intellectual outlook and my personal engagement with the subject of technological transformation. I was drawn to the stark contrast between China's soaring economic aspirations and the acute deficiencies of its telecommunications infrastructure, a sector then emblematic of national backwardness yet charged with modernisation dreams.

Over eight intensive months, I conducted 63 in-depth interviews across a wide spectrum of stakeholders: workers, engineers, senior managers, government officials, and research scientists. Key sites included Shanghai Bell, the Sino-Belgian joint venture responsible for localising the advanced System-12 digital switching system (see Section 3.3), and the Luoyang Telephone Equipment Factory (LTEF), the state-owned manufacturer of the indigenous HJD-04 system (see Section 3.4). Gaining access, especially to LTEF, required multiple journeys between Luoyang and Beijing and careful navigation of institutional gatekeeping and political sensitivities.

My research approach was adaptive and exploratory, constantly redefined in response to emergent insights. The fieldwork was far from straightforward. It became a deeply immersive experience, requiring strategic negotiation, sustained engagement, and continuous reflection. This groundwork laid the empirical foundation for my first book, *The Chinese Road to High Technology* (Shen, 1999), and shaped my enduring commitment to understanding the socio-technical entanglements of innovation in latecomer contexts.

From the angle of strategic imitation, adopting the most advanced Western technologies to build a modern telecommunications infrastructure, China's achievements were remarkable. Learning by doing extended from elite system designers, engineers, and technicians to low-skilled workers on shop floors, from software to basic components like screws, cables, and assembly-line tasks (see Section 3.3). The stories I documented conveyed a sense of glorious success.

Yet, in writing this book, I was constantly taken back to the individuals I had interviewed. Their excitement at the new opportunities was tempered by the bewildering logic of market competition. For many, the greatest challenge was not

https://doi.org/10.1515/9783110757576-009

foreign rivals but their own peers. Without a clear understanding of the emerging dual-track system, people competed by imitating one another, sometimes fairly, sometimes not. As one LTEF manager put it, “It’s not the way we would like to go, deep in our hearts, but it is ’a way’ against ’no way’. We have so many mouths to feed” (Personal communication, 22 April 1993). His words capture the common experience of the time. Competition-induced corruption and moral decline saddened many, even as they recognised its inevitability.

China’s utilitarian approach, *liǎng tiáo tuǐ zǒulù* (两条腿走路), stirred not only its industries but also the wider society. People were inspired by new opportunities but also learned that there was a heavy price to pay. This dual-track trajectory put the state before new challenges: managing institutional reforms, balancing the competing logics of planned and market systems, and confronting the proliferation of imitation in its many regulated and unregulated forms (see Section 3.5).

3.1 Introduction

Framing the Cases: Public Digital Switching Systems, the Heart of Telecommunications Infrastructure

Public Digital Switching Systems (PDSS) are central components of national telecommunication infrastructures. These systems act as the “traffic controllers” of telephone networks, automatically connecting callers to recipients and managing multiple simultaneous calls. They control how voice and data traffic are routed (directed through the network) across different locations, enabling fundamental services such as telephone calls, data transmission, and digital connectivity. Digital switching systems represented a major advance over earlier analogue systems. Whilst analogue switches used mechanical or electrical connections to physically link callers, digital systems converted voice into computer data, allowing more efficient routing and enabling features like call forwarding and conference calling.

In the 1980s and 1990s, when mobile communication was still nascent and the internet largely inaccessible in China, digital switching systems were the invisible backbone of modern communication. Without them, a society could not modernise its information infrastructure, let alone participate in the global economy.

This chapter focuses on two systems that became focal points of China’s efforts at technological catch-up: System-12, a sophisticated foreign platform introduced through the Sino-Belgian joint venture Shanghai Bell, and HJD-04, an indigenous system initiated by a domestic research institute and produced at the Luoyang Telephone Equipment Factory (LTEF). These systems represent two distinct routes into digital modernisation, one through international technology transfer, the other through local initiative and institutional negotiation.

China's Technology Choices

The introduction of System-12 and the emergence of HJD-04 must be situated within the broader reform-era principle of *liǎng tiáo tuǐ zǒulù* (两条腿走路), pursuing foreign technology transfer whilst simultaneously cultivating indigenous development. This dual strategy reflected the dilemmas of reform: China urgently needed advanced infrastructure, but it also sought to build domestic capabilities to avoid long-term dependence.

System-12 represented the foreign technology leg. Developed over eight years by Bell Labs in collaboration with European partners, System-12 consumed vast financial and human resources across the Atlantic. Yet its immaturity was soon apparent, particularly in software design. Unlike hardware, which could be standardised, the software of digital switches required extensive customisation for country-specific networks and for the diverse configurations of individual exchange offices. Eventually, Bell Labs decided to sell the system, thereby passing on both its promise and its limits.

For China, however, System-12's very newness was part of its appeal. A decisive consideration was that it incorporated cutting-edge microchips, specifically, Large Scale Integration (LSI) chips, advanced semiconductors that could pack thousands of electronic components onto a single chip. These represented cutting-edge technology that was precisely the kind of components restricted under COCOM-Coordinating Committee for Multilateral Export Controls sanctions (Cold War-era Western export controls on strategic technology to socialist countries). Choosing System-12 thus offered more than a switching platform: it provided an entry point into the semiconductor domain. This ambition was institutionalised in the creation of Shanghai Belling, a joint venture tasked with establishing local integrated circuit production. System-12 was therefore not just about telecommunications; it was a strategic bet on positioning China within the frontier of global electronics.

By contrast, HJD-04 exemplified the indigenous leg of the strategy. It did not begin as a state-sponsored project. At the time, the Ministry of Posts and Telecommunications (MPT) had invested in the DS series[7] as the official domestic line of

7 The DS series was launched by the Ministry of Posts and Telecommunications in the early 1980s as China's official domestic development programme for digital switching systems. Despite sig-

R&D. HJD-04 instead originated from the Centre for Information Technology (CIT), a military research institute redirected towards civilian applications. Led by Professor Wu Jiangxing, a computer design specialist, the team approached switching from a computational rather than a telecom perspective. This interdisciplinary framing enabled them to bypass entrenched traditions of telecom engineering, reconceptualising a digital switch as a large-scale computing system.

Through alliances with the Luoyang Telephone Equipment Factory (LTEF) and later the Posts and Telecommunications Industrial Corporation (PTIC), HJD-04 gradually moved from prototype to production. Its path, however, was fraught with institutional resistance. MPT, committed to its DS series, initially refused to recognise HJD-04. Only after multiple evaluations and political negotiations did it win official approval, eventually entering production in the early 1990s.

Both carried enduring implications: System-12 by linking telecom modernisation to semiconductor development, and HJD-04 by demonstrating the possibilities of indigenous coalition-building in an era of uncertainty.

Together, System-12 and HJD-04 reveal the logic of *liǎng tiáo tuǐ zǒulù* (两条腿走路). The former brought China face-to-face with the most advanced global technologies, despite their immaturity, whilst the latter embodied a domestic improvisation that leveraged interdisciplinary knowledge to meet local needs. Their broader significance will be drawn out in the comparative analysis at the end of this chapter. The following analysis examines first the System-12 case (Section 3.3), then HJD-04 (Section 3.4), before comparing their implications (Section 3.5).

3.2 Aspirational Imitation and the Desire for Modernity

The technological choices described above were not made in a vacuum. They were shaped by a powerful cultural and political undercurrent: the desire for modernity. French sociologist Gabriel Tarde provides a useful conceptual lens here. In his *Laws of Imitation* (1903), Tarde argued that imitation is the essential social action from which innovation proceeds. He emphasised what he termed the "imitation of the superior by the inferior" as a fundamental driver of social change. For latecomer societies, imitation is less a matter of passive copying than of aspiration, an active engagement with external models as a way of projecting new futures.

In reform-era China, this *aspirational imitation* was palpable. After decades of isolation, the West appeared both as a model and as a stimulus Technologies like

nificant investment, progress was slow and performance limited, making room for alternative initiatives such as HJD-04 (Shen, 1999, pp. 121–126).

digital switching systems embodied not just technical utility but also symbolic value: they represented efficiency, modernity, and global integration. Imitation in this context was not reducible to technical transfer; it was bound up with a collective longing to overcome backwardness and achieve recognition on the global stage.

This aspiration manifested across multiple layers of society. For policymakers, importing advanced systems like System-12 was a way to fast-track entry into the global technological order. For engineers and managers at Shanghai Bell, it provided exposure to international standards of design, quality control, and project management, knowledge that could be adapted and redeployed in Chinese contexts. For ordinary citizens, the spread of telephones transformed daily life: to own a telephone in the early 1990s was not merely convenient, but a marker of status and modern identity.

At the same time, *aspirational imitation* took different forms depending on the pathway. System-12 represented direct engagement with the most advanced Western practices. Its adoption was a form of *learning by emulation*, where Chinese actors observed, adapted, and sometimes contested the organisational routines and technical protocols imported alongside the system. The goal was not only to use the system but also to absorb its embedded socio-technical practices.

By contrast, HJD-04 illustrates a different mode of aspiration. Although not officially supported at first, the project was driven by a determination to demonstrate that a domestic alternative was possible. Its initiators at the Centre for Information Technology (CIT), led by Professor Wu Jiangxing, brought a computer engineering background into the traditionally telecom-dominated domain of switching. This interdisciplinarity allowed the team to bypass entrenched legacies and conceptualise the switch as a large-scale computing system rather than a conventional exchange. The full implications of this cross-disciplinary approach will be developed in later chapters, but it is important to note here that it exemplifies how *aspirational imitation* could generate novel pathways, rather than mere replicas, in latecomer innovation.

In both cases, imitation was not blind reproduction. It was mediated by comparison, negotiation, and selective appropriation. Chinese engineers and policymakers were acutely aware of their country's technological inferiority, but this awareness acted as a spur to action, not paralysis. They constantly asked: *What can we learn from foreign systems? What must we adapt to Chinese conditions? What can we create ourselves?*

From a Science and Technology Studies (STS) perspective, these cases highlight that the line between imitation and innovation is inherently unstable. System-12 and HJD-04 both began in imitation, one of foreign systems, the other of broad technical principles, but in practice they catalysed learning, institutional experimentation, and hybridisation. In this sense, imitation was not the opposite of innovation but its condition of possibility.

The desire for modernity thus played a dual role. It justified the pursuit of foreign technologies despite their immaturity, and it energised indigenous efforts that initially lacked official recognition. Both pathways were saturated with aspiration, but aspiration refracted through different institutional settings and technical traditions. Together, they show how imitation, when driven by desire and embedded in reform-era politics, became a productive force in China's technological transformation.

3.3 System-12 and the Joint Venture Experience

Joint Venture as a Socio-Technical Platform

In conventional thinking, technologies appear as finished artefacts: machines designed abroad, shipped, and then simply installed in the receiving country. Yet Science and Technology Studies (STS) show that technologies are not static objects but unfinished systems. They must be adapted, reconfigured, and continually maintained within specific social and infrastructural contexts (Fleck, 1993; Williams & Edge, 1996). This was particularly true for System-12, one of the most advanced public digital switching systems of its day, introduced into China through the Shanghai Bell joint venture.

The transfer of System-12 was not simply the delivery of equipment. It marked the beginning of a complex socio-technical journey in which engineers, managers, policymakers, and even end-users became entangled. At stake was not just whether the machines worked but how they could be made to fit into one of the most heterogeneous telecommunications environments in the world. Success required not only technical expertise but also contextual knowledge: understanding local practices, institutions, and expectations.

The institutional form chosen to mediate this transfer was the joint venture, a new experiment in China's reform-era economy. Shanghai Bell was established in 1984 as a joint venture between the Belgian company Bell Telephone Manufacturing Company (BTM), later absorbed into Alcatel, and the Ministry of Posts and Telecommunications (MPT), China's government body responsible for telecommunications. BTM held a 50 % share, whilst Chinese stakeholders, through MPT's industrial arm, the Posts and Telecommunications Industrial Corporation (PTIC), held the other 50 %.

For China, the joint venture model promised more than just access to imported technology. It offered a platform for structured technology transfer: production capacity, training of engineers, and exposure to advanced management systems. For BTM and Alcatel, it provided entry into a vast, underdeveloped market at precisely the moment when System-12 needed global expansion to recoup its enormous development costs.

The stakes were high. System-12 had taken more than eight years to develop and had consumed immense financial and human resources across Europe and the United States. By the time it was offered to China, it was a technology in need of a market. For China, it was a rare opportunity to gain access to advanced microelectronics, including Large Scale Integration (LSI) chips at the heart of the system, components that were otherwise restricted under the Coordinating Committee for Multilateral Export Controls (COCOM), the Cold War-era alliance of Western countries that regulated sensitive technology exports to socialist states.

In this sense, Shanghai Bell was more than a company: it was a laboratory of socio-technical entanglement. Its Belgian engineers and managers had to learn to work within China's unique institutional and cultural environment, whilst its Chinese engineers, many of whom initially felt daunted by the complexity of System-12, had to master unfamiliar technical routines and management practices. Each side had to adjust, compromise, and learn.

From the outset, therefore, the joint venture was never a neutral site. It was a vantage point where the politics of reform, the economics of international trade, and the technicalities of digital switching converged. It was simultaneously a production facility, a school of engineering, a diplomatic tool, and a testing ground for new forms of industrial organisation.

Win-Win Situations and the Political Economy of Transfer

Whilst the day-to-day life of Shanghai Bell centred on technical problem-solving and production routines, its very existence was the product of a delicate political economy of technology transfer. In the 1980s, at the dawn of China's reform era, joint ventures in strategic sectors were not simply business contracts. They were statecraft in action, combining diplomacy, industrial policy, and technological ambition.

China's Call for Partners

By the early 1980s, China's leadership recognised the acute backwardness of its telecommunications system. Catch-up required not only incremental upgrades but also access to the most advanced digital switching technology available. To that end, Beijing extended invitations to leading multinational corporations in Europe, North America, and Japan, hoping to attract joint ventures that would bring both capital and know-how.

Most companies were cautious. Some saw China as too politically risky; others were unwilling to part with cutting-edge technology. The exception was Bell Telephone Manufacturing Company (BTM) of Belgium, then part of the ITT/Alcatel group. For BTM, entering China aligned with its broader European expansion strategy, whilst also offering a chance to recoup the immense costs of System-12 development.

System-12 at a Crossroads

System-12 itself was a product of massive investment. Developed in the 1970s by Bell Labs under ITT, it had consumed more than eight years of research and billions of dollars. When ownership passed to Alcatel in the mid-1980s, the system needed new markets to justify its sunk costs.

China's interest came at the perfect moment. For Alcatel, securing a foothold in the world's largest untapped telecom market promised not only sales but a platform for global expansion. For China, System-12 was attractive precisely because it was new, modular, and chip-based, features that offered entry into domains otherwise restricted by Cold War technology controls.

The COCOM Barrier

The most sensitive issue was the Large Scale Integration (LSI) chip at the heart of System-12. At the time, semiconductor technologies were tightly controlled by the Coordinating Committee for Multilateral Export Controls (COCOM), a Cold War body of Western nations that restricted the export of "strategic" technologies to socialist states.

To move forward, diplomatic negotiations were required. The Belgian government took the lead, lobbying the United States and other COCOM members to allow an exception. These discussions were lengthy and fraught, reflecting broader tensions between Western governments that feared aiding China's technological rise and those who saw commercial opportunity.

Eventually, after nearly four years of negotiations, the restrictions were relaxed. Approval was granted for the transfer of LSI chip technology to Shanghai Bell. The justification was that the technology would be integrated into a monitored joint venture rather than transferred wholesale to China's domestic industry.

State Loans and Financial Engineering

Alongside diplomatic manoeuvres, financing was critical. The Belgian government extended a long-term loan to China, providing the capital required to establish Shanghai Bell's facilities. BTM, in turn, agreed to transfer not just assembly operations but significant production know-how, including chip integration and circuit board design.

This arrangement reflected the triangular nature of the deal: The Belgian state acted as guarantor, securing political approval. BTM/Alcatel provided technology and management expertise. The Chinese state, through the Ministry of Posts and Telecommunications (MPT) and its industrial arm the Posts and Telecommunications Industrial Corporation (PTIC), provided land, labour, and market access.

Production Quotas and Market Expansion

Initially, MPT attempted to regulate the number of different foreign digital switching systems allowed in China to avoid fragmentation. But international pressure, particularly from the United States during World Trade Organisation (WTO) negotiations, led to a gradual opening of the market to multiple foreign suppliers.

Even before that opening, however, MPT repeatedly raised production quotas for System-12 beyond the original plan, responding to explosive demand from provincial telecom administrations. By the mid-1990s, System-12 had become the dominant digital switch in China, and Shanghai Bell's revenues exceeded those of Alcatel's European operations.

Mutual Benefits

For Alcatel-BTM, the venture was highly profitable, securing a stable and expanding market just as System-12 was struggling in Europe. For China, the benefits went beyond the immediate expansion of telephone lines. The joint venture provided access to advanced chip technology, international engineering practices, and the organisational discipline of quality management.

This was the essence of the "win-win" arrangement: each side pursued its own interests, commercial profit for Alcatel, technological catch-up for China, yet the structure of the joint venture created a shared space where these interests aligned.

Analytical Reflection

From an STS perspective, Shanghai Bell exemplifies how technology transfer is never purely technical. It is entangled in global geopolitics, trade negotiations, and institutional bargains. The fact that System-12 entered China at all was the product of years of diplomatic lobbying, state loans, and compromises between national interests.

At the same time, the political economy of the transfer shaped the socio-technical dynamics inside Shanghai Bell. Belgian managers were aware that their presence in China depended on state-to-state agreements; Chinese engineers recognised that their access to advanced technology was mediated by political negotiation as much as technical capacity.

Thus, the joint venture was not just a site of technological adaptation but also a node in a global network of power, commerce, and diplomacy.

Learning by Doing and the Stage Machinery

Gabriel Tarde, in his *Laws of Imitation* (1903), distinguished between what he termed the "optical point" of imitation (see Section 2.2), where observers see only visible surface practices, and the deeper "stage machine," the hidden mechanisms revealed only through immersion and sustained practice. This distinction captures the trajectory of learning within the Shanghai Bell joint venture.

From Surface Routines to Hidden Mechanisms

In the early years, Chinese engineers largely operated at the "optical point." They observed Belgian experts, copied visible routines, and followed prescribed manuals. Many expressed modesty and even self-doubt in interviews, worrying that their limited exposure to advanced digital systems left them ill-prepared. Belgian staff often reinforced this perception by retaining control over sensitive processes, particularly in kernel-level programming.

Yet as daily operations unfolded, the limits of surface imitation became clear. Simply copying routines was not enough to resolve the unforeseen challenges of China's telecommunications environment. When systems crashed under heavy usage, when CAE software failed to adapt to local exchanges, or when quality issues disrupted production, Chinese engineers were forced to go deeper. They had to engage with the hidden mechanisms of the technology, working not only with what was visible but with what was originally off-limits.

The Emergence of Reciprocal Learning

Through this immersion, Chinese staff gradually moved into the "stage machine." They rewrote CAE software, learned to handle kernel processes, and adapted System-12 to environments far beyond those envisioned in Europe. These acts of deep learning transformed their status within the joint venture. No longer merely apprentices, they became co-producers of knowledge, shaping the future trajectory of the system.

At the same time, Belgian engineers were also forced into new learning. They encountered a telecommunications environment that defied their assumptions: overloaded public lines, heterogeneous infrastructure, and shifting regulatory standards. Troubleshooting in China required abandoning certain European habits and learning from local engineers who understood the social and technical texture of the network.

Thus, imitation was not one-way. It was reciprocal, producing new forms of expertise on both sides.

Learning by Doing as the Core of Joint Ventures

This process exemplifies the broader lesson of joint ventures as laboratories of learning by doing. Manuals and formal training could only take engineers so far. The real breakthroughs came from grappling with problems in practice, discovering the "stage machinery" of technology by working through its failures and adaptations.

For Chinese engineers, learning by doing provided not only technical mastery but also a new sense of agency. They discovered that foreign technologies, however advanced, were not infallible; they required local expertise to function in China. For Belgian engineers, learning by doing brought humility: they realised that local practices and conditions carried forms of knowledge just as valuable as formal technical expertise.

Analytical Reflection

From an STS perspective, the Shanghai Bell experience shows that innovation often emerges not from invention in isolation but from engagement with technologies in use. The process of working through breakdowns, blind spots, and quality disputes created new capacities on both sides.

In this light, Tarde's distinction helps us see that imitation was never passive. What began at the "optical point", copying visible routines, evolved into mastery of the "stage machine," where deeper mechanisms were revealed through practice. The joint venture thus became not a site of replication but of transformation, where both foreign and local actors advanced their understanding through entangled socio-technical learning.

Blind Spots: Hidden Design Assumptions and Embedding Social Reality

One of the most revealing episodes in the early history of Shanghai Bell was the discovery of a fundamental mismatch between the design assumptions of System-12 and the social reality of telephony in China. This episode nearly doomed the project in its infancy and stands as a vivid reminder that technologies are always embedded in particular social practices.

When System-12 was first introduced to Shanghai in the late 1980s, China's telecommunications landscape bore little resemblance to that of Western Europe or North America. Telephone penetration was among the lowest in the world, fewer than one line per 100 people in 1990 (IDRC & SSTC, 1997). Private household telephones were rare, especially outside elite urban residences. Instead, the backbone of urban telephony was the public telephone booth, a manned kiosk often operated by neighbourhood committees or local service centres.

These booths were not simply technical installations; they were social infrastructures. Staffed from early morning until late evening, they provided access to telephony in a communal, often noisy setting. Callers would line up, sometimes for hours, to place or receive calls. To reach recipients, booth staff used loudspeakers or sent runners into nearby alleys, calling out names in public spaces until the intended party emerged. Taking a call often meant excusing oneself from domestic tasks, changing clothes, and walking to the booth. Conversations unfolded in a collective atmosphere, observed by staff and neighbours alike.

From a design perspective, this created an extreme usage profile. In Western contexts, where System-12 had been conceived, each subscriber line was assumed to be active only intermittently, on average 0.1 Erlang (a telecommunications measurement unit where 1 Erlang equals continuous use for one hour), equivalent to six minutes of use during the busiest hour of the day. In Shanghai's public booths, however, demand was continuous. A single line might be in use 100 % of the time, or 1 Erlang per line, ten times the expected load.

The consequences were immediate and dramatic. In its first "cut-over" trial in Shanghai, the newly installed System-12 switch passed technical inspection but collapsed within minutes of real operation. Designed for sporadic private calls, it simply could not cope with the relentless demand of communal public telephony.

For over a year, Belgian engineers struggled to identify the cause. Their troubleshooting was thorough but ultimately fruitless, as they approached the problem within the design frame of European usage. Frustration grew, and confidence in the project waned.

The breakthrough came not from the foreign experts but from a Chinese engineer, who quietly pointed out that the problem lay not in hardware or software bugs but in the very assumptions built into the system's design. System-12 had been calibrated for one social world but was being forced to operate in another. The mismatch between design expectations and social reality was the true blind spot.

Once this was recognised, the solution became clearer: the system had to be reconfigured to match China's telephony patterns, not the other way around. The recognition was humbling for the Belgian engineers, who realised that their state-of-the-art system was not universally applicable. For the Chinese engineers, it was empowering: their intimate knowledge of local social practices proved indispensable to the adaptation of advanced foreign technology.

This episode underscores a key point in STS: technologies carry within them assumptions about their users and environments. When exported, these assumptions may be invisible until they collide with new social realities. The collapse of System-12 in Shanghai revealed how deeply telecommunication design had been shaped by Western norms of private ownership and intermittent use. Its resurrection depended on recognising and valuing the local socio-technical knowledge of Chinese engineers and administrators.

In interviews, some Chinese engineers admitted they had felt hesitant to voice their insights at first, given their limited exposure to such an advanced system. Yet once their perspective proved correct, they shifted the dynamics of collaboration within Shanghai Bell. Belgian and Chinese staff alike became more attentive to each other's knowledge. The blind spot had not only been technical; it was also social, rooted in asymmetries of confidence and authority.

The "Shanghai breakdown" therefore became more than a troubleshooting episode. It was a turning point in the joint venture, showing that successful technology transfer required recognising the interplay of technical design and social context. Far from being passive recipients, Chinese engineers demonstrated that they could diagnose and solve problems that Western experts had overlooked. The lesson would resonate throughout the subsequent trajectory of Shanghai Bell: that innovation in China would emerge not from wholesale copying, but from the fusion of imported systems with embedded local realities.

This episode underscored the importance of local knowledge for making imported technologies workable. For Shanghai Bell, it marked the beginning of a more grounded process of mutual adjustment, where technical expertise and contextual experience had to be combined if the venture was to succeed.

Adaptation and the Treasure Core of the System

The Shanghai breakdown was a wake-up call. It showed that technological artefacts cannot be separated from the contexts in which they operate. But solving that immediate crisis was only the beginning. To make System-12 truly work in China required years of painstaking adaptation, not only to technical conditions but also to the institutional, cultural, and environmental contexts of Chinese telecommunications.

The Layered Architecture of System-12

At the heart of System-12 lay the **kernel**, a closely guarded "treasure core" that managed operating functions such as memory, database operations, system maintenance, and error handling. Above this were two layers of application software: Country Development Engineering (CDE) tailored System-12 to national regulations, signalling standards, and infrastructure conditions and Customer Application Engineering (CAE) customised software for each exchange office, with specific trunk line connections, subscriber volumes, and local transmission quality.

In Europe, these layers were relatively stable because infrastructures were standardised. In China, however, each layer demanded constant reconfiguration.

Adapting to China's Complex Telecommunication Environment

Chinese networks were fragmented and uneven, featuring a patchwork of analogue and digital exchanges from different generations. In some regions, poor line insulation caused interference during humid summers, whilst in northern provinces, extreme cold affected signalling reliability. Voltage fluctuations were common, requiring additional safeguards.

One engineer recalled how heavy monsoon rains in southern provinces degraded copper transmission lines to the point that switches struggled to maintain connections. System-12 had never been tested in such conditions in Europe, and its software had to be modified to tolerate signal "noise" far beyond Western norms.

In addition, signalling protocols varied between local networks. Where Western systems assumed uniformity, Chinese operators encountered a mosaic of standards. This meant CAE software could not simply be imported; it had to be rewritten for each exchange office, adapting to the idiosyncrasies of local configurations.

From Patching to Re-writing: The CAE Breakthrough

At first, Shanghai Bell engineers relied on CAE software provided by BTM in Belgium. But it proved cumbersome and ill-suited to China's demands. System configuration was slow, error-prone, and could not keep pace with the rapid rollout of exchanges across the country.

Chinese engineers began by writing small patches to fix immediate issues: correcting data mismatches, automating repetitive steps, and adjusting algorithms for heavy line usage. These patches accumulated into more than 300 separate modifications. At that point, the team concluded that piecemeal fixes were no longer sufficient; they needed a full rewrite of CAE.

This decision was momentous. Only a few years earlier, Chinese engineers had felt insecure handling System-12's complexity, often deferring to their Belgian counterparts. Now they took ownership of one of the most critical layers of the system. The rewritten CAE not only worked more smoothly but also automated the conversion of specifications into programmed data tapes, speeding up deployment and reducing system downtime.

Exporting Chinese Software: The SESA Deal

The new CAE package did not just solve Chinese problems; it outperformed its European counterpart. Alcatel's Spanish subsidiary, SESA (Sociedad Española de Sistemas de Automática), had struggled to adapt CAE to its own needs. After repeated failures, SESA turned to Shanghai Bell, requesting access to its rewritten version.

Initially, Shanghai Bell's management hesitated. The joint venture agreement restricted unilateral technology exports. But when BTM's own attempts to improve CAE failed, SESA returned with a more serious offer. In late 1992, a deal was struck: Shanghai Bell would license its CAE software in exchange for an annual business commitment worth US$1.8 million over five years (Shen, 1999, p. 117).

The symbolism was striking. A Chinese joint venture, once a passive recipient of foreign technology, had now become a technology provider to Europe. This marked a reversal of the usual direction of innovation flows and signalled the beginning of China's role as a contributor, not just consumer, of advanced telecommunications software.

Learning from Environmental Complexity

The very conditions that made China's telecommunications infrastructure so challenging also became a school of learning. Engineers had to grapple with fluctuating transmission quality, mixed signalling systems, and rapidly changing regulatory demands from the Ministry of Posts and Telecommunications (MPT).

As a result, they developed exceptional problem-solving skills and an ability to innovate under pressure. By the early 1990s, Shanghai Bell engineers were performing 80 % of CDE work themselves, ensuring compliance with constantly updated MPT standards. Belgian engineers increasingly took on supervisory roles.

For Chinese engineers, this transition represented a profound confidence shift: from hesitant apprentices to indispensable system architects. For their Belgian counterparts, it was a lesson in humility, proof that local engineers, when confronted with complex conditions, could produce solutions that advanced the technology as a whole.

Analytical Reflection

The adaptation of System-12 demonstrates that technology transfer is never linear. It is a process of negotiation, improvisation, and sometimes reversal. What began as dependence on foreign expertise evolved into Chinese contributions that were indispensable to the global System-12 ecosystem.

The treasure core of the system, the kernel, remained under Belgian control. But in mastering and transforming the application layers, Chinese engineers learned to navigate the hidden "stage machine" (Tarde, 1903). They discovered that the key to technological success lay not only in hardware or design but in the capacity to adapt systems to local realities.

In this sense, China's infrastructural complexity, once viewed as a liability, became a source of strength. It forced Chinese engineers into a steep learning curve, which in turn accelerated their move from imitation to innovation.

Transferring and Developing Expertise

One of the central promises of the Shanghai Bell joint venture was technology transfer. But in practice, this was never a simple act of handing over designs. It was a long and contested process of building expertise, learning not only how to assemble parts but how to master the inner workings of the technology.

Hardware and Software Training

At the outset, Belgian managers and engineers organised intensive training sessions for their Chinese counterparts. These covered assembly-line operations, component testing, and quality inspection for hardware, as well as programming routines and troubleshooting for software.

The aim was to enable Chinese engineers to manage Customer Application Engineering (CAE) and Country Development Engineering (CDE) independently. This meant not only learning how to use pre-prepared tools but also acquiring the conceptual knowledge to adapt and extend them.

Belgian staff often emphasised discipline and precision, values they considered essential to high-quality production. For Chinese engineers, who came from a background of looser state-enterprise practices, this was a demanding adjustment. Yet the exposure to these standards laid a foundation for more rigorous approaches to engineering in China.

The Treasure Core: Accessing the Kernel

Perhaps the most sensitive area of knowledge transfer concerned the system kernel, the "treasure core" of System-12. This kernel contained the fundamental operating system routines, database management, and error-handling logic. In theory, access to it was tightly restricted; foreign companies were reluctant to expose such knowledge, both for reasons of intellectual property and competitive advantage.

Yet in practice, the complexity of China's network made it impossible to adapt System-12 successfully without Chinese engineers learning at least part of the kernel. Over time, through persistent involvement in troubleshooting and adaptation, Chinese staff began to penetrate the deeper layers of the system. By the early 1990s, they were not merely patching code at the application level but engaging with kernel processes to optimise performance in demanding local conditions.

This was a milestone in the joint venture's trajectory. What had begun as guarded training turned into deep transfer of expertise, creating a generation of Chinese engineers who could handle the very heart of an advanced digital switching system.

Developing Local Capacity

As engineers gained confidence, Shanghai Bell began to take on more responsibility. By 1992, Chinese staff were handling 80 % of all CDE tasks: adapting System-12 software to comply with the MPT's frequently updated national standards. Belgian staff increasingly took on supervisory or advisory roles.

This shift was not only technical but also institutional. It signalled the gradual localisation of expertise, in which Chinese engineers were no longer mere recipients of knowledge but active participants shaping how System-12 evolved in practice.

Shanghai Bell also became a training ground for broader skills: project management, systems integration, and cross-cultural teamwork. Engineers learned to communicate across linguistic and institutional boundaries, blending Belgian discipline with Chinese flexibility. For many, this experience was transformative, preparing them for later leadership roles in China's expanding telecommunications sector.

Management and Organisational Learning

Technology transfer also extended to management. The joint venture's organisational structure mirrored that of BTM, with departments for productivity, quality control, engineering, and marketing. Chinese managers were expected to adopt these practices, which contrasted sharply with the looser hierarchies of traditional state-owned enterprises.

For example, Shanghai Bell established a Department of Productivity and Quality Management in 1989, led initially by a Belgian specialist. Its function was to introduce systematic quality assurance routines, including statistical sampling and defect tracking. These methods were new to most Chinese staff, who were accustomed to reactive inspection rather than proactive prevention.

Adopting these routines was not easy. Chinese engineers and managers often struggled with the cultural assumptions behind them, for instance, the insistence on rejecting entire batches of components that failed international standards, even when local suppliers considered them acceptable. Yet over time, these practices took root, instilling new expectations about what counted as "quality."

STS Perspective: Knowledge Transfer as Co-Production

From an STS perspective, what occurred at Shanghai Bell was not one-way "transfer" but co-production. Knowledge was shared, negotiated, and redefined in practice. Belgian staff learned that success in China required flexibility, patience, and attentiveness to local realities. Chinese staff learned to master foreign systems by intervening in their hidden layers and by incorporating new routines into their own work culture.

In the process, Shanghai Bell became not just a factory but a school of socio-technical learning. It trained a generation of Chinese engineers in advanced digital switching whilst simultaneously reshaping Belgian engineers' understanding of what it meant to operate in a vast, heterogeneous, and rapidly changing environment.

Quality, Culture, and the Perception of Standards

If mastering the software layers of System-12 represented one frontier of learning, another emerged in a domain that might appear more mundane: quality control. For Shanghai Bell, quality was not a side issue but a central challenge. The success of the joint venture depended not only on installing advanced switches but also on ensuring that every component, from microchips to screws, met the standards required for reliable long-term operation.

The Problem of Quality in Rapid Expansion

In the late 1980s and early 1990s, Shanghai Bell scaled up production at a remarkable pace. Demand for digital switching systems far outstripped initial projections, and the Ministry of Posts and Telecommunications (MPT) repeatedly raised production quotas to meet the surge in telephone subscribers.

Yet rapid expansion came at a cost. Local suppliers struggled to keep up, both in volume and in consistency. Belgian managers, accustomed to strict European quality regimes, often found the components delivered by Chinese factories unsatisfactory. Even minor defects, slightly uneven threading, inconsistent surface finishes, or microscopic flaws in contacts, were flagged as unacceptable, since they could undermine system reliability.

The Screw Incident

One episode, recounted by several interviewees, crystallises the issue. Shanghai Bell placed an order for a large batch of screws, a simple and standardised component. Detailed specifications were provided, and the local supplier delivered the order on time. To the Chinese manufacturer, the screws were perfectly serviceable: they matched the standards the company had used for years and had passed domestic inspection.

But when the screws arrived at Shanghai Bell, Belgian quality controllers rejected the entire batch. The threads were deemed too shallow, the surface finish too rough, and the dimensions slightly off. From a European engineering perspective, these flaws were unacceptable; they threatened the long-term stability of the system.

The supplier was stunned. His company had a long-standing reputation in Shanghai and had never faced such complaints. To him, the demand for rejection seemed arbitrary, even insulting. The screws, after all, had always worked fine in Chinese applications.

During an interview, the Belgian quality manager reflected on this incident whilst gazing out of his office window overlooking Shanghai's ageing residential quarters. His conclusion was striking: *"Quality is perceptive."* (Personal communication, 15 March 1993).

By this, he meant that quality is not an objective measure but a socially and historically shaped concept. What counted as "acceptable" in one environment was considered inadequate in another.

Cultural Dimensions of Quality

The screw incident exemplified how quality standards are shaped by cultural and institutional histories. In Belgium, a long tradition of precision engineering and customer accountability had produced stringent norms. In China, decades of central planning, resource scarcity, and looser tolerances had fostered a different culture: one that valued meeting production targets and "good enough" reliability.

These divergent traditions clashed in the joint venture. Belgian managers insisted on strict compliance with international standards, sometimes rejecting entire batches of components. Chinese suppliers, used to more flexible criteria, were frustrated by what they saw as excessive rigidity.

For Shanghai Bell's Chinese staff, this created difficult tensions. On the one hand, they recognised the necessity of higher standards for advanced telecommunications equipment. On the other, they empathised with local suppliers, who lacked both the equipment and the mindset to meet European tolerances immediately.

Institutionalising Quality Control

In response, Shanghai Bell created a Department of Productivity and Quality Management in 1989, led by a Belgian specialist. Its role was not only to inspect but also to train suppliers and employees in systematic quality practices. Statistical process control, defect tracking, and preventive maintenance became part of daily routines.

Over time, these practices took root. Chinese engineers began to internalise the idea that quality was not just about meeting quotas but about ensuring reliability across time and space. Suppliers, too, gradually adjusted, upgrading equipment and adopting stricter controls.

Yet the cultural dimension never disappeared. What counted as a "defect" continued to vary depending on perspective. The process of aligning expectations was as much about mutual negotiation as about technical improvement.

Analytical Reflection

The screw incident illustrates that quality is not an abstract technical property but a socio-technical construct. It is defined by expectations shaped through culture, history, and institutional frameworks. For Shanghai Bell, achieving "quality" meant bridging two worlds: the European insistence on precision and the Chinese tradition of pragmatic adequacy.

From an STS perspective, this episode shows that technology transfer involves not only hardware and software but also epistemic frameworks, ways of knowing and valuing what counts as acceptable. The challenge was not only to raise Chinese standards but also to create shared understandings between foreign and local actors.

In this sense, quality control at Shanghai Bell became a site of cultural as well as technical learning. It reshaped how Chinese engineers thought about reliability, precision, and accountability, whilst also teaching Belgian managers that "quality" could not be assumed to have universal meaning. It had to be negotiated across contexts.

3.4 HJD-04 and the Politics of Indigenous Innovation

The Hybrid Alternative: Interdisciplinarity as a Pathway

In the 1980s, China's Ministry of Posts and Telecommunications (MPT) placed its confidence in the DS series of digital switches as the official domestic R&D line. The DS programme embodied the state's planned approach to indigenous development: centrally directed, institutionally sanctioned, and heavily resourced. Against this backdrop, the emergence of HJD-04 was highly unusual. It did not begin as part of the state plan, nor did it come from within the telecommunications establishment. Instead, it arose from the Centre for Information Technology (CIT), a military-affiliated research institute better known for computer systems than for telephone exchanges.

The project's intellectual architect was Professor Wu Jiangxing, a computer scientist with a background in digital architectures and military computing applications. Wu and his colleagues approached switching from a very different epistemic starting point. Where telecom engineers typically saw a switch as a specialised piece of telephony hardware, Wu conceived of it as a large-scale computer. Switching, in his view, was essentially a matter of data processing: inputs, outputs, and control logic could be organised through modular architectures, just as in computing.

This re-imagination was not a superficial metaphor but a genuine design principle. Drawing on modular computing logics, Wu's team sidestepped many of the traditional skills, routines, and incremental learning pathways that had constrained indigenous PDSS efforts in China. Instead of painstakingly replicating foreign telecom systems component by component, they treated the switch as a programmable system that could be built from the ground up using computing expertise.

The HJD-04 became a cornerstone of China's telecommunications network in the 1990s, marking a significant step in the country's digital transformation (Shen, 1999, pp. 12–56; Shen, 2019). Unlike earlier analogue automatic switches, the HJD-04 was a digitally controlled software-based exchange, allowing China to leapfrog outdated technologies and enter the digital era. Its distributed modular design offered scalability and adaptability, enabling exchanges to expand based on local demand and infrastructure capacity. The result was a system that was smaller, simpler, modular, and significantly cheaper than its foreign counterparts. It required fewer resources to install and maintain, could be deployed incrementally in modest local exchanges, and scaled up as needed. In a country like China, where infrastructure varied enormously between dense urban centres and remote rural areas, the system was particularly well-suited. China's telecommunications networks were often a patchwork of outdated technologies, including manual exchanges, step-by-step switches, and electro-mechanical systems, interspersed with newer digital elements. In these regions, transmission lines were frequently bare open wires, making them vulnerable to fluctuating signalling conditions due to weather and environmental factors. Whilst sophisticated foreign systems like System-12 struggled in such unpredictable network conditions, the HJD-04 proved more resilient, delivering reliable connectivity to underserved areas and playing a crucial role in expanding China's telecommunications reach (Shen, 1999, pp. 142–148).

The advantages of this approach soon became clear. HJD-04 was designed and prototyped in just 18 months, a pace that astonished many in the sector, given that comparable systems typically required years of iterative development. In interviews, engineers emphasised both the boldness and the outsider status of the CIT team. One research scientist remarked to me:

"CIT did not know the old traditions of telecom, but maybe that was their strength. They thought differently. Where others copied, they reimagined." (Personal communication, April 1993).

This interdisciplinarity, the crossing of disciplinary boundaries between computer science and telecommunications, was the hallmark of HJD-04. It generated what might be called a hybrid alternative: a system that was neither a product of telecom orthodoxy nor a simple derivative of computing, but a novel synthesis of the two.

Yet this hybrid position also entailed risks. Without MPT's official endorsement, the project operated in a precarious space, lacking the institutional legitimacy enjoyed by the DS line or by foreign joint ventures such as Shanghai Bell. To many in the telecom establishment, HJD-04 was an oddity, a peripheral experiment at best.

Nevertheless, the project pressed ahead, propelled by the conviction that China's technological future required more than imitation or state-sanctioned orthodoxy. By treating switching as a computational problem and leveraging knowledge from outside the telecom field, HJD-04 embodied the creative potential of interdisciplinarity in latecomer contexts. It was a hybrid pathway, opening a space for indigenous innovation even amid institutional resistance.

Building Alliances: LTEF as a Socialist Enterprise in Transition

For the HJD-04 project to move from concept to reality, the Centre for Information Technology (CIT) could not work alone. Wu Jiangxing's team brought vision and technical expertise in computer-based architectures, but they lacked the industrial base to produce and deploy a working switch. This made the search for a manufacturing partner essential.

After an aborted attempt by the Luoyang Telephone Equipment Factory (LTEF) to form a joint venture with Belgium's Bell Telephone Manufacturing Company (BTM), the factory turned to CIT. This unlikely partnership, between a military research institute and a struggling state-owned enterprise, gave HJD-04 its industrial foundation.

LTEF was more than just a production facility; it was a microcosm of China's broader reform-era dilemmas. Established in the 1970s under the Ministry of Posts and Telecommunications (MPT), LTEF had once thrived under state protection, producing crossbar telephone switches based on designs freely transferred from a state R&D institute. But by the mid-1980s, with China's "foreign technology fever" introducing advanced Public Digital Switching Systems (PDSS) from abroad, demand for LTEF's low-tech products collapsed. The factory faced the challenge of survival in a newly competitive market.

Like many state-owned enterprises, LTEF functioned not only as a workplace but as a self-contained community. Located on the outskirts of Luoyang, it provided housing, schools, a hospital, post office, guest houses, canteens, even its own bus services. Workers joked to me during fieldwork that, *"Here we have everything except for a crematorium"* (Personal communication, April 20, 1993). When I stayed in the factory's guesthouse and dined with staff, I experienced firsthand this community-like atmosphere, where enterprise and livelihood were deeply intertwined.

By 1992, LTEF employed more than 2,700 people, with a total community of around 7,000 when families were included. Jobs were permanent, and managers were expected to act as caretakers as much as supervisors. They arranged hospital visits, organised community support during family crises, and even played matchmaker when employees struggled to find partners. The factory director described his role as one of both industrial leadership and social stewardship.

But market reforms strained this model. Digital switch production was capital-intensive and required far fewer workers, leaving LTEF with a bloated workforce and mounting financial pressure. Mass layoffs were politically and morally unthinkable. As the director explained to me:

"The market economy is the market economy, whether you call it socialist or capitalist. But I have lived with these people for years, I can't bear to see them jobless. If we just kick them out after they have served this country for so long, where is justice and humanity?" (Personal communication, 22 April 1993).

To cope, LTEF experimented with an internal labour market. Surplus workers were paid 70 % of their salary and reassigned to temporary or long-term work elsewhere, or enrolled in training courses to prepare them for redeployment.

Younger engineers often worked long hours and returned in the evenings to refine designs. These measures reflected what Deng Xiaoping famously called *mōzhe shítou guò hé* (摸着石头过河, crossing the river by touching the stones), a pragmatic, adaptive approach to reform in uncertain times.

For HJD-04, LTEF's involvement was decisive. The factory provided not only manufacturing capability but also a workforce willing to adapt, experiment, and learn. Collaboration was not easy, factory staff had to grapple with CIT's unfamiliar computing-based design logics, whilst researchers had to translate conceptual models into workable hardware. But through this co-production process, HJD-04 gained credibility as a real system rather than a research experiment.

In this sense, LTEF was both a partner in technological innovation and a case study in institutional transformation. Its struggles reflected the broader challenges of reform-era state-owned enterprises: balancing social responsibility with market competitiveness, and finding pragmatic pathways between old structures and new imperatives. For Wu Jiangxing and his team, LTEF was not simply a manufacturing base but an institutional ally navigating the same uncertain terrain.

Market Pressures and Distorted Competition

During China's economic reforms, market competition was celebrated as the driving force of technological dynamism. In practice, however, the case of HJD-04 reveals a more ambivalent picture. Market reforms stimulated survival strategies and efficiency improvements, but they also undermined the collaboration needed to consolidate indigenous alternatives.

By the time HJD-04 entered the scene, foreign PDSS such as System-12 had already secured over half the Chinese market (Shen, 1999). Provincial telecommunications administrations, under pressure to expand services quickly, often preferred foreign systems, which carried prestige and appeared more reliable. Against this backdrop, HJD-04 struggled for attention and credibility.

The Luoyang Telephone Equipment Factory (LTEF), the earliest and most experienced producer of HJD-04, could have led a national effort to pool expertise, improve product quality, and scale up production. Instead, fearing loss of market share, LTEF resisted wider collaboration with other domestic manufacturers. Knowledge was withheld rather than shared. As one engineer explained in retrospect, "we were competing with each other when we should have been competing with the foreigners" (Personal communication, April 1993).

Market competition also drove LTEF into unfamiliar and ethically ambiguous territory. Its marketing team began adopting aggressive sales strategies to persuade provincial purchasing officials. At first, this meant hosting banquets and organising sightseeing tours of Luoyang, the ancient capital of many dynasties. But before long, these practices escalated into fully sponsored trips to destinations such as Hong Kong and Thailand. Such incentives, inconceivable under earlier socialist management, became an accepted way of "doing business." These market-driven adaptations reveal the double-edged nature of reform. Competition pushed firms like LTEF to innovate, but it also introduced behaviours that undermined trust, discouraged cooperation, and distorted the technological trajectory.

Institutional Conflicts and Bureaucratic Fragmentation

If the market presented one obstacle, the bureaucratic politics of the telecommunications sector presented another. Within MPT, officials were reluctant to recognise HJD-04 because of the ministry's heavy investment in the DS series. Acknowledging HJD-04's viability risked undermining this official line of indigenous development. As a result, HJD-04 was subjected to multiple rounds of evaluation and field testing, where political negotiation mattered as much as technical performance.

Institutional rivalries extended beyond MPT. Different HJD-04 producers were affiliated with different ministries, some with MPT, others with the Ministry of Machinery and Electronics Industry (MMEI). Instead of cooperating, these enterprises became rivals under competition, each seeking to protect their own institutional sponsors. MPT resisted allowing HJD-04 systems produced under the Ministry of Machinery and Electronics Industry (MMEI) to be integrated into the national network, fragmenting the project's potential and weakening domestic capacity.

A parallel case illustrates the same problem: Shanghai Belling, a joint venture semiconductor company established in 1988 by Shanghai Bell and the No. 14 Shanghai Radio Factory. Originally intended to manufacture custom LSI chips for System-12, it struggled with poor quality. The lack of coordination between its Ministry of Machinery and Electronics Industry (MMEI) parent and its Ministry of Posts and Telecommunications (MPT)-linked partner might be one of the issues. By contrast, Shanghai Bell, with unified support and clearer institutional channels, flourished. These contrasting trajectories underscore how ministerial fragmentation hindered indigenous innovation.

Recognising the inefficiencies of this system, the State Council intervened. In 1995, it created *Great Dragon* (*Jùlóng* 巨龙), a national telecommunications entity designed to consolidate HJD-04 production across ministries. But bureaucratic resistance and entrenched rivalries blunted its effectiveness. Only in 1998 did the government take decisive action, merging the Ministry of Posts and Telecommunications (MPT) and the Ministry of Machinery and Electronics Industry (MMEI) into the Ministry of Information Industry (MII), in an attempt to streamline oversight and eliminate duplication.

Analytical Reflection: Indigenous Innovation as Improvisation

HJD-04's success lay not only in institutional perseverance but also in its technical architecture. By leapfrogging over traditional telecom design and reimagining the switch as a computer system, it achieved a modularity and simplicity that matched China's infrastructural realities far better than the bulky, complex systems developed elsewhere. Its trajectory demonstrates how latecomer innovation can thrive by exploiting interdisciplinarity to bypass stages of technological evolution, producing solutions that are "good enough" yet transformative in their local setting.

The HJD-04 story illustrates how indigenous innovation in reform-era China was less a matter of planned progress than of improvisation under uncertainty. Emerging outside the official DS series programme, initiated by a military computer science team rather than telecommunications specialists, and developed through alliances with a struggling state-owned enterprise, the system was a hybrid creation. Its distinctiveness lay not in its technical superiority over foreign systems, but in the way it mobilised interdisciplinary knowledge, institutional negotiation, and pragmatic adaptation to carve out a space within China's shifting telecommunications landscape.

Two lessons stand out. First, interdisciplinarity mattered. By reframing the switch as a large-scale computer, Wu Jiangxing and his team sidestepped entrenched telecom orthodoxies and accelerated the development cycle. This move highlights how borrowing from adjacent fields can generate fresh solutions, particularly in latecomer contexts where conventional knowledge regimes are already dominated by foreign incumbents.

Second, indigenous innovation was never a purely technical affair. The fate of HJD-04 depended on institutional recognition, market positioning, and political negotiation. LTEF's role demonstrates how innovation was co-produced within reform-era enterprises that were themselves navigating contradictions between socialist responsibility and market discipline. MPT's repeated resistance showed how bureaucratic loyalties could slow adoption even when technical viability was proven. And the rivalry with System-12 underscored how legitimacy was shaped by symbolic hierarchies as much as by engineering.

From an STS perspective, HJD-04 exemplifies innovation as co-production. It was the outcome of interactions between disciplines (computer science and telecom), organisations (CIT, LTEF, PTIC, MPT), and social practices (factory communities, marketing tactics, bureaucratic negotiations). Far from being linear, its trajectory was improvisational, constantly adapting to pressures from market competition, institutional silos, and shifting state priorities.

In this light, HJD-04's legacy is not simply that of a "successful" or "failed" project. Rather, it is a reminder that indigenous innovation in latecomer contexts thrives in the margins, in the spaces where improvisation bridges gaps between disciplines, institutions, and markets. It was precisely in these liminal zones, rather than in the centre of official planning, that China's technological creativity flourished.

3.5 Comparative Analysis: Lessons from Two Paths

Two Legs, One Trajectory

System-12 and HJD-04 exemplify the two legs of China's catch-up strategy, representing contrasting but complementary trajectories. They also reveal the interplay between foreign transfer and indigenous initiative. System-12 brought China face-to-face with the most advanced global technology, providing a platform through the Shanghai Bell joint venture for day-to-day interaction, technical training, managerial innovation, and production engineering, exposing engineers to international standards and learning through entangled collaboration. HJD-04, by contrast, emerged from a bottom-up, cross-military-civil sector initiative, embodying the improvisational creativity of domestic actors. Through interdisciplinarity and persistence, HJD-04 carved out a space for indigenous innovation.

Neither path was straightforward, and neither can be judged by static criteria of success or failure. Instead, both show how imitation, when embedded in aspiration and practice, became a productive force, not the opposite of innovation but its precondition. Together, the cases suggest that China's technological rise was not the result of a single model but of plural trajectories. The joint venture and the indigenous initiative were not rivals but interdependent elements of reform, each exposing different socio-technical entanglements and historical contingencies.

Imitation as a Collective Endeavour in an Era of Transition

What united both cases was the centrality of imitation. Both pathways reveal that imitation was not confined to senior officials or research institutes. It was a mass participatory practice, involving engineers, factory managers, provincial telecom bureaus, suppliers, and even users. In Shanghai Bell, Chinese engineers learned by rewriting CAE software, by absorbing quality management routines, and by gradually penetrating the "treasure core" of System-12. In Luoyang, the HJD-04 team leveraged computing knowledge from military research to reimagine switching, whilst factory workers and local administrators contributed to its adaptation and deployment.

This collective dimension underscores that imitation is not passive copying by elites but an active process of engagement across social strata. Reform made imitation both possible and precarious. Market competition opened space for experimentation but also introduced distortions. LTEF, facing pressure to survive, withheld knowledge from other domestic producers to protect its market share, whilst provincial administrators often preferred the prestige of foreign systems. Salesmanship edged into banquets and sponsored trips, signalling how quickly socialist norms gave way to market improvisations. At the ministerial level, rivalry between the Ministry of Posts and Telecommunications (MPT) and the Ministry of Machinery and Electronics Industry (MMEI) produced duplication rather than synergy.

Imitation, in other words, unfolded within a hybrid order, part socialist legacy, part emerging market. The result was intense internal competition, fragile collaboration, and uneven outcomes. Yet even in this fragmented environment, imitation remained a powerful engine of learning: Chinese engineers acquired not only technical know-how but also organisational and managerial knowledge that would shape later successes.

The Experimentalist State: Keeping Balance of Multiple Seesaws

Hovering above both cases was the state, confronted with unprecedented challenges. Both cases illustrate that the Chinese state was not a monolithic planner but a pragmatic experimentalist. It could not simply command, nor could it leave matters to the market. Instead, it acted as it could, adjusting by trial and error, seeking balance rather than perfection.

System-12 was treated "as if" it were indigenous, ensuring rapid diffusion despite its foreign origins. At the same time, subsidies were extended to encourage the purchase of HJD-04, regardless of whether it was made by private or state-owned companies, under MPT or MMEI, keeping the domestic project alive long enough to gain legitimacy. When fragmentation threatened to undermine the sector, the State Council created *Jùlóng* (巨龙, Great Dragon) in 1995 and later merged

MPT and MMEI into the Ministry of Information Industry in 1998, attempting to consolidate oversight and reduce duplication.

The lesson is not of a state that planned everything in advance, but of one that improvised in its own way, containing destructive competition, sustaining multiple pathways, and steering reform without losing control.

Geopolitics, Co-Production, and Historical Ironies

Neither System-12 nor HJD-04 can be understood apart from the shifting geopolitics of the late Cold War. The lifting of COCOM sanctions opened the way for System-12's microchip transfers, a breakthrough that epitomised co-production: China gained access to frontier technology, whilst European firms gained access to a vast new market where they gained experience for operating in an environment that differed substantially from home. For a moment, it seemed possible that technological development could be a genuine win-win.

Young engineers expressed this optimism vividly: China, they told me, could become "a tree in the global forest", learning, contributing, and growing as part of a larger ecosystem. Yet history carried its ironies. By prioritising chip imports over the uncertain path of indigenous development, China deepened its dependency. Decades later, new waves of sanctions on semiconductors exposed the long shadow of those choices. What was once a triumph of pragmatic adaptation has become a cautionary tale of strategic vulnerability.

Conclusion

Viewed together, System-12 and HJD-04 reveal that China's technological catch-up was never linear. It advanced through plural trajectories, foreign transfer and indigenous initiative, joint ventures and factory improvisation, woven together by imitation, negotiation, and state experimentation. Success and failure were always provisional, shifting with time and perspective.

The deeper lesson is that in latecomer contexts, innovation is rarely born from grand design. It emerges from co-produced improvisations, shaped as much by institutions and geopolitics as by technology itself. In this sense, imitation was not a sign of weakness but the generative ground from which China's innovation capacity was built. The two cases foreshadow themes that recur throughout this book: the blurred boundaries between imitation and innovation, the state as an experimentalist regulator rather than a central planner, and technological catch-up as a process of improvisation rather than linear progress.

4 A Dilemma for All

Preamble

My exploration of Linux and software piracy in the early 2000s mirrored China's experiments with intellectual property: both my research and China's reforms revealed the entanglement of ideals of openness with the realities of lock-in and critical mass.

At the beginning of 2003, I returned to China to explore the development of the Linux open-source operating system. I had long been fascinated by software developers, often called "hobbyists" or "hackers" in the West, who were driving the open-source movement. Projects like Linux, the GNU initiative, and the Apache Web Server, along with the "copyleft" concept pioneered by Richard Stallman at MIT (Stallman, 1999; Raymond, 1998), convinced me that a technological revolution was underway.

Having lived in Europe, I was accustomed to the idea that all technologies and creative products with commercial value came with a price tag. In contrast, Linux was offered as a free PC operating system, a radically inspiring concept. Enthralled by its potential, I purchased a Linux installation disk for less than £50 and installed it on my own computer. Yet I soon realised that I could not integrate it into my daily work, since I already relied on Microsoft Windows, the system I was most familiar with.

Compared to Microsoft Windows, the Linux operating system was free or required only a minimal fee. The copyleft framework encouraged users to study, modify, and share the software, offering what I believed was an ideal solution for developing countries, especially with the anticipated expansion of personal computers (Stallman, 1999; Weber, 2004). I envisioned a future where this model might democratise technology, enabling access and innovation on an unprecedented scale.

By the late 1990s, major multinational corporations such as IBM, Oracle, and Intel had publicly announced their support for Linux and open-source software. In the West, many regarded Linux as the "people's software," a grassroots technological movement (Smith, 2000). This fuelled my curiosity about how China might seize this unique opportunity, adapting Linux to produce innovative and unexpected outcomes (Shen, 2005a).

What I encountered, however, was a different reality: the power of critical mass (see Section 4.3). The widespread sale of pirated Windows discs in China was not an act of intellectual resistance, nor a deliberate rejection of state calls to protect intellectual property. It was simply a collective act of pragmatism, tak-

https://doi.org/10.1515/9783110757576-010

ing advantage of the new computing technologies available. Although Linux may have been the "better" technology by expert criteria, Microsoft's systems created a lock-in effect by amassing the overwhelming majority of users. For me, this was an exciting learning moment: the entanglement of technology and social practice had produced a synergy that sustained one technology whilst marginalising another, effectively creating a de facto standard, contrary to the intentions of both state planners and technical elites (see Section 4.2).

The different ethics of knowledge sharing between China and the West was also striking. I began to wonder how the top-down imitation of Western science and technology could extend to the embrace of the IP protection system and its cultural underpinnings. How far would China go? Revisiting this research today, it is clear that commercial companies adopt diverse strategies to secure market share and revenue. Intellectual property protection is one such strategy, but its significance must be differentiated across technologies (see Section 4.4). Protecting public interest requires careful case-by-case management, which in turn depends on the availability of infrastructures for visibility and traceability.

4.1 A Wrong Presumption

Upon conducting field research in China, I quickly realised that reality did not align with my expectations. Whilst numerous projects, funded by both the state and private companies, were working on local adaptations of Linux, and many programmers and academics shared my enthusiasm, the widespread adoption I had envisioned simply did not materialise. Companies offering free Linux-based operating systems bundled with Chinese office software reported limited uptake. Many users who initially installed these systems soon abandoned them due to a lack of technical expertise to troubleshoot issues. The technical challenges of Linux adoption were particularly acute for non-technical users who lacked access to the support services commonly available for proprietary software. The problem was especially pronounced in smaller cities, counties, and rural areas, which were key target markets for one of the state-owned companies. Even in large cities and government organisations, where Linux adoption was officially required, Microsoft Windows remained dominant in practice.

What I observed instead was the rampant use of pirated Microsoft Windows operating systems. Illicit copies were widely available, openly sold in black markets, and could be purchased from street vendors on compact discs. Windows was the default operating system installed on personal computers by individuals and even organisations. Simultaneously, Microsoft was actively pursuing legal action, securing victories in court against major companies for violating intellectual property (IP) regulations (People's Daily, 1999). These high-profile cases were still a topic of conversation at dinner tables when I arrived.

It was at this juncture that my interest in IP protection took root. This period saw intellectual property issues gaining significant media and government attention. Even state media frequently reported China's lack of IP protection and Western portrayals of China as the world's leading violator of IP rights through large-scale technology theft (Yang, 2003). Microsoft's legal victories in China represented some of the first successful IP enforcement actions by a foreign company in Chinese courts. Yet at the grassroots level, only a limited number of Chinese people had acquired familiarity with the term "intellectual property."

The term "intellectual property" translated to Chinese as *zhīshì chǎnquán* (知识产权) means "ownership or rights of creation of knowledge". The concept was alien to most Chinese people at the time. Indeed, it is hard to imagine how Chinese (or any other) society could have arisen if throughout several thousand years of history had knowledge been strictly privately owned. Nevertheless, people were eagerly adopting Western ideas, not only technologies but also concepts of protecting technology-related IP. Some Chinese scholars diligently tried to demonstrate with evidence that social norms and practices in ancient China were similar to this IP protection (Shen, 2005a).

Working in management schools, I witnessed China's rise as the top destination for foreign direct investment. Concurrently, an influx of academic papers, aligned with media reports, emphasised the supposed link between weak IP protection and reduced investment and technology transfer (Maskus & Penubarti, 1995; Park & Ginarte, 1997). The dominant argument suggested that without strict IP enforcement, developing countries would struggle to advance technologically and achieve economic growth. Yet this conclusion stood in stark contrast to my research on China's past experiences with technological catch-up.

The World Intellectual Property Organisation insisted that IP protection promotes innovation and knowledge creation. My investigation in China sought to critically examine the claimed causal relationship between IP protection and innovation, and explore the complications surrounding this policy prescription, particularly from a developing country's perspective, with China serving as a compelling case study (World Trade Organisation, 2003).

Already a Heated Debate About Intellectual Property (IP) Protection

At the time of my research, the global structure of IP ownership showed a stark divide. On one side were the powerful multinational enterprises (MNEs) and their host developed countries, which held the majority of IP rights. On the other side were developing countries, which had limited IP assets to protect and were eager to learn from the West, thus often being perceived as major potential violators of international IP regulations.

A common critical argument was that stringent IP protection could significantly hinder developing and underdeveloped countries from acquiring the technological know-how necessary for industrialisation and economic growth (Chang, 2002; Drahos & Braithwaite, 2002). This led to the theoretical controversy about whether there was a positive link between IP protection and the acquisition of technological capabilities in developing countries? Some argued that stronger IP protection could remove barriers to foreign investment and technology transfer, fostering innovation. Others feared that global IP harmonisation would disproportionately benefit developed economies whilst restricting developing nations' access to essential technologies. In response, some developing countries, along with academic scholars, proposed measures to mitigate the anticipated negative impact of strict IP enforcement.

At this time, my primary interest was in open-source Linux, which led me to focus specifically on software-related IP issues, including copyright and the copyleft framework. I immersed myself in academic literature on the subject, particularly the ongoing debate surrounding IP protection in developing countries. It became increasingly clear that the push to strengthen IP protection on a global scale was largely driven by the interests of multinational corporations. Whilst these companies sought to expand into emerging markets by outsourcing manufacturing, they also faced growing concerns about technology leakage. Protecting their intellectual assets became a top priority, fuelling efforts to enforce stricter IP regulations worldwide.

IP and Developing Countries (DCs)

The issue of IP protection emerged alongside the rapid expansion of globalisation, driven by multinational enterprises (MNEs) competing to enter new markets. This coincided with a wave of economic transitions in many developing countries, including former socialist bloc nations. Throughout this era, numerous countries, particularly those in Eastern Europe, previously part of the Soviet Union and Warsaw Pact, sought to join the World Trade Organisation (WTO). One of the key preconditions for WTO membership was adherence to international IP protection standards. Aligning the IP regimes of developing countries with those of the developed world became a central objective, as major technology holders in developed economies sought stronger safeguards for their intellectual assets in emerging markets.

In 1995, the WTO introduced the Trade-Related Aspects of Intellectual Property Rights (TRIPS) agreement, setting the pace for global IP harmonisation. Under TRIPS, all WTO members were required to implement minimum standards of IP protection, extending beyond traditional areas such as patents and trademarks to newer fields, including software (World Trade Organisation, 2003).

Governments in many developing countries, including Brazil and Mexico in Latin America, China, India, Vietnam, and Indonesia in Asia, as well as several Eastern European nations, worked to rapidly build or upgrade their IP protection systems. The prevailing assumption was that since strong IP protection had contributed to technological and economic growth in developed countries, replicating such mechanisms at home would be a necessary step for development.

Despite these efforts, most developing countries still fell short of meeting the IP protection standards demanded by MNEs and Western economies. Countries such as China frequently appeared on the "top offenders" lists compiled by the United States Trade Representative (USTR) and international organisations advocating strict IP enforcement, such as the Business Software Alliance (BSA) and the International Federation of the Phonographic Industry (IFPI). According to a 2003 BSA study on software piracy, regions outside North America and Western Europe had an average piracy rate exceeding 50 %, with Vietnam, China, and Indonesia identified as the worst offenders (Business Software Alliance, 2003). The software piracy rate was defined as the proportion of business application software installed without a proper licence.

In practice, IP regimes in developing countries remained weak. The primary issue was the limited number of domestic IP rights holders. Additionally, enacting IP laws was one thing; effectively enforcing them was another. Some countries inherited their IP frameworks from former colonial rulers, whilst others implemented IP laws under international pressure. In both cases, enforcement mechanisms were often inadequate. Several factors contributed to this challenge: a shortage of IP expertise in academic institutions, a lack of trained legal professionals in national litigation systems, and, perhaps most crucially, low awareness and understanding of IP rights among key stakeholders, let alone the general public (Leesti & Pengelly, 2002).

Overall, as I entered the field, my central concerns were twofold: Could the IP protection mechanisms originally developed in the West genuinely benefit developing countries like China? And if so, could a country like China, which had no tradition of IP protection, successfully establish and enforce a strict legal regime? I believed that the new international initiative of open-source Linux software and the copyleft legal framework would be more suitable for China. As my fieldwork progressed, these initial questions evolved, leading me to reassess the very assumptions behind them.

4.2 Case Studies

Software Piracy in China

Throughout my fieldwork, purchasing a pirated disc, whether for music, video, or software programs, cost between 5 and 12 yuan RMB (approximately US$1–2), with slight variations depending on city location (Shen, 2005a). The price was largely determined by the cost of copying materials onto a compact disc. Vendors selling pirated software often operated from registered businesses within electronic shopping malls or designated street markets in cities and towns. Whilst publicly offering licensed and locally produced products, they kept unauthorised foreign software CDs hidden under the counter.

I was astonished by the vast range of products available when I was allowed into the backroom of a small shop. The selection included computer games, plug-in applications, internet software, desktop office applications, professional design tools, and even entire operating systems. Most pirated software CDs were of poor quality and often failed to work properly. Yet, given their low cost, customers could afford to purchase multiple copies from different vendors until they found one that functioned.

According to a study released by the US Business Software Alliance (BSA) and the Software & Information Industry Association, 95% of China's newly installed business software in 1998 was pirated. The 2003 BSA report estimated that in 2002, China's software piracy rate stood at 92%, the second highest in the world after Vietnam. For the first time, China, driven by the rapid expansion of its economy, was identified as the country with the largest financial losses due to software piracy, estimated at US$2.4 billion in 2002 (Business Software Alliance, 2003). BSA's methodology for calculating losses from piracy assumed that each pirated copy represented a lost sale at full retail price, an assumption widely criticised by economists.

I could see how widespread piracy was in China and agreed with this assessment. Yet the report about financial losses was misleading. Most Chinese people who did not buy the expensive Microsoft software systems could not afford them. In 2001, Microsoft released Windows XP operating system and upgraded its Office suite to Microsoft Office XP. The full version of the former cost about US$300 and the latter about US$600.

Since its economic reforms, the Chinese government had worked rapidly to establish an intellectual property (IP) protection framework, passing a series of IP-related laws (iSinoLaw Research Centre, 2001). This legal development occurred in several phases.

In the early phase of IP legislation during the 1980s and early 1990s, China enacted its first comprehensive trademark regulation, the Trademark Law, in 1982, which took effect on 1 March 1983. This was followed by the Patent Law, adopted in 1984 and later amended in 2000, though it notably excluded computer programs. The Copyright Law, which took effect on 1 June 1991, aimed to bring China closer to international standards.

During the 1990s, China also acceded to multiple international IP agreements. These included the Paris Convention for the Protection of Industrial Property in 1992, the Berne Convention for the Protection of Literary and Artistic Works on 15 October 1992, the Universal Copyright Convention on 30 October 1992, the Patent Cooperation Treaty on 1 October 1993, and the Nice Agreement on International Classification of Goods and Services on 15 April 1994 The Trademark Law was subsequently amended on 22 February 1993, granting trademark owners stronger legal rights.

Under mounting pressure from the US government, which repeatedly threatened trade sanctions, and in response to the requirements for WTO accession, China took increasingly stringent measures to combat domestic piracy.[8] The government established IP research institutions and organised workshops and seminars for senior officials to enhance their legal expertise in IP rights and protection. In an unprecedented move, public hearings of IP court cases were widely broadcast to raise public awareness. Authorities also conducted high-profile crackdowns in major cities, with police raids confiscating pirated software CDs, which were then publicly destroyed. In many cases, businesses involved in piracy were forcibly shut down, without formal legal proceedings.

Determining whether government actions effectively raised Chinese people's awareness of IP protection was challenging. I once saw a policeman purchasing pirated discs in a shop. He explained that his four-year-old son loved watching children's videos, and he regularly bought from that vendor because the discs were of reasonably good quality (Shen, 2005a).

I couldn't help but wonder whether this same policeman would participate in official raids on black markets for pirated goods. For many Chinese people, such crackdowns seemed like a pointless waste, as the government indiscriminately destroyed entire stockpiles of discs, regardless of whether they contained pirated or legally produced content.

China was diligently rebuilding its legal system from scratch to meet Western expectations for IP protection. Nevertheless, as many observers noted, the funda-

8 U.S. trade pressure, including threats of sanctions, played a crucial role in accelerating China's IP reform efforts.

mental challenges surrounding China's weak IP regime were deeply rooted in its cultural traditions and legal framework despite legislative efforts (Alford, 1995; Yang, 2003). Enforcement remained problematic due to inefficiencies in the court system, administrative offices, and most critically the attitudes of the public and businesses towards intellectual property (Shen, 2005a). Popular support for IP protection was largely absent, and the systemic issues ran too deep to be resolved through legislative quick fixes alone.

Microsoft's Legal Victories and Market Strategy

Microsoft established its representative office in Beijing in 1992, which later became Microsoft (China) Ltd. in 1995. Over time, the company expanded its presence, opening offices in Shanghai and Guangdong and steadily increasing its investments in China.

Outside China, Western media frequently portrayed Microsoft as a major victim of China's weak IP enforcement. However, Microsoft dominated the Chinese market, holding an estimated 95 % market share. Due to rampant software piracy, revenue from individual user sales accounted for only about 10 % of its total software earnings in the country (Kanellos, 2002).

China was the world's leading OEM computer manufacturer, with mass production driving down PC hardware costs. In China, one could purchase a PC without built-in operating system for about 1,000–2,000 yuan RMB or even lower, whilst having a set of licensed versions of Microsoft Windows and Office software cost at least approximately 6,000 yuan RMB, triple the price of the hardware itself (Shen, 2005a, p. 29). Much PC hardware was sold separately from operating systems, especially the non-branded ones, many of which were shipped without pre-installed software. As a result, most individual users opted to install pirated versions of Windows and Office rather than pay the high licensing fees.

China was the second or third-largest PC market in the world, and Microsoft's Windows operating system was installed on approximately 97 % of all computing devices, reflecting its near-monopoly status across the globe. Recognising the scale of the piracy problem, Microsoft initially took an aggressive approach to protect its investments. The company hired local staff to pay unannounced visits to large businesses and organisations to inspect their office computers. Unsurprisingly, many of these companies were found to be using unauthorised copies of Microsoft software.

Microsoft's crackdown on piracy led to one of the first high-profile IP lawsuits in China. In May 1998, the company successfully sued Beijing Hai Si Da Science and Technology Development Company and Beijing Min An Investment Consulting

Company for copyright violations (Lewis, 2001). According to People's Daily (18 December 1999), the two Chinese companies were ordered to pay Microsoft 790,000 yuan (about US$95,000) in compensation and issue public apologies in designated publications. This legal victory, the first of its kind in a foreign-related IP case since the founding of the People's Republic of China, was likely approved by the Chinese government, signalling a shift towards stricter IP enforcement.

Whilst Microsoft's victories were welcomed by Western media, governments, and multinational enterprises (MNEs), they did little to improve the company's public image in China. Despite Microsoft China's claim that its primary goal was to raise awareness about IPR and educate consumers about the value of software, many Chinese viewed its pricing policies as unjustifiable (Shen, 2005a, p. 30).

Public Perception: The Case Against Microsoft

To many Chinese consumers, Microsoft's pricing strategy was a major point of contention. Many young Chinese software developers felt that its high prices and proprietary restrictions stifled creativity and innovation, making it difficult for local developers to compete.

Through both formal interviews and casual conversations, I encountered widespread scepticism about Microsoft's actions. One common sentiment was:

"Why should we pay such high prices for Microsoft products when the company has already made billions (US$30 billion at the time) from its software monopoly in wealthier markets?" (Personal interview, 2003.[9]

Another frustration was tied to China's role in global computer manufacturing:

"Our cheap labour has contributed to producing computers for the global market, yet they charge us the same high prices as richer countries" (Shen, 2005a).

These remarks reflected a deep sense of economic disparity, where consumers in a developing country were expected to pay prices set for wealthier nations, despite their role in producing the very technology they struggled to afford. Public frustration was evident when Microsoft lost a 1.5 million yuan (approximately US$181,000 at the time) lawsuit in another piracy-related case, a ruling that was widely cheered amongst Chinese consumers.

9 I conducted a range of interviews, which captured widespread resentment about pricing disparities between developed and developing markets.

Around the same period, Mr Liu Bo (*Liú Bó* 刘博), who served as Vice General Manager of Microsoft (China) Co., Ltd. and the Director of OEM Department for Microsoft Mainland and Hong Kong regions, left Microsoft to run Chinese Linux Red Flag as President and CEO of Zhongke Hongqi Software Technology Co., Ltd. Microsoft (China)'s former general manager, Ms. Juliet Wu (*Wú Shìhóng* 吴士宏), became a heroine after resigning from her position and wrote a memoir, "Flying Against the Wind" (《逆风飞飏》) (Wu, 1999), criticising Microsoft's pricing policies and arrogant attitudes in China.

Chinese consumers understood why the government wanted to push IP protection, but many were unwilling to follow the rules. One vendor in an electronic shopping mall voiced the sentiment directly:

"Authentic Microsoft products are simply out of reach for most Chinese consumers," he told me. "More and more people are buying computers for home use. Young people buy PCs for themselves, whilst parents buy them for their only child, hoping they will master computing skills to stay competitive in school and future jobs" (Personal interview, 2005).

This vendor, who only sold software, proudly explained his business strategy:

"I don't do music or video DVDs, only software discs, by word of mouth. Good quality ones... everyone in here knows. I have a good reputation for it" (Personal interview, 2003).

His justification was simple: "I am a parent and not rich, but I want my son to have a workable computer. It's a necessity rather than a luxury." Then, as if to prove a point, he added: "Ask any government official, if they are parents like me, they would agree with me too" (Personal interview, 2005).

At this time, living standards in China were still low, and the market was highly price-sensitive. Buying a licensed Microsoft product costs perhaps as much as a month's salary for an average office worker (Smith, 2000). Whilst PC prices gradually decreased, making them increasingly affordable household goods, the high price of software meant that for many Chinese, buying pirated copies felt like a necessity rather than a crime.

Beyond software piracy, Microsoft also faced serious security concerns worldwide. The company was criticised for alleged hidden backdoors in its software, raising cybersecurity concerns in both developed and developing countries.

Despite these challenges, Microsoft's biggest long-term threat was the rise of the global "open-source" movement and the emergence of Linux as an alternative to the Windows operating system.

Linux in China: Open-Source Momentum, Market Competition, and Government Dynamics

Linux began gaining recognition in China in 1998 and saw rapid growth from 2000 onwards (Marketing News, 2002). Its development accelerated significantly, advancing both operating systems and applications. Many believed that the free software/open-source philosophy aligned with China's socialist ideals, framing Linux as "the people's software". With a combination of grassroots enthusiasm, government backing, and interest from major international IT players, initiatives emerged from diverse communities, including software developers, universities, research institutions, and private enterprises. Soon after, China became one of the world's strongest advocates for Linux.

Xteam (*Chōnglàng* 冲浪), founded in February 1998, was China's first Linux R&D group, established by enthusiastic software developers working in rough conditions with limited resources. Despite this, on 1 March 1999, they released Xteam-Linux Chinese Version 1.0, the first-ever Chinese Linux distribution, selling 100,000 copies in four months. In the following year, they released Chinese Version 3.0 and subsequently developed Linux server OS for internet services, e-commerce and SMEs. XteamLinux 4.0 included versions for desktop PCs and server administrators.

The Chinese government saw Linux as a strategic alternative to proprietary software, particularly Microsoft Windows, for several key reasonsSecurity concerns and technology dependency were paramount: adopting Linux would lessen reliance on Microsoft, ensuring greater domestic control over critical IT infrastructure. There were also significant economic advantages, as a Linux desktop OS cost only 98 yuan RMB, compared to over 3,000 yuan RMB for Microsoft Windows. To promote Linux adoption, the Ministry of Information Industry established an Open Source Alliance to support Linux adoption (Marketing News, 2002).

Linux's appeal extended beyond government circles. China's strong software developer community, leading universities, and key IT companies all played important roles in Linux adoption and localisation. Competition between them became intensified. For example, Xteam, which was strong at the beginning, struggled to compete with larger, government-backed players and eventually ceased operations as a commercial entity.

Meanwhile, China Software & Service Co., Ltd., a state R&D institute, together with the Software Institute of the Chinese Academy of Sciences, developed COSIX, a Chinese UNIX-based OS and released COSIX32 Linux V1.0 in September 1999, followed by multiple desktop and server versions. The Software Research Institute of the Chinese Academy of Sciences also set up another project, Red Flag Linux, which became a commercial company launching Red Flag Software Co. Ltd. in August 1999. The former Vice General Manager of Microsoft (China) Co., Ltd., Mr Liu Bo, took the role as CEO of Red Flag.

In the early 2000s, both CS&S Linux OS and Red Flag Linux Desktop software became key forces in China's Linux ecosystem and won major government contracts, including e-government platform contracts. My personal interviews with programme developers and high-level managers of these companies, including Mr Liu Bo at Red Flag and Mr Han Naiping at CS&S, showed their determination and confidence in open-source software development. This was confirmed by the results of a survey carried out by Evans Data Corp. in China in July 2002, which suggested that Chinese developers favoured Linux and were strongly confident about using Linux for mission-critical applications. A significant number of programmers in China were beginning to develop applications for Linux. The survey also showed that the level of confidence in open-source operating systems was greater in China compared to North America (Evans Data Corp., 2002).

4.3 Critical Mass and Network Effects

The contrasting trajectories of Microsoft and Linux in China converge on a crucial insight: infrastructure depends on critical mass. Microsoft achieved this infrastructure, through informal, even illegal channels, whilst Linux, despite formal state backing, never did.

Critical mass here is not just a quantitative threshold, but a qualitative turning point. It marks the moment when a technology begins to sustain itself, when it attracts developers, standardises practices, builds social support systems, and becomes embedded in everyday life. Microsoft reached this point through sheer ubiquity, largely driven by mass piracy. Linux never crossed this threshold.

In this sense, piracy did more than violate IP law, it functioned as a mass literacy programme, embedding Microsoft systems into the daily routines of users and developers alike. The state's formal support for Linux, by contrast, lacked the necessary user base to generate comparable feedback loops.

The divergence between Microsoft and Linux reveals a broader misalignment of rationalities. The Chinese state acted strategically, promoting Linux as a tool of digital sovereignty. Yet this top-down logic failed to align with the practical logic of users, who prioritised ease of use, application availability, and peer support.

Microsoft, paradoxically, benefited from this misalignment. Whilst users flouted IP norms, and the state pressed for enforcement, Microsoft adapted, converting informal usage into de facto standardisation. The company thrived not because of aligned strategy, but because of a convergence of divergent actions: the state's legitimacy project, the users' need-driven practices, and the firm's infrastructural recalibration.

Linux, by contrast, suffered from formal alignment without practical traction. It represented the state's ideals, but lacked a social base. Without users, even state-supported alternatives with technical merit can wither.

The Software Lock-In Effect

Despite the growth of Linux, it never reached critical mass. Linux failed to generate the volume of users necessary to establish feedback loops, support networks, or application ecosystems. Whilst Linux was legal, flexible, and ideologically consistent with state aims, it was structurally fragile. It remained isolated, technically viable, but socially marginal. The absence of mass uptake proved fatal to its infrastructural potential.

Linux's openness, its core strength in theory, became a practical liability. Without standardisation or strong user communities, openness translated into uncertainty and inconsistency. In an environment where users valued functionality and familiarity, the decentralised and fragmented nature of Linux made it appear unreliable. In contrast, Microsoft offered a coherent experience, even if illegally obtained.

Linux failed not only because Microsoft was dominant, but because it lacked the conditions to become infrastructure. Without user mass, without community, and without reinforcement, Linux remained a peripheral project. Its failure underscores a larger lesson: the lock-in effect helped Microsoft to take a dominant position in the market.

From a traditional economic perspective, the situation might appear paradoxical: Microsoft's dominance emerged from market failure, whilst Linux failed despite strategic support. If we shift the lens from markets to infrastructures, the picture clarifies.

Piracy enabled Microsoft to dominate because it allowed users to engage, learn, adapt, and build routines. This created the conditions for network effects, where each additional user enhanced the value of the system for others. Linux, lacking that foundational base, could not benefit from such dynamics.

The lesson is clear: copyright protection and suppressing piracy are not the only pathways to market success (and as this case shows, may not be the best strategy) when it comes to infrastructure formation. What matters is whether the system gains traction among users, creating the momentum required for it to persist and evolve.

These dynamics carry broader implications for digital strategy and policy.

4.4 Discussion and Reflections

When I conducted this fieldwork, the main debates regarding adopting the WTO TRIPS IP protection regime centred around several key issues. One heated debate related to developing countries was whether weak IP protection would deter foreign direct investment in the country. The other was the emergence of open-source software accompanied by the free software movement and novel copyleft legal framework, which was supposed to provide the best opportunity for developing countries to adopt and excel without depending on proprietary software like Microsoft.

Whilst these debates emphasised institutional and legal architectures, they often overlooked a key shaping force: the actions and preferences of ordinary users, the masses, who adopted, adapted, or rejected systems based on immediate needs, not formal rules.

The case study in China exhibited a range of complex issues, and the research did not provide straightforward answers. The paradoxical phenomenon in China was especially complicated by China's tradition that did not have an equivalent conception of "intellectual property," not to mention legal framework to protect intellectual properties.

In this gap between official policy and local practice, the masses played a constitutive role in shaping technological infrastructures. Their widespread use of pirated Microsoft software, despite legal risks, created a base of functionality, familiarity, and learning that formal actors would later depend on.

As research outcomes, I produced two papers. The early paper "Developing Country Perspectives on Software: Intellectual Property and Open Sources, A Case Study of Microsoft and Linux in China" (Shen, 2005b), focused on the benefits of open-source Linux and argued against the high hopes of promoting Linux software system and copyleft concepts. The second paper "A Dilemma for Developing Countries in Intellectual Property Strategy? Lessons from a Case Study of Software Piracy and Microsoft in China" (Shen, 2005a) critiqued the view that a weak IP regime like China would deter foreign direct investment and argued there are many issues that need to be taken into consideration. Other issues become clear with hindsight.

The Paradoxical Phenomenon in China

The case studies of Microsoft and Linux in China reveal a paradoxical phenomenon in the country's approach to intellectual property protection. Whilst China appeared committed to aligning with Western IP frameworks, rampant software piracy persisted, shaping market outcomes in ways that contradicted the intended goals of these reforms.

Software piracy, despite violating IP laws, played a crucial role in entrenching Microsoft's dominance in China. Widespread illegal copying allowed Microsoft products to become the de facto standard, creating an informal infrastructure through uncoordinated collective action by millions of users. Simultaneously, the Chinese government promoted open-source software to reduce dependency on foreign proprietary technologies, yet Linux-based alternatives struggled to achieve mass adoption because Microsoft's ecosystem had already become deeply embedded in everyday workflows. Even in government offices where Linux was officially required, Microsoft products remained widely used due to compatibility concerns and established user habits. These "user habits" were not incidental but system-shaping: accumulated through classroom learning, peer support, and informal IT help, they constituted the very infrastructure the state was trying to regulate.

This paradox underscores a fundamental contradiction: whilst a weak IP regime facilitated rapid software adoption, it also impeded the growth of indigenous alternatives, creating a technological landscape where foreign monopolies thrived under conditions that were theoretically unfavourable to them.

Software as Socio-Technical System Understanding the Distinctive Social and Technological Characteristics of Software Systems

The case studies of Microsoft and Linux in China highlight the unique socio-technical nature of software systems, distinguishing them from traditional industrial technologies (Williams & Edge, 1996; MacKenzie & Wajcman, 1999). In particular, software operates within interconnected digital ecosystems where adoption, usability, and long-term sustainability depend on reaching a critical mass of users. This embeddedness is not created by designers alone but is socially constructed through the everyday decisions of ordinary users navigating affordability, usability, and access.

Software becomes more valuable as more people use it, adapt it to different contexts, and integrate it into their daily workflows. This self-reinforcing cycle of adoption, driven by network effects, interoperability, and diverse usage patterns, ultimately determines whether a software technology thrives or fails (Katz & Shapiro, 1985).

In the case of Microsoft in China, this networked nature played a critical role in reinforcing market dominance. Microsoft's proprietary file formats (.doc, .xls, .ppt) became the de facto document exchange standard, making it difficult for users to switch to alternative software without encountering compatibility issues. Given IP protection, proprietary software producers can keep their source codes closed from the public. Even when Linux-based operating systems were introduced as government-backed alternatives, the dominance of Microsoft's ecosystem meant that many users continued to install Windows alongside Linux to ensure seamless interaction with other software and users.

A defining characteristic of software systems is network externalities, the phenomenon where the value of a product increases as more people use it (Cowan, 1992). In China, software piracy, whilst technically undermining Microsoft's IP protection, actually reinforced its network effects. As more users adopted pirated versions of Windows and Office, Microsoft's software became deeply embedded in workplaces and educational institutions, ensuring its long-term market dominance.

These network effects created lock-in effects (Samuelson, 1995), where the cost of switching to an alternative system became prohibitively high. Such lock-in effects are sustained and amplified by user mass. Each additional user, by creating documents, learning skills, or requesting support, reinforces the system's dominance. Users had already developed skills and workflows around Microsoft products, businesses had structured their operations based on Microsoft's ecosystem, and software developers prioritised creating applications for Windows rather than for alternative platforms like Linux.

The Chinese government's push for Linux adoption in public institutions faced significant resistance due to these lock-in effects. Even when Linux-based PCs were procured, many government offices continued using Microsoft Office because document exchange with external users required compatibility with Microsoft formats. This demonstrates how early adoption decisions can constrain future choices, making it difficult for new entrants, even state-backed ones, to disrupt an entrenched system. Resistance here was not only technical but infrastructural: it reflected the fact that Linux had not passed the threshold of critical mass needed for collective learning, support, and everyday fluency.

Policy Implications

The success of software technologies depends not just on technical superiority but on achieving widespread adoption, being used in diverse contexts, and continuously evolving to meet user needs. A critical mass of users is what transforms software from a product into a platform, from a tool into a standard. For both businesses and policymakers, understanding this dynamic is essential.

The case studies of Microsoft and Linux in China provide valuable insights into the challenges of intellectual property adoption policies in developing countries. Whilst strong IP protection is often portrayed as necessary for fostering innovation and attracting foreign direct investment (FDI), China's experience reveals a more complex reality. Mass engagement with pirated software served, ironically, as a vector for digital literacy, building the skills and expectations that later supported formal market adoption.

This raises critical questions: How should developing countries adopt IP regimes originally designed in and for advanced economies? Should IP protection prioritise safeguarding proprietary rights, or should it focus on enabling technological diffusion and indigenous innovation?

China's experience challenges the assumption that strong IP protection encourages innovation. Despite formally adopting IP laws to comply with TRIPS, enforcement remained weak and inconsistent (Yu, 2007). Developing countries typically have weak IP enforcement mechanisms. China's experience highlights several contributing factors: limited initial enforcement capacity, widespread public resistance, and economic realities where the high cost of licensed software relative to income levels made piracy a necessary alternative for both individuals and businesses.

China's IP reforms were largely driven by government interests in trade agreements and foreign investment, but these policies did not reflect grassroots perspectives. The general public navigated the system pragmatically, creating alternative pathways to software access that bypassed legal and institutional constraints. Whilst the state sought to strengthen IP laws, the general public and domestic businesses largely ignored them. For ordinary consumers, software was seen as a basic tool for education, business, and communication, rather than a commodity that required strict licensing.

The State's Role in Regulating Lock-In Monopoly in the Software Technology Market

Examining open-source development in China provides further insight into the relationship between state intervention and market success. Even in open-source initiatives, the absence of a critical mass of end-users undermined long-term success. Without widespread uptake, Linux distributions failed to gain resilience. Unlike Microsoft, which benefited from mass adoption driven by piracy and market forces, Linux-based open-source systems struggled to gain a critical mass of adoption in the PC market, despite multiple initiatives from academic institutions, private enterprises, and government programmes.

This phenomenon was not unique to China but was observed globally. Many had hoped that China, with its vast market size and strong government intervention, would be able to break the monopoly of proprietary software systems. This expectation did not materialise. Despite the global appeal of the copyleft philosophy and the free software movement, proprietary software continued to dominate the PC market.

In China, Linux-based open-source software gained a strong foothold in the enterprise and government sectors, supported by multiple private and public initiatives. Large technology firms such as IBM (China) and Hewlett-Packard (China), along with various government institutions, adopted Linux-based systems. Key ministries, including the National Ministry of Science, the Ministry of Statistics, and the National Labour Unit, integrated Linux into their servers. Furthermore, critical industrial sectors such as finance, telecommunications, transport, education, and railways also adopted Red Flag Linux, a Chinese-developed distribution of Linux (Smith, 2000; Kanellos, 2002).

Despite these successes, Linux struggled to gain traction in the PC market. One key reason lies in the market dynamics of emerging technology adoption. Software technologies require a critical mass of users to achieve sustainability. This mass is not just a passive user base; it is an active infrastructure, generating compatibility demands, feedback, peer learning, and market responsiveness. Once a software system reaches widespread adoption, it begins to exhibit network externalities, meaning that its value increases as more people use it. Microsoft's dominance in the market created lock-in effects, making it difficult for new entrants to compete and eventually leading to monopolistic control.

Today, market failure caused by monopolistic practices is widely recognised, and economic theories advocate for regulatory intervention to protect market equilibrium and public interest (Stiglitz, 2000). There remains a gap between recognising diverse market failures and developing effective regulatory tools for market correction. Many economic theories treat technology as an abstract entity, failing to account for the socio-technical specificities of different technologies. Without a deeper understanding of these dynamics, policymakers struggle to implement regulations that effectively balance market power and promote fair competition.

To address the power imbalances in the software technology market, governments must mitigate the effects of network externalities and lock-in monopolies. Regulation alone cannot create adoption. What Microsoft achieved through informal mass uptake, Linux failed to achieve through official policy. This contrast highlights the infrastructural agency of the masses: their power to normalise or marginalise technologies, regardless of legal standing. One of the most effective tools for achieving this is the enforcement of rules ensuring compatibility and interoperability. By mandating that dominant software providers maintain open standards and support alternative platforms, regulators can keep the market open for emerging technologies and ensure that local software solutions can thrive alongside global giants.

Returning to China's approach during this period, it is interesting to analyse the government's policy stance on software market regulation. The 10th Five-Year Plan (2001–2005) outlined a strategy to promote technological independence and reduce costs by supporting Linux and other open-source platforms. It underestimated the unique challenges posed in the PC market, particularly the dominance of proprietary systems, interoperability barriers, and entrenched user habits.

I recall an interview with an official from the Ministry of Information Industry, who explained the government's "neutrality" policy regarding software adoption. He used a well-known Chinese proverb:

"Wǒmen bùnéng ràng zìjǐ zài yī kē shù shàng diàosǐ" (我们不能让自己在一棵树上吊死, We cannot hang ourselves on a single tree until death) (Personal communication, Ministry of Information Industry official, Beijing, October 2003).

This expression was so vivid and funny and easy to comprehend as I was brought up in China, which made me laugh then, and remember the scene till today.

Though the literally translated, *"We cannot hang ourselves on a single tree until death"*, may seem unusual in English, in Chinese, it expresses the idea of keeping multiple options open rather than relying on a single path, a wisdom of rules for life. This philosophy reflects China's broader strategy of learning from multiple sources and avoiding dependence on any single technological model.

Whilst revisiting China's software market strategies, it is evident that the government recognised the complexity of global technological competition. To build sustainable digital ecosystems, governments must not only craft regulations but also mobilise mass participation, through education, public access, and shared design standards. As the field of Science and Technology Studies (STS) gains prominence, it is becoming increasingly clear that effective market regulation requires a nuanced understanding of the socio-technical dynamics of different technologies.

To correct market failures and maintain a competitive marketplace, public regulation must go beyond IP enforcement and actively mitigate lock-in monopolies by enforcing rules of compatibility and interoperability. This crucial issue will be further elaborated and discussed in subsequent chapters.

5 Impossibility of Indigenousness

Preamble

China's increasing involvement in international ICT standardisation to support indigenous innovation brought me into a new area. My learning curve was as steep as that of the Chinese policymakers and industrial innovators; as newcomers, we all struggled to navigate arenas dominated by long-established industrial alliances from the developed world.

Between 2008 and 2010, I joined a research project funded under the European FP7 Socio-economic Sciences and Humanities programme: the China-EU Information Technology Standards Research Partnership. Together with colleagues at the University of Edinburgh's Institute for the Study of Science, Technology and Innovation (ISSTI) and Tsinghua University's Centre for Science and Society, we investigated China's role in international ICT standardisation.

The project opened a new chapter in my academic journey, ushering me into the commercial world of standards and standardisation. Until then, I had regarded standards as straightforward mechanisms to ensure collaboration, reduce costs, and raise quality. What I encountered instead was a highly complex ecology where technical merit was only one dimension. Commercial interests, industrial alliances, institutional strategies, and political considerations were often more decisive in shaping outcomes (see Section 5.1).

The deeper I looked, the clearer it became that China, as a latecomer, faced profound disadvantages: little familiarity with long-standing industrial consortia, limited experience with the norms of international committees, and linguistic barriers that constrained participation. Its one counterweight was the magnetism of its domestic market, which global actors could not ignore (see Section 5.2).

This realisation was reinforced as I engaged more actively with the field. I became involved in workshops and conferences organised by the European Academy for Standardisation (EURAS),[10] presenting our findings and contributing to wider debates. The experience convinced me that standards were not simply technical artefacts but socio-technical constructs, entangled with power, legitimacy, and global competition (see Section 5.3).

---

10 EURAS (*European Academy for Standardisation*) is a learned society established in the 1990s to promote research and dialogue on standardisation, bringing together academics, practitioners, and policymakers.

https://doi.org/10.1515/9783110757576-011

Our project was proposed in 2007, at a moment when the 3rd Generation Partnership Project (3GPP)[11] was consolidating its role as the primary global forum for mobile communications standards. 3GPP is not a single organisation but a partnership of regional standards bodies, including ETSI in Europe and ATIS in North America, through which companies participate as members. These industry-backed organisations effectively serve as gatekeepers, each with long histories of consortia-building and insider networks. From China's perspective, this was never a level playing field: without decades of prior involvement in such alliances, and with limited experience in international rule-making, China's only leverage lay in the size and growth of its market (see Section 5.3).

The research formally ran from 2008 to 2010, but its influence extended well beyond that period. It not only generated academic publications but also reshaped my thinking: standards were no longer invisible background rules but central arenas where technological futures were contested and negotiated (see Section 5.4).

5.1 Introduction: Illustration of the Background

China's ICT development over the past few decades has undergone a remarkable transformation from a latecomer nation into a key global player. In the first two generations of mobile telephony, for example, China was primarily a technology adopter, relying on foreign innovations and paying substantial costs in patent licensing and equipment purchases (Shen, 1999). This highlighted the country's initial limitations in developing advanced ICTs. However, recognising the strategic significance of telecommunications and the need to strengthen domestic technological capabilities, China embarked on an ambitious path of catching up and integrating with global technological and industrial ecosystems. The phrase "connecting with international tracks" (和国际接轨) became a widely used slogan, reflecting the national drive towards learning and adaptation. This applied whether it was individuals, including retirees, entering the stock market or firms preparing for IPOs—many concepts of which were even unheard of by generations living under socialism.

The state itself became an integral part of this learning club. Moving away from its traditional role as a rigid planner, it evolved into more of a project manager—monitoring, convening, directing adjustments, and providing funding. Whilst the role of the state is often viewed with scepticism, particularly in the

11 3GPP (*3rd Generation Partnership Project*) is a global collaboration between seven regional Standards Development Organizations (SDOs).

West, the Chinese state apparatus has undergone continuous reform, engaging in learning by doing alongside other stakeholders in society. It functioned as a visible hand, sometimes making mistakes, but also executing strategic manoeuvres in response to external opportunities and pressures (Shen & Naughton, 2013).

The case of China's 3G mobile standard provides a unique lens through which to examine the dilemmas of state intervention in technology development. The debates over whether China's approach was a success or a failure persist, underscoring the complexities of balancing state involvement, market forces, and global integration in the evolution of ICT industries.

After the huge success of the landline telecommunications network in China, mobile technology rapidly replaced or overtook fixed-line phones. The number of mobile subscribers in China surpassed that of the United States in 2003, and it has been the largest mobile phone market ever since.[12] At the same time, China was the biggest producer of mobile handsets. In 2002, 120 million handsets or 27 % of the world's total were produced in China. The proportion increased to 33 % in 2003, and 35.1 % (233.5 million) in 2004. China's handset exports increased from 22.75 million in 2000 to 55 million in 2002. During the first half of 2003, China exported 37 million handsets (MII, 2004).

In the early stages, China's mobile phone sector was primarily characterised by its role as a global manufacturing hub, leveraging its substantial manufacturing capacity and large pool of relatively cheap labour to produce mobile handsets and telecommunications equipment for both domestic and international markets. As China's production volume of mobile devices surged, so did its obligation to remit "hundreds of millions of dollars every year for 2G patent licensing fees" (Shen, 2019, p. 505). According to our calculations at that time, compared to 1G, the 2G licensing fees increased for each mobile phone unit and ranged from around 5 % to 10 % of the wholesale price of the phone. Assuming China produced 40 million mobile phones and each phone's wholesale price was $100, thus $280 million would go to the companies holding the intellectual property. In many cases, because of intensive competition (especially in mobile handset markets), these fees substantially eroded the already thin profit margins of producers.

This financial outflow underscored the inherent limitations China faced as a technology follower, hindering its ability to fully capitalise on its immense production capabilities and further innovate in advanced mobile ICTs. The sheer scale of its investment in purchasing foreign 2G equipment reached "five hundred billion US dollars" (Shen, 2019, p. 505).

---

12 China's Ministry of Information Industry produced a range of *statistical reports on the telecommunications industry, which include, (2004).* .

Concurrently, the global landscape of the Information and Communication Technology (ICT) sector witnessed a significant trend where standardisation activities became one of the top agendas in the developed world (Jakobs, 2014). This period saw the rise of influential standard-setting bodies and the emergence of dominant technological standards. In the realm of 3rd Generation (3G) mobile technology, this manifested in the development and promotion of standards like the "European-centred WCDMA" and the "US-centred CDMA 2000" (Funk & Methe, 2001). These standards, backed by significant intellectual property and the established technological prowess of Western nations, began to shape the future of mobile communications globally, creating a context where latecomer nations like China faced the challenge of navigating a technological terrain largely defined by others.

As China rapidly ascended to become the largest mobile producer and home to the largest number of mobile users in the world, this dependence on foreign mobile technologies became increasingly salient and economically burdensome (Shen, 2019). The sheer volume of mobile handsets manufactured in China meant that Chinese producers had to pay escalating licensing fees to the owners of the core 1G and 2G mobile technologies. As one source explicitly states, "for Chinese manufacturers, the more devices they have produced, the more licence/royalty fees they have to pay to the technology owners" (Shen et al., 2011, p. 15). In a fiercely competitive market, especially in mobile handsets, these fees often eroded the already thin profit margins of Chinese enterprises. This growing awareness of the financial implications of technological dependence fuelled a national imperative to shift from being merely a manufacturer and user of foreign technologies to becoming a genuine innovator and standard-setter in the ICT sector.

In response to this imperative, several local initiatives for developing Chinese ICT standards emerged across various sub-sectors (Suttmeier & Yao, 2004). Beyond the prominent case of mobile technology, China also initiated efforts to create its own standards in areas such as audio and wireless local area networks, with WAPI being a notable example in the latter domain (Hong & Huang, 2014). The ambition to develop a proprietary 3G mobile standard became a central and strategically crucial component of this broader national aspiration for technological self-reliance and global competitiveness. The development of TD-SCDMA (Time Division Synchronous Code Division Multiple Access) standard for 3rd Generation mobile technology was thus not an isolated event but part of a larger movement aimed at establishing China's own technological footing in key ICT domains and reducing its reliance on foreign intellectual property and standards.

Crucially, the formal articulation and prioritisation of this strategic direction can be traced back to the 10th Five-Year Plan (2001–2005) (State Council, 2001). Whilst the 11th Five-Year Plan (2006–2010) further emphasised "endogenous innovation" (State Council, 2006), the 10th Five-Year Plan holds the distinction of being the first official policy document to explicitly mention the concept of "indigenous standards" (自主标准) (State Council, 2001). This marked a significant policy shift, formally recognising the strategic importance of developing national technological standards as a means to enhance innovation capabilities, promote industrial upgrading, and secure a more advantageous position in the global technology landscape. The inclusion of this concept in the highest level of national policy provided strong impetus and clear direction for subsequent initiatives aimed at developing China's own technological standards, with the pursuit of a Chinese 3G mobile standard becoming a flagship endeavour in this national strategy.

However, the very notion of "indigenous" later became a heated topic with competing views on government support for China's 3G standard development. Proponents framed this 3G standard as "indigenous innovation", a claim which opponents disputed as the overwhelming majority of its IP was foreign-owned. As TD-SCDMA encompassed various existing techniques developed in industrially advanced countries, it was "far from being an entirely 'indigenous' Chinese technology" (Shen et al., 2011, p. 18). This underscores the hybrid nature of standards development (Egyedi & Spirco, 2011), where global and national elements are intertwined. This prevalent understanding, which equated a "Chinese own standard" with technology and IP developed entirely within China, divided governments and industries and sowed the seeds for a long-lasting and heated debate. Competing views on TD-SCDMA's true "indigenousness" arose due to the reality that the standard incorporated existing techniques and intellectual property not solely originating in China (Gao, 2014), which we will discuss further in the rest of this chapter.

Against this backdrop of significant manufacturing capacity, a burgeoning domestic market attracting foreign investment, the dominance of Western-developed ICT standards, the increasing burden of licensing fees, and a national policy explicitly prioritising the development of indigenous standards, China's pursuit of TD-SCDMA as its own 3G mobile standard took shape (Stewart et al., 2011). This endeavour was driven by a confluence of strategic objectives: to break free from technological dependence, reduce substantial royalty payments, gain recognition as a global innovator, foster the growth of domestic ICT industries, and ultimately secure a more influential position in the future trajectory of mobile communications technology. The case of TD-SCDMA therefore serves as a vivid illustration of China's strategic response to the existing global ICT order and its determined effort to gain "membership" in the "prestigious club" of global mobile innovators, a journey fraught with both technological and socio-political complexities.

5.2 The Initiatives

The development of TD-SCDMA was a complex process that involved both domestic efforts and international collaboration. Unlike the widely held perception that it was a purely indigenous Chinese technology, TD-SCDMA emerged as a hybrid innovation, shaped by foreign expertise, state intervention, and the broader latecomer strategy in mobile telecommunications (Shen et al., 2011; Stewart et al., 2011). Our case study explores how various actors aligned their initiatives, the learning process involved in bringing TD-SCDMA to standardisation, and the role of international collaboration in its development.

Local and Global: A Multi-Layered Innovation Landscape

TD-SCDMA was born from the convergence of two key initiatives. One was the effort initiated by a group of overseas Chinese IT academics in the United States, who worked on projects developing smart antenna technologies. The other was a European consortium led by Siemens that had been working on time-division multiple access (TD-CDMA) standards (Shen et al., 2013).

In the early 1990s, Chinese IT professionals in the United States, led by Dr Guanhan Xu, were conducting research on smart antennas and joint detection systems. Xu had completed his PhD in 1991 at Stanford University Information Systems Lab, specialising in smart antenna technology. After one year of post-doctoral research, Xu took a position as an assistant professor at the University of Texas in Austin and established his own laboratory to research the use of smart antennas in civil wireless telecommunications. He drafted a blueprint for Synchronous Code Division Multiple Access (or SCDMA) as an interface for wireless devices to connect to networks. Recognising the potential for applying these technologies in China, together with his two colleagues, Xu engaged with the Chinese Academy of Telecommunications Technology (CATT) under the Ministry of Posts and Telecommunications, leading to the establishment of Xinwei Telecommunications Inc. in 1995, a joint venture, which later played a role in TD-SCDMA's technical framework (Shen et al., 2013).

At the same time, Siemens and its partners in Europe, including Nortel, Alcatel, Motorola, Italtel, Bosch and Sony Europe, were exploring the development of a TD-CDMA (Time Division CDMA) based 3G standard. Their efforts aligned with China's growing interest in establishing an independent mobile standard (for details, see Shen et al., 2013). In 1998, liaised through a Chinese professional working for Siemens, a delegation from the China Academy of Telecommunications Technology (CATT) visited Siemens, which led to a collaborative agreement that merged

China's research on synchronous code division multiple access (SCDMA) with Siemens' TD-CDMA expertise. This partnership formed the basis of what later became TD-SCDMA.

TD-SCDMA's early development illustrates the interconnected nature of global innovation. The involvement of both Chinese research individuals, institutions and foreign multinationals highlights the extent to which technological advancements often rely on transnational knowledge exchange (Ernst, 2009).

Learning by Doing: Development and Standardisation

Chinese domestic players experienced enormous difficulties in participating in international standardisation activities. As newcomers in this prestigious club, they often felt lost. At the negotiation table, they could only admire their rivals' beautiful presentations, elegant manners, and sophisticated approaches. One company representative responsible for standard matters illustrates the situation vividly:

"We have a good number of participants in these meetings, but hardly any would speak out. Most of them, especially those from small companies, just sit and listen. Bigger players like us are not much better. We want to express our views, but lack knowledge and skills. We don't even have sufficient language skills to make our points clearly without good preparation beforehand. Compared to their documents, I would say, our ones are very 'basic', frankly speaking, 'poor'. We really need to learn from scratch, the concepts, terminologies, phrases... those are norms expected there. But, it is not something that, in one day, two day, we can achieve" (Personal communication, Beijing, 14 April 2009).

The development of ICT infrastructural technologies is to a great extent dependent on previous development achievements, which are difficult to bypass (David, 1985; Teece, 1986). For China as a latecomer, bringing the TD-SCDMA 3G mobile standard was an "entry point" for gaining "membership" in this prestigious "club" of global mobile innovators. However, to confront other well-established competing standards—the European-centred WCDMA and the US-centred CDMA 2000—China had to overcome enormous hurdles, which were social and political as much or more than technical (Shen et al., 2011). The knowledge and skills that Chinese players most lacked were organisational and cultural ones—how to behave and operate effectively within that prestigious "club", in which the culture is unfamiliar and the rules were made by others.

The TD-SCDMA mobile system was developed by the Datang Technology Group and based on techniques already existing and initially championed by Siemens. Technically, it is far from being an entirely 'indigenous' Chinese technology (Gao, 2014). Within China, the implementation process for the TD-SCDMA technology represents a huge socio-technical engineering project, which requires a large array of financial and technical resources and considerable coordination between stakeholders along the supply chain. For ICT infrastructural technologies, these capabilities are essential. However, this is not a task that a single company in China could have.

Once TD-SCDMA was established as a potential 3G standard, it faced the challenge of gaining recognition both internationally and domestically. The first major step in its legitimisation came in June 1998 when China's Ministry of Posts and Telecommunications (MPT) approved the standard for submission to the International Telecommunication Union (ITU). By May 2000, ITU formally accepted TD-SCDMA as one of the three global 3G standards, alongside W-CDMA and CDMA2000 (ITU, 2000). China's engagement with the 3GPP consortium in 2001 further solidified TD-SCDMA's place within the international telecommunications framework (3GPP, 2001).

Despite these achievements, TD-SCDMA struggled to gain domestic support. Chinese mobile operators, particularly China Mobile, initially showed little enthusiasm for adopting the new standard, as they were more inclined towards the more established W-CDMA and CDMA2000 technologies (Xia, 2011). Without a strong industrial base or widespread market adoption, TD-SCDMA remained a standard on paper rather than a viable commercial technology.

In response to this challenge, the Chinese government launched a series of strategic initiatives to support TD-SCDMA's development. In 2003, the government facilitated the formation of the TD-SCDMA Industry Alliance, which brought together key domestic firms such as Datang, Huawei, ZTE, Lenovo, and others (TDIA, 2003). This alliance was crucial in coordinating the industrial and financial resources necessary to build a TD-SCDMA ecosystem. At the same time, the government allocated RMB 708 million in R&D subsidies through the National Development and Reform Commission (NDRC), the Ministry of Information Industry (MII)[13], and the Ministry of Science and Technology (MOST) (Stewart et al., 2011). These financial and institutional interventions were critical in sustaining TD-SCDMA's development, demonstrating the importance of state support in large-scale infrastructure projects.

The TD-SCDMA initiative was a prime example of the "learning by doing" approach in China's technology strategy. By engaging in the process of developing a national standard, Chinese firms and research institutions not only gained experience in telecommunications innovation but also deepened their participation in global standardisation efforts. The process provided them with insights into regu-

13 Later became the Ministry of Industry and Information Technology (MIIT).

latory negotiations, intellectual property management, and the industrial coordination required for large-scale technological implementation.

The Chinese government was eventually convinced that China should put forward its TD-SCDMA 3G standard to the International Telecommunications Union (ITU) (Stewart et al., 2011). In June 1998, China formally proposed the TD-SCDMA blueprint to ITU, which was accepted in May 2000. It was also accepted as one of the three international 3G Standards by the 3GPP consortium in March 2001 (3GPP, 2001).

The TD-SCDMA project did not gain momentum until October 2002, when the TD-SCDMA Industry Alliance (TDIA) was formed. Behind the scene was the government, which put key players from Public Sector Research and Development and industries together and provided the political and financial support needed for the project. The newly formed Ministry of Information Industry—MII (the outcome of the reorganisation of ICT sectors including the Ministry of Electronic Industry and the Ministry of Post and Telecommunications) assigned 155MHz radio spectrum previously in a military band to the TD-SCDMA project. With these resources, the project started rolling. In 2004, MII, the Ministry of Science and Technology (MOST) and the National Development and Reform Commission (NDRC) granted an R&D subsidy of RMB 708 million for launching the TD-SCDMA R&D and an Industrialisation Programme to turn the prototype standard into marketable technology systems (Stewart et al., 2011). The Industry Alliance was growing day by day with newly joined enterprises from various component technological fields: core network capabilities, Radio Access Network, terminals, chips, testing instruments, antennas and direct amplifier stations. By that stage, the project had become the "national flagship" with "the full support from the highest level of the government" (Stewart et al., 2011, p. 22), which thus did not allow any fall-back route.

Engaging with International Partners

In the run-up to the provision of TD-SCDMA services to Chinese users, 2006 saw the official approval of the TD standard by MII for nationwide networks. A series of public tenders were organised for the supply of network equipment, terminals, mobile systems, and other components beginning 20 March 2007. These attracted major domestic players, such as ZTE, Datang, Huawei, Potevio, Fiberhome, and Newpostcom, as well as joint ventures and foreign companies including Alcatel-Shanghai Bell, Ericsson, Nokia, and Siemens (Stewart et al., 2011). Later, major vendors of mobile systems and component manufacturers also joined forces. In 2008, a major reorganisation of the industries was completed resulting in the creation of a super-ministry, the Ministry of Industry and Information Technology (MIIT). Compared to the sceptical attitudes of the previous MII, the new MIIT committed itself to TD implementation.

On 23 May 2008, the Ministry of Finance, the NDRC, and MII jointly issued the "Announcement on Deepening the Reform of the Structure of the Telecommunications Sector" which indirectly criticised China Mobile, stating that China Mobile had no choice other than to devote itself to the implementation of TD-SCDMA (MOF, NDRC, & MII, 2008). Following that, the new Minister, Li Yizhong, appeared publicly, meeting with TD-SCDMA technical experts and discussing further advances of TD-SCDMA's implementation. The president of China Mobile responded to this with a sharp turn, declaring that China Mobile would "make every effort" to ensure the excellent service of TD-SCDMA during and after the Beijing 2008 Olympic games. China Mobile finally made the critical manoeuvre—belated but decisive—formally becoming a member of the TDIA. At the ministerial level, MIIT and other related government departments formed a cross-ministry coordinating group to oversee the implementation of thirty-four TD-related special work packages. In August 2008, the first licences for TD-SCDMA handset production were issued by MIIT, and the subsequent schemes for commercialisation were laid out (MIIT, 2008).

Before the roll-out of the 3G licences, a structural reform/reorganisation was carried out in the telecommunications sector in 2008. Previously, six state-owned operators were consolidated into three key players to compete in all telecommunications services: China Mobile, China UNICOM and China Telecom. In the beginning of 2009, three 3G licences were formally issued by MIIT. China Mobile was awarded TD-SCDMA, the Chinese home-grown standard, and China UNICOM and China Telecom took on WCDMA (European-centred standard) and CDMA (US standard) respectively (Stewart et al., 2011). In the face of competition from WCDMA and CDMA2000 that had already matured and been widely adopted worldwide, questions arose whether the new Chinese TD-SCDMA would eventually succeed in the market. Observing the most recent developments, we see major Chinese companies including ZTE and Huawei have become heavily involved in LTE standardisation (Personal communication, 28 April 2010). Huawei supplied a TD-LTE system for the Shanghai Expo in April 2010, and conducted large-scale tests in at least 2 cities with over 100 base stations from the second quarter of 2010 (Stewart et al., 2011). ZTE was actively involved and participated in TD-LTE tests organised by MII and China Mobile. MIIT's TD-LTE initially included not only Chinese flagship companies but also global players, such as Nokia, Siemens, Ericsson, Motorola, Alcatel-Lucent, Aeroflex, and others (TD Forum, 2010).

The TD-SCDMA 3G mobile standard case again demonstrates that the Chinese government possesses means, power and abilities to influence the technology process, from R&D to adoption/implementation (Shen, 2019). However, this does not intimate that the Chinese government had wisely pre-planned and carefully orchestrated the whole process. It is rather a combination of the routine mechanisms installed for supporting technology and innovation in the country and a gamut of contingent activities and measures devised in response to the needs of the R&D and industrial players at specific times and circumstances (Breznitz & Murphree, 2011). Compared to governments in Europe and North America, the Chinese government can exercise its influences effectively by adopting direct or indirect measures. With its hierarchical structure and socialist legacy, when necessary, it could hand-pick the CEO for a state-owned company, restructure and reorganise industries—in this case pulling all the players in the supply chain together and having the resources from different government departments made available for implementing the TD standard. It also appears that despite being generally bureaucratic like most others, the Chinese government is nevertheless a learning organisation, whose policies and strategies of intervention have been changing/adjusting over time. When many outside China expected that China would endorse one standard, TD-SCDMA, the government implemented three international standards, each with an operator allocated.

It is interesting to note the change in government attitudes and rationale towards the TD standard on the issue of indigenous technology and also in embracing the involvement of foreign companies in the implementation and commercialisation of TD for the Chinese market during the process. It is however difficult to determine whether this should be seen as simply the outcome of the pragmatism of the Chinese government or as the result of a better understanding of the innovation of ICT infrastructural technologies. As discussed above, ICT technologies become increasingly complex, and technology-related international communities and organisations—for example, IPR regimes and standardisation organisations/consortiums—become increasingly proactive and powerful (Weiss & Sirbu, 1990; Shapiro & Varian, 1999). In the context where technologies are becoming increasingly globalised, it could be a mistake to over-emphasise indigenous technological capabilities (and treat indigenous and foreign technologies as wholly distinct). It is impossible for an R&D institution or business corporation (or even a country) to possess every single technology of the entire package of a complex infrastructural technology. The key is perhaps who takes control institutionally of the rules of play within the current framework of international industrial activities (Suttmeier & Yao, 2004).

By 2005, reports suggested that foreign companies, including Nokia, Qualcomm, Motorola, and Alcatel-Lucent, held approximately 66 % of TD-SCDMA's intellectual property rights (Gao, 2014). This reliance on foreign patents challenged the narrative of TD-SCDMA as a fully indigenous innovation. It also reflected a broader reality in the telecommunications sector—complex technology systems often require collaboration and cross-border knowledge exchange, making it nearly impossible for any single nation to develop a mobile standard entirely in isolation (Ernst, 2009).

Beyond technical collaboration, market challenges forced Chinese stakeholders to engage with international players to ensure TD-SCDMA's commercial viability. Unlike W-CDMA and CDMA2000, which had extensive global adoption, TD-SCDMA lacked an established supply chain and user base. To address this gap, the TD-SCDMA Industry Alliance worked closely with global telecom companies to improve compatibility and interoperability. This experience proved invaluable for Chinese firms, enabling them to acquire the industrial and managerial expertise necessary for future technological leadership (Mu & Lee, 2005).

Through these interactions, China not only strengthened its domestic telecommunications capabilities but also positioned itself as a more influential player in the global technology landscape. The lessons learned from the TD-SCDMA experience would later be applied to the development of TD-LTE and 5G, where Chinese firms such as Huawei and ZTE played a much more influential role (Kshetri et al., 2011).

Summary: The Latecomer Dilemma and Competing Views on Indigenousness

The TD-SCDMA initiative exemplifies the complexities of technological development in a latecomer country. On one hand, China pursued TD-SCDMA as a means of reducing reliance on foreign technologies and avoiding costly royalty payments. On the other hand, the process of developing the standard revealed the limitations of a purely indigenous approach, as global collaboration and foreign expertise were essential to TD-SCDMA's realisation (Shen et al., 2011).

Whilst some viewed TD-SCDMA as a symbol of national technological sovereignty, others saw it as an intermediate step in China's broader technological trajectory. The experience of developing TD-SCDMA exposed Chinese firms to the realities of global telecom governance, supply chain management, and standardisation politics. It also reinforced the idea that national innovation efforts must be accompanied by industrial alliances, market development, and ongoing collaboration with international stakeholders.

The next section (Section 5.3) will examine how China attempted to build industrial alliances and an ecosystem to support TD-SCDMA's commercial success, moving beyond the technical standard itself to consider the broader industrial and economic forces at play.

5.3 Challenges and Learning by Doing in Building the TD-SCDMA Mobile Standard

The development of TD-SCDMA was not a straightforward technological advancement but a deeply complex and contested process. As a latecomer in mobile telecommunications, China faced significant challenges at multiple levels—technological, institutional, and political. Yet, these very challenges provided critical opportunities for learning by doing, shaping the country's capabilities in standardisation, industrial coordination, and strategic market positioning (Stewart et al., 2011).

Navigating the Global ICT Standards Landscape

One of the biggest hurdles was understanding and operating within the global ICT standards community, where China was still an outsider. Standardisation was as much about politics and negotiation as it was about technology, and Chinese companies initially found themselves at a disadvantage. Major standard-setting bodies, such as the 3rd Generation Partnership Project (3GPP), were dominated by experienced players from Europe, the US, and Japan, who had long-established influence in shaping the direction of mobile technology (3GPP, 2001; Ernst, 2011).

For Chinese participants, the environment was not only unfamiliar but also intimidating. A representative from a Chinese company recalled how many Chinese attendees at international meetings would sit silently, struggling with language barriers and lacking the strategic understanding to contribute meaningfully. Their documents, when compared to those of established players, were often considered "basic" and insufficiently persuasive (Personal communication, 14 April 2009). Learning to operate in these arenas meant grappling with technical norms, business strategies, and cultural expectations that were second nature to Western firms but new to China (Shen et al., 2013).

Over time, through persistent engagement, China began to adapt and develop its own strategies. By closely observing how alliances were formed and decisions were made, Chinese firms learned to navigate the political and technical dimensions of standardisation. It was a slow and often frustrating process, but as Deng Xiaoping famously described China's economic reforms, it was like "crossing the river by feeling the stones"—gradual, adaptive process, reliant on experience rather than predetermined plans (Breznitz & Murphree, 2011).

Balancing Domestic Development and Global Market Commitments

Even as China pushed for an indigenous 3G standard, its domestic telecommunications industry was deeply intertwined with global markets. By the late 1990s, Chinese firms like Huawei and ZTE were already producing and exporting 3G products based on existing foreign standards (Shen, 2019). The American CDMA2000 and European WCDMA standards were well-established, and Chinese network equipment makers had invested heavily in developing and supplying these technologies for foreign markets (Gao, 2014).

At the same time, China's own mobile service providers, including China Mobile, were actively testing 3G networks based on these mature standards. For companies and operators accustomed to these existing technologies, switching to TD-SCDMA posed enormous risks. The technology was still in its infancy, unproven on a large scale, and lacked the robust ecosystem that WCDMA and CDMA2000 already enjoyed (Stewart et al., 2011).

Despite frustrations over high licensing fees paid to foreign IP holders, many Chinese companies were reluctant to abandon established technologies unless the state provided a clear commitment and active coordination to ensure the viability of TD-SCDMA (Shen et al., 2013). The risk of investing in a new, untested standard was too great without government backing.

Forming the TD-SCDMA Industry Alliance

Recognising the need for coordination, the Chinese government stepped in as an active organiser. In October 2002, the TD-SCDMA Industry Alliance (TDIA) was established, bringing together major network providers, chipmakers, handset manufacturers, and research institutions to work collaboratively on advancing the technology (TDIA, 2003). This alliance helped address critical issues, including intellectual property rights, financial investments, and supply chain development.

The TDIA served as a bridge, ensuring that different stakeholders—many of whom were competitors—worked together rather than against each other. It also provided a platform for resolving practical challenges, such as ensuring component compatibility, optimising system performance, and preparing for commercial deployment.

Without this structured support, TD-SCDMA might never have progressed beyond an experimental technology. The alliance provided a mechanism through which China could consolidate its fragmented efforts and push for large-scale adoption (Kshetri et al., 2011).

The Technology Neutrality Decision: A Strategic Surprise

Just when many expected the government to fully back TD-SCDMA as China's sole 3G standard, a surprising policy shift occurred. Instead of exclusively promoting the homegrown standard, the government announced a technology-neutral approach, allowing all three major international 3G standards to operate in China (MIIT, 2009).

In early 2009, China formally allocated licences as follows:
- China Mobile was assigned TD-SCDMA
- China Unicom was given WCDMA
- China Telecom was awarded CDMA2000

This decision took many by surprise. Until then, it had been widely assumed that China would commit entirely to TD-SCDMA in a bid for technological independence. However, divisions within the government itself played a key role in shaping this outcome (Shen, 2019).

The Ministry of Science and Technology (MOST) had strongly supported TD-SCDMA, viewing it as a symbol of indigenous innovation (MOST, 2004). In contrast, the Ministry of Industry and Information Technology (MIIT), which was responsible for telecommunications infrastructure and industry policy, had been more sceptical. MIIT officials were pragmatic, recognising the technical limitations and commercial risks of relying solely on TD-SCDMA when mature alternatives were readily available.

Moreover, international pressures also influenced this decision. Both European and American telecom industry leaders were eager to secure China's massive market, knowing that widespread adoption in China would provide a crucial competitive advantage for their respective standards (Ernst, 2011). Seeing this competition play out, China realised it could leverage its market size to its advantage, a lesson drawn from observing previous "standards wars" in the global industry.

By choosing to adopt all three standards, China achieved multiple objectives:
1. It gained bargaining power, as foreign technology holders saw access to the Chinese market as a major incentive to negotiate technology transfers.
2. It forced domestic companies to develop expertise in multiple standards, ensuring they remained competitive in global markets.
3. It accelerated China's learning curve in standardisation and telecommunications infrastructure development, laying the foundation for leadership in 4G and 5G (Stewart et al., 2011).

The Indigenous Innovation Controversy

Despite government backing, TD-SCDMA faced significant scepticism even within China. The debate over whether it truly represented an "indigenous innovation" exposed divisions between different stakeholders (Shen, 2019).

Much of the core technological foundation of TD-SCDMA had originated from Siemens, which had been working on a similar concept in Europe. Critics argued that labelling it as purely Chinese innovation was misleading (Shen et al., 2013). Others pointed out that innovation is rarely a purely national endeavour—technological advancements often result from cross-border collaborations and adaptations (Ernst, 2011).

This controversy reflected a broader tension in China's technological strategy—how to balance domestic innovation with global integration. Whilst China wanted to assert greater control over its technological future, it also had to engage with international firms and standards to stay competitive.

Lessons Learned and the Road to 4G and 5G

Regardless of TD-SCDMA's commercial success, the learning process it enabled was invaluable. By participating in standardisation and developing its own mobile technology ecosystem, China gained the experience needed to play a leading role in the 4G and 5G eras (Stewart et al., 2011).

Chinese companies learned to navigate global standardisation bodies and advocate for their interests. The government refined its ability to coordinate industry efforts whilst balancing international pressures. China's market leverage was effectively used to secure technology transfers and establish a more competitive domestic industry.

In hindsight, TD-SCDMA was less about achieving dominance in 3G and more about learning the socio-technical specificities of ICT networked technological systems and preparing for the future, which we will discuss in Section 5.4 (Shen, 2019). By the time 4G and 5G arrived, Chinese companies were no longer just learning the game—they were helping to write the rules (Kshetri et al., 2011).

These learning processes depended on more than firm-level strategies. They relied on dense social ecologies of engineers, users, and consumers who collectively tested, refined, and normalised practices (Breznitz & Murphree, 2011). Critical mass in usage created feedback loops that made learning stick. Without such collective reinforcement, imitative learning would have dissipated rather than accumulating into innovation capacity (Ernst, 2011).

5.4 Discussion: Reconciling Long-Standing Debates with Pragmatism

In January 2015, I received an email from a journalist from Hong Kong's *The Phoenix Weekly* (凤凰周刊), which asked me to help with a range of questions about TD-SCDMA development. The interview topic given was: How to Evaluate the Merits and Drawbacks of TD-SCDMA. Despite the long list of questions, the main issues were based on the controversial views, particularly the critical ones from domestic and international professional communities. The result of the long-lasting debate has been inconclusive until now. In most recent years, because of US administrations, such as Trump, Biden and Trump 2.0, China was pushed to face a series of technological sanctions, mirroring COCOM during the Cold War, the voices of criticism died down.

Two consistent issues were based on the original controversies: one was technical and the other relevant to the role of the Chinese government. The former raised again the proportion of the "indigenousness" of TD-SCDMA standard, with some domestic critics complaining about the cost regarding the return-on-investment for the TD project. International professional communities also raised complaints that China deviated the efforts of global community from existing standards.

Redefining "Indigenousness" in the Era of Complex Innovation

The question of whether TD-SCDMA can truly be regarded as an "indigenous" Chinese innovation has remained a source of debate and controversy. On the surface, when judged by the criteria of intellectual property (IP) ownership, TD-SCDMA falls far short of being a purely indigenous technology. Much of its technical foundation, including crucial components and design principles, can be traced to pre-existing work by foreign firms, most notably Siemens TD-CDMA and prior to it, Xinwei's SCDMA and even smart antenna research in Stanford University's lab (Shen et al., 2013). However, this narrow lens, judging indigenousness solely by the origin of IP, misses the more substantive and dynamic dimensions of technological development today.

In reality, very few modern technologies, especially complex infrastructural systems like mobile communication standards, are entirely indigenous to any one nation. Innovation in these sectors is cumulative and layered, building upon decades of global research, design, and iterative development (Rosenberg, 1982; Nelson & Winter, 1982). As such, trying to isolate a "pure" national origin often obscures the collaborative and international nature of technological evolution.

The global IP regime itself was constructed to address the limitations of market incentives for innovation. This was in a context where the market system might fail to reward innovation, especially where up-front investments in R&D are high and outcomes uncertain. Similarly, the rise of standardisation as a major force in modern technological development reflects an even broader shift: from competition over proprietary invention to collaboration over shared systems, designed to foster interoperability, large-scale adoption, and ongoing improvement (David & Greenstein, 1990).

In this context, TD-SCDMA represents something more nuanced, and arguably more important: a learning process. The case of TD-SCDMA offers a compelling example. China's real achievement was not in claiming IP origin but in the pragmatic process of learning how to build and evolve a standard into a commercially viable infrastructure. Through the process, China acquired the capabilities to translate a protocol into market-ready technologies, developing terminals, chips, network equipment, and operational services. The government successfully orchestrated industrial alliances across the supply chain, enabling collaborative innovation amongst fragmented actors. The stakeholders across industries learned through hands-on experience with technical integration, market rollouts, and user feedback, paving the way for future iterations of standard-building.

It reflects the cultivation of capabilities, institutions, and industrial coordination mechanisms needed to take part in a new era of technology-making, one where the ability to build, manage, and evolve standards collaboratively is as critical as the invention of individual technical components (Teece, 1986; Pisano & Shih, 2012).

A key part of this learning process was China's growing exposure to and participation in the international standardisation arena. Chinese firms and institutions had to learn the norms, procedures, and "rules of the game" that governed international standard-setting bodies, most notably 3GPP. This included everything from terminology and document formatting, to technical negotiations, strategic alliances, and even lobbying practices. For many Chinese participants, this was a steep learning curve, and the early stages were marked by cultural and organisational dissonance (Shen et al., 2011). But it was precisely through this process that China began to acquire the tacit, institutional knowledge necessary to influence standardisation, not just to follow it.

This transition, from being outsiders to active players in standardisation, has long-term implications. Modern standards, especially in ICT, are not just technical blueprints; they are governance structures, platforms for ongoing evolution (Russell, 2014). In this light, IP ownership is only the seed. The real work begins in nurturing that seed, building ecosystems of adopters, managing contributions from multiple players, negotiating shared rights, and ensuring broad and sustainable implementation.

TD-SCDMA, therefore, offered a practical entry point for China into this emerging institutional terrain. Through it, China learned that:

- Standards require markets to thrive, and market size can be a powerful bargaining chip, as seen when both European and American standards bodies competed to attract Chinese adoption (Funk & Methe, 2001).
- Standardisation is inherently collaborative, demanding tools and mechanisms for fair contribution and benefit sharing, something that had to be constructed and internalised by Chinese stakeholders.
- Technological evolution depends on ongoing institutional engagement, not just one-off innovation. Once a standard is deployed, its relevance and competitiveness must be maintained through continuous feedback, revision, and alignment with changing technical and market demands (Egyedi & Blind, 2008).

Thus, the indigenousness of TD-SCDMA should be understood not through a static lens of IP origin, but through the dynamic lens of learning and institutionalisation. What made TD-SCDMA meaningful for China was not that it was "all Chinese", but that it was the first serious project through which China began to understand and engage with the global system of technology governance on its own terms. It laid the groundwork for more confident and competent participation in future standardisation processes, most notably in 4G and 5G, where Chinese firms like Huawei and ZTE have become central players (Kshetri et al., 2011).

The TD-SCDMA case underscores a broader truth: in the age of complex and collaborative technology systems, indigenous innovation is less about origin and more about capacity—the capacity to participate, shape, and co-evolve within global systems of technology and knowledge. The learning derived from building TD-SCDMA, technical, organisational, and institutional, was China's real innovation (Shen, 2019).

The Learning State: Being an Active Enabler

The development of TD-SCDMA was far from a centrally pre-planned initiative. Instead, it evolved as a story of distributed innovation, where early initiatives from individuals and institutions, many at the grassroots level, sowed the seeds for what would eventually become a national technological project. The government's role in this process was not fully formed at the outset. Rather, it emerged and matured through learning by doing, shaped by internal debates, institutional adaptation, and engagement with external pressures (Heilmann & Perry, 2011).

The initial technological foundation came from collaborative efforts between overseas Chinese researchers and domestic R&D bodies like CATT. These actors explored opportunities in a fragmented policy landscape, often without clear endorsement from the state. In fact, within the government itself, there was no unified view about the viability or necessity of a homegrown standard. Departments like the Ministry of Posts and Telecommunications (MPT) remained sceptical, largely due to their pragmatic preference for tried-and-tested foreign technologies that could rapidly support infrastructure expansion. The Ministry of Science and Technology (MOST), by contrast, took a more enthusiastic stance on promoting "indigenous innovation" (Shen et al., 2011).

Amidst these divergent perspectives, the state gradually developed a more coherent and proactive role. This shift was part of a broader institutional transformation in China's ICT governance. In 1998, the State Council restructured the ICT-related ministries, dissolving the MPT and the Ministry of Electronics Industry (MEI) and merging them into a new body, the Ministry of Information Industry (MII) (State Council, 1998). This institutional overhaul signalled an attempt to remove bureaucratic fragmentation, facilitate coordination, and support the increasingly convergent needs of telecommunications and information technology.

Through MII, the government began to play a more strategic and integrated role in supporting TD-SCDMA. One key intervention was the assignment of 155 MHz of radio spectrum, previously used for military purposes, to the TD-SCDMA project (MII, 2003). This allocation was not only a significant material resource but also a strong political signal of commitment. The government also took the unusual step of creating a controlled competitive environment by choosing to support all three 3G standards. When 3G licences were formally issued in 2009, China Mobile was assigned TD-SCDMA, whilst China Unicom received WCDMA and China Telecom took on CDMA2000 (MIIT, 2009). This approach of "technology neutrality" was initially shaped by international pressure and internal hesitancy, but ultimately allowed China to keep multiple pathways open, ensure learning from mature global standards, and guarantee a testing ground for its indigenous standard (Shen, 2019).

Critically, the state's decision to back TD-SCDMA did not come overnight, nor was it based on an inherent capacity for innovation governance. Rather, it was the result of institutional learning, built through engagement with both domestic actors and international developments. The Chinese government came to understand that the size of its market was a valuable bargaining chip, something both US-based and European standards consortia had been keenly aware of (Funk & Methe, 2001). Observing the dynamics of global "standards wars",

China learned that the value of a standard is not only in its technical merit or IP ownership, but in its adoption, its market uptake. This recognition allowed Chinese policymakers to recalibrate their strategies from a position of passive adaptation to active participation.

This learning was reflected in the establishment of the TD-SCDMA Industry Alliance (TDIA) in 2002, which the government initiated to orchestrate collaboration across the supply chain, including component makers, device manufacturers, network equipment providers, and service operators (TDIA, 2003). The alliance became a vital mechanism for aligning fragmented capacities, enabling experimentation, and facilitating knowledge sharing. The government, through MII and later the Ministry of Industry and Information Technology (MIIT), offered political backing, R&D funding, and institutional coordination to address practical bottlenecks, from IPR allocation to equipment testing and pilot deployments (Stewart et al., 2011).

Vertical coordination was just as critical. Recognising that adoption was central to the success of TD-SCDMA, the government moved to ensure buy-in from major operators, particularly China Mobile. Initially reluctant, given their reliance on more mature WCDMA and CDMA technologies for their existing infrastructure and international markets, these firms would not have committed to TD-SCDMA without strong and unambiguous state backing. Eventually, MIIT exercised direct intervention, assigning China Mobile the responsibility for rolling out TD-SCDMA with no fallback option (MOF, NDRC, & MII, 2008). This move effectively eliminated hesitation and secured a pathway for deployment, ensuring that the homegrown standard would be more than a paper achievement.

In this broader process, the role of the State Council became pivotal. It functioned not simply as a planner, but as a high-level coordinator, capable of re-aligning ministries, resolving bureaucratic gridlocks, and creating institutional frameworks that allowed experimentation to flourish. Whilst Western commentary at the time often depicted the Chinese state as monolithic and authoritarian, the TD-SCDMA case reveals a more nuanced reality: an evolving, learning state that responded pragmatically to external challenges and domestic initiatives (Breznitz & Murphree, 2011). The Chinese government did not always lead from the front; instead, it became an enabler, sometimes reluctantly, sometimes assertively, of a complex innovation process unfolding across multiple levels.

This process also helped lay the foundations for China's future advancements in mobile technology. The institutional capabilities, collaborative mechanisms, and market strategies honed during the TD-SCDMA experience paved the way for the country's rapid progression to 4G (TD-LTE) and eventually 5G technologies. Industrial players like Huawei and ZTE, having gained valuable technical and organisational experience, were now better positioned to lead and influence global standardisation processes (Kshetri et al., 2011). The state, for its part, had become smarter and more strategic, capable of coordinating actors, managing uncertainty, and leveraging national strengths to shape global technological futures.

In sum, the Chinese state's role in the development of TD-SCDMA was emergent rather than preordained. It was shaped by distributed initiatives, contested ideas, and ongoing institutional learning. The success of the process lies not merely in the commercial fate of TD-SCDMA itself, but in the innovation ecosystem that it helped build, one where state, industry, and research co-evolved in pursuit of long-term technological sovereignty (Shen, 2019).

"Technology Neutrality"? The Outcomes of Encompassing Three 3G Standards

The Chinese government's decision to adopt all three internationally recognised 3G standards—TD-SCDMA (TDD), WCDMA (FDD), and CDMA2000 (FDD)—was, at the time, viewed by many observers as an act of expediency. Facing considerable international pressure from both European and American stakeholders who had heavily invested in their respective standards, China's posture of "technology neutrality" was a carefully calibrated strategy to delay commitment whilst learning from the international landscape (Shen, 2019). However, what emerged from this cautious stance was far more impactful than expected.

Whilst some may have regarded this multi-standard policy as representing indecisiveness or lack of confidence in domestic innovation, the outcomes tell a different story. This approach fostered an environment for deep learning, capability accumulation, and eventually, technological leadership. Despite the well-known drawbacks of TD-SCDMA, such as slower data transmission, poor compatibility with international roaming, and a relatively limited ecosystem for devices and services, its role in China's mobile telecommunications history should be viewed through the lens of long-term capability building and strategic positioning (Xia, 2011; Gao, 2014).

TD-SCDMA as a Stepping Stone to TD-LTE and 5G

TD-SCDMA was based on Time Division Duplexing (TDD), a technique that allows bidirectional communication on a single frequency band by separating transmission and reception into different time slots. Whilst TDD was not a mainstream global standard at the time, China's commitment to TD-SCDMA provided its industry with early, exclusive expertise in this domain (3GPP, 2001).

When the transition to 4G began, China Mobile's choice of TD-LTE as its primary 4G technology leveraged both the technical infrastructure and human capital developed through the TD-SCDMA project. With TD-LTE, the benefits of accumulated TDD experience came to fruition, allowing for rapid rollout of one of the world's largest 4G networks, supported by over four million base stations by 2019 (China Mobile, 2019). Moreover, as 5G began to take shape, TDD once again became central, particularly in the mid- and high-frequency bands. The competence developed through the 3G phase uniquely positioned China to lead the world in 5G deployment by 2023.

Comparative Understanding of TDD and FDD

The coexistence of all three 3G standards within the same national market gave Chinese actors a rare opportunity to compare TDD and FDD technologies in practice. Telecom operators, equipment suppliers, and handset manufacturers were forced to engage with the technical, operational, and economic dimensions of both duplexing methods (Shen et al., 2013).

This comprehensive experience yielded a generation of engineers, researchers, and corporate decision-makers who not only understood how to implement these technologies but also how to integrate and improve upon them. This dual expertise was particularly valuable in the 4G and 5G eras, where multimode capability became a competitive advantage in global markets (Kshetri et al., 2011).

Innovation in Multi-Mode Equipment

The policy of supporting all three standards inadvertently accelerated the development of multi-mode devices. Domestic handset manufacturers had to design and produce phones capable of operating across all standards. This demand for versatility soon evolved into a core strength, with companies like Huawei, ZTE, Xiaomi, and Oppo gaining the engineering know-how to build globally compatible devices (Ernst, 2011).

Likewise, equipment makers developed base stations and network infrastructure that could support both TDD and FDD modes. This flexibility made Chinese firms more attractive in international markets, where telecom operators often operate across diverse spectrum allocations.

Infrastructure Reuse and Accelerated 4G/5G Transition

The physical and organisational infrastructure developed for TD-SCDMA, though often criticised for underperforming, was not wasted. Many of the TD-SCDMA base station sites, spectrum allocations, and operational teams were transitioned directly into the deployment of TD-LTE (Stewart et al., 2011). This significantly lowered the cost and time required for the 4G rollout. The same applied to human resources and institutional experience, which could now be redirected towards emerging 5G projects without starting from scratch.

Strategic Lessons and Capability Building

Perhaps the most profound benefit of adopting three standards was the strategic learning it enabled. Chinese stakeholders learned, often through trial and error, how to manage and negotiate within a globalised technology regime, ranging from IPR complexities and global patent pools to standardisation politics and supply chain collaboration (Suttmeier & Yao, 2004). The metaphor of Deng Xiaoping's phrase, "crossing the river by feeling the stones", is particularly apt here. The technology neutrality policy was not a calculated bet in the traditional sense, but rather a flexible approach to learning by doing, allowing China to accumulate experiential knowledge without locking itself prematurely into one technological path (Heilmann & Perry, 2011).

This process also highlighted the limits of IP ownership as the sole metric of technological sovereignty. Whilst TD-SCDMA did not originate entirely from indigenous Chinese IP, the value lay in mastering the process of turning a standard into a product, a market, and ultimately an industrial ecosystem. The importance of institutional coordination, cross-sector collaboration, and iterative learning proved more critical than initial ownership of technology (Pisano & Shih, 2012).

Government's Role in Orchestrating the Process

Throughout this multi-standard experiment, the Chinese government evolved its role from a hesitant observer to a strategic orchestrator. Initially driven by a desire to delay commitment under international pressure, it later embraced an active coordinating role, ensuring spectrum allocation, funding, and regulatory alignment. The Ministry of Industry and Information Technology (MIIT), emerging from earlier institutional restructuring, provided consistent support for innovation, particularly for TD-SCDMA (MIIT, 2008).

The State Council and MIIT not only facilitated vertical alignment between ministries and enterprises but also enforced horizontal coordination, assigning China Mobile to champion TD-SCDMA and ensuring the system would be deployed on a national scale, despite early resistance from the operator and scepticism from parts of the industry (MOF, NDRC, & MII, 2008). The state, whilst still criticised in some quarters for its top-down style, had in fact learned and adapted, becoming a more sophisticated actor in technology governance (Breznitz & Murphree, 2011).

In retrospect, China's policy of technology neutrality during the 3G era may have appeared overly cautious, even fragmented. To many outside observers at the time, it seemed as though China lacked a clear direction or was hedging its bets in the face of uncertainty. The decision to adopt all three 3G standards—TD-SCDMA, WCDMA, and CDMA2000—was met with scepticism both domestically and internationally. Critics viewed it as a sign of indecision, a lack of confidence in homegrown innovation, or even an avoidance of hard choices.

However, this cautious stance masked a deeper strategic logic. Rather than committing too early to one standard under external pressure, China chose a path of experimental pluralism, a deliberate learning process guided by pragmatism rather than ideological or technological conviction (Shen, 2019). By embracing the coexistence of multiple standards, the country created a unique environment for developing institutional capabilities, market flexibility, and technological understanding across the board.

The real payoff came not from TD-SCDMA alone, but from the accumulated knowledge and infrastructure across all three standards, which laid the groundwork for China's remarkable ascent in 4G and 5G technologies. What initially appeared fragmented turned out to be a foundation for integration and coordination, enabling a generation of engineers, firms, and institutions to gain broad, comparative experience and build robust innovation systems. In this sense, China's 3G policy was less about hedging and more about learning, and ultimately, about positioning itself to lead in the next technological era.

6 Imitative-Innovation and/or Innovative-Imitation

Preamble

Teaching Chinese case studies to Western students forced me, like China itself, to confront stereotypes of "copying" and to demonstrate how imitation could be reframed as creativity and adaptation.

This chapter brings together a series of case studies I originally developed for teaching purposes. As I described in Chapter 1, teaching British students about innovation in China was often challenging. Many arrived with deeply ingrained preconceptions of China as a "copycat" economy, where imitation was equated with theft or inferiority (Abrami et al., 2014; Peng, 2013). These assumptions, while rarely malicious, reflected a worldview shaped by Western media, technological dominance, and a narrow understanding of innovation (Keane, 2007).

In response, I would begin classes with a simple reminder: *"We are all biased, one way or another, by the conditions of our upbringing."* This is not a personal failing; it is, as Karen Barad puts it, an outcome of our onto-ethico-epistemological situatedness—our ways of being, knowing, and valuing are co-constituted (Barad, 2007, p. 185). Knowledge is never neutral. Teaching innovation, then, requires not only new content, but also new ways of seeing.

To support this re-seeing, I brought not only case texts but also photos, advertisements, and design visuals. These helped challenge students' assumptions by showing the specificity and ingenuity of Chinese adaptations. While not all of these images can be reproduced here due to copyright restrictions, the visual strategy was integral: to make the unfamiliar visible, not through abstraction but through granular detail.

While collecting these materials, I was fascinated by the energy and creativity on the ground. Though I was dismayed by the money worship and hyper-consumerism of the time, these cases also convinced me of a distinctive culture of resilience and resourcefulness. From the ground up, people engaged in imitative innovation and adaptive creativity, generating a wide range of products that met the needs of different social groups—urban and rural, young and old, manual labourers and professionals alike.

I was deeply moved when told that even "old ladies picking up trash on the street also use mobile phones daily." Such stories crystallised the pervasive reach of China's technological transformation. Equally striking were the "washing machine that can wash potatoes" (see Section 6.2), Alibaba's triumph over eBay

https://doi.org/10.1515/9783110757576-012

(see Section 6.3), and the *shanzhai* phones that democratised access to mobile technology (see Section 6.4). The state had built the telecommunications infrastructure, but it was small companies and grassroots actors who provided the handsets and applications that embedded it into everyday life. These different forms of imitation, top-down and bottom-up, were complementary. Without the latter, China's rise would not have taken the shape it did.

6.1 Introduction

At the heart of this chapter is a broader claim: that innovation in a globalising world is deeply intertwined with imitation. Globalisation, at its core, is a vast and complex tapestry woven through countless acts of imitation. As Gabriel Tarde argued more than a century ago, imitation is not the antithesis of innovation; it is the medium through which social and technical change unfolds (Tarde, 1903, p. 7).

Yet imitation is never a mere act of copying. In the global arena, what begins as imitation often ends as transformation (Ernst & Kim, 2002). Whether subtle or radical, these transformations emerge through the interaction of imported models and local conditions. Sometimes they are deliberate: strategic adaptations made to fit new markets, meet regulatory demands, or match user practices. Other times, they are emergent: shaped by misperceptions, misalignments, resource constraints, cultural frictions, and infrastructural realities (Shen & Williams, 2005).

In this sense, imitation is less a mirror than a prism, refracting and reshaping ideas through the filters of lived experience. To make sense of these dynamics, I coined two conceptual terms to help us navigate the complex relationship between imitation and innovation:

Imitative-innovation: This occurs where the initial goal is imitation, but the process generates adaptations, recombinations, or local innovations that depart from the original. Here, copying becomes a starting point for creative problem-solving, as local constraints and opportunities reshape the imported model.

Innovative-imitation: This recognises that even seemingly novel solutions are embedded within a frame of imitation, drawing from existing forms while blending in new elements to meet local practicalities or aspirations. Innovation here builds consciously on what came before, adapting and extending rather than rejecting precedent.

These concepts exist on a spectrum rather than as rigid categories. Both unfold within what I call the *existing frame*, the structured socio-technical environment in which actors operate. This frame includes the availability of resources (technical skills, infrastructure, capital), the strategic priorities of actors (balancing survival and ambition), and the surrounding ecosystems (legal rules, standards, user expectations, cultural norms) (Williams & Edge, 1996). In many cases, even the objectives of actions may be blurred or hidden, intentionally or unintentionally.

The existing frame is not fixed. It evolves through feedback, learning, and contestation (Fleck, 1993). A regulation might be challenged or reinterpreted; a design standard might be bent; a user habit might shift slowly, then suddenly. Actors work not in a vacuum but in negotiation with these frames, sometimes reinforcing them, sometimes stretching them, and sometimes transforming them.

Thus, the outcomes of imitation and innovation are not determined by originality alone. They are shaped by how people—engineers, entrepreneurs, regulators, and users—navigate the space between imitation and invention. Just as earlier chapters highlighted how Microsoft's dominance and Linux's failure hinged on the actions of millions of ordinary users, this chapter insists that the "masses" are central to the story of innovation (Shen, 2019b). They do not simply consume innovations made elsewhere; they actively refashion technologies, practices, and infrastructures. Without their participation, no system, whether proprietary or open-source, can reach viability. The masses generate the critical mass on which innovation depends.

The case materials that follow explore this space. From washing machines adapted for rural Chinese life that wash potatoes, to the construction of Alibaba's digital ecosystem, to the rebellious ingenuity of *shanzhai* phones, these illustrate different trajectories of imitative-innovation and innovative-imitation. Together, they invite us to rethink the assumptions we bring to global innovation: where it happens, what it looks like, who gets to be part of it, and why ordinary people are the lifelines of social and technological development.

6.2 The Washing Machine That Can Wash Potatoes

In the 1990s, multinational giants such as Whirlpool, Siemens, and Bosch turned their attention to China, eager to tap into what was fast becoming one of the world's largest emerging consumer markets (Nolan, 2012). With white goods markets in the West largely saturated, these firms brought not only their products but also their expectations, chief among them, that Chinese consumers would soon follow Western aspirations towards front-loading washing machines and integrated kitchen aesthetics.

For a time, this appeared true. In urban centres, Western-style front-loaders gained traction. Chinese developers and consumers alike embraced the trend, reshaping domestic architecture to include washing machines beneath kitchen countertops. But in the countryside, a different logic prevailed, one rooted in practicality, not prestige.

While international brands competed for urban middle-class consumers, domestic Chinese manufacturers, facing limited access to top-tier urban markets, shifted their focus to the underserved rural population (Shen, 2017). Among these manufacturers, Kelon, a lesser-known but agile company, made a critical observation: rural users were repurposing their top-loading washing machines not just to clean clothes, but to rinse muddy vegetables, especially potatoes. This improvised use reflected local priorities: durability, simplicity, and the ability to adapt technology to multipurpose routines in resource-constrained settings.

What followed was a quiet but powerful act of imitative-innovation. Kelon did not invent a new machine from scratch. Instead, it adapted the existing top-loader design, already itself an import from Japanese models, to better meet rural needs (Shen, 2017). Engineers modified the drainage system to handle silt and debris, reinforced internal parts to support irregular and heavier loads, and enhanced control options to accommodate more flexible cycles. These changes were incremental, but meaningful. They reflected attentiveness to real use, not hypothetical scenarios drafted in urban design labs.

This innovation was not driven by marketing vision or research and development (R&D) breakthroughs, but by pragmatic engagement with emergent user practices (Silverstone, 1993). The washing machine was reimagined not because of a shift in global technological paradigms, but because farmers had started using it to wash root vegetables. It was a transformation that no global company had anticipated, and one that few would have noticed without being embedded in local contexts.

This process highlights a recurring theme in China's industrial rise: that innovation is not always about invention. Sometimes, it is about noticing, listening, and adapting (Lundvall, 2010). What appears as a minor adaptation here reveals a deeper truth: innovation emerges when ordinary users—farmers, households, small entrepreneurs—improvise new uses for existing technologies. Their everyday experiments generate insights that manufacturers can stabilise into design (von Hippel, 2005). Without this feedback from the ground, the innovations of Kelon and others would not have been possible. The critical mass of rural users gave weight and legitimacy to such design shifts, making them commercially viable rather than isolated curiosities (Shen, 2019b). The potato-washing washing machine did not disrupt the industry. But it flourished, precisely because it fit the rhythms of rural life better than any glossy, urban-centric front-loader.

As I discussed in an earlier talk on Chinese innovation for the History and Sociology of Technology (HST) programme, companies like Kelon exemplify how imitative adaptation, when shaped by cultural practices and local constraints, can yield designs that are both functionally successful and socially embedded (Shen, 2017). Unlike high-end Western appliances that were ill-suited to the material realities of China's countryside, Kelon's machine was embraced not because it was cheaper, but because it was smarter for the context in which it operated.

This case reminds us that technological success is not universal; it is situated. And in that situatedness, imitation becomes a site of invention.

6.3 Alibaba: Adaptive Innovation in China's Platform Ecosystem

In 2002, eBay acquired a 33 % stake in China's leading online auction platform, EachNet, and subsequently acquired it fully in 2003, aiming to replicate its global success in the burgeoning Chinese market (Chen, 2006). However, eBay's strategy underestimated the distinct socio-technical conditions of China, particularly the lack of a widespread credit system and consumer habits rooted in face-to-face transactions (Shen, 2016).

That same year, Alibaba launched Taobao, directly competing with eBay by tailoring its platform to the specific needs of Chinese consumers. Instead of relying on credit cards or PayPal, Taobao introduced Alipay, a prepaid escrow system that held funds until buyers confirmed receipt and satisfaction with their purchases (Greeven & Wei, 2018). This innovation addressed trust issues prevalent in a market rife with counterfeit goods and inconsistent product quality.

Taobao also implemented real-time chat functions, enabling direct communication between buyers and sellers, replicating the trust-building practices of local markets. Unlike eBay, which charged listing fees and restricted direct communication to maintain its auction structure, Taobao offered free listings and fostered open interaction, allowing sellers to build credibility over time (Shen, 2016).

By 2005, Taobao had captured the dominant share of the Chinese e-commerce market, while eBay's presence declined significantly. eBay eventually shut down its Chinese operations in 2006 (Chen, 2006). While some Western analysts attributed Taobao's rise to its free listings policy, the broader success lay in what scholars identify as "adaptive innovation", small but systemic transformations deeply integrated into the socio-economic fabric of a locale (Ernst & Kim, 2002).

Alibaba's success exemplifies what I have termed "mass and momentum" (Shen, 2019b, p. 508). Unlike eBay's strategy, which focused on the premium market segment, Alibaba targeted the wider population, continuously adjusting its business model to accommodate diverse demands. This approach allowed all interested parties—buyers, sellers, and service providers—to interact and negotiate directly, finding workable solutions within existing contexts.

As latecomers in a new market system, participants began experimenting by enrolling themselves on the platform, mutually reinforcing pragmatic commercial practices. Consumers learned to shop for satisfactory outcomes by voicing complaints about poor-quality goods or unethical seller behaviour. Sellers, in turn, experimented with marketing methods, leveraging affordable digital techniques previously inaccessible to small businesses (Karippacheril et al., 2013).

During this period, China's market was filled with counterfeit and poor-quality goods, some of which appeared on Taobao. When the government intensified efforts to clamp down on counterfeits and demonstrate compliance with intellectual property (IP) protection rules, platforms like Taobao faced scrutiny (Alford, 1995). Upon receiving complaints from original brand companies, Taobao would swiftly remove infringing products. However, similar goods could still be sold on Taobao without involving further counterfeiting behaviour. Some products were listed as "clones" of known brands, with user reviews often comparing them to authentic items and assessing their "value for money."

Moreover, Taobao's iterative design and continuous improvement fostered a mass-participatory ecosystem. The platform became a space for co-learning between consumers and traders, engaging not only service sector actors but also producers and product designers (Ardolino et al., 2020). For instance, in 2009, after receiving a faulty electric converter, I requested a return. The seller promptly contacted me, offered a replacement, and possibly relayed my feedback to the producer. Over time, I observed a gradual improvement in product quality on Taobao.

Initially, online shopping had to compete with vibrant physical stores, shopping centres, and malls in cities like Beijing and Shanghai. These shopping districts attracted enthusiastic consumers, especially during weekends and national holidays. During my visits between 2008 and 2012, I would often bring electronics or garments for repair or replacement. At that time, my Chinese academic colleagues anticipated that these shopping districts would eventually be replaced by online shopping. Initially sceptical, my subsequent experiences convinced me of the convenience and efficiency of online shopping in China.

This dynamic is crucial to understanding China's technology landscape. Imitation here does not denote passivity or lack of creativity. Rather, as Gabriel Tarde's sociology of imitation suggests, imitation can be a generative social force when combined with deviation and transformation (Tarde, 1903). Taobao imitated eBay's e-commerce model, but only as a point of departure. Its purpose was not to replicate but to reformulate digital commerce for Chinese realities.

Alibaba's ecosystem strategy did not stop with Taobao. Over the years, it evolved into a multi-sided platform integrating online and offline services, incorporating Ant Financial, logistics networks, credit systems like Sesame Credit, business financing, entertainment, and more (Kshetri, 2016; Shen, 2019d). These services emerged not from a central plan but as extensions of emergent needs from Chinese society. This bottom-up dynamic exemplifies how latecomer innovation can develop through local adaptations rather than radical disruption. Here again, it was not Alibaba alone that displaced eBay, but the mass participation of millions of consumers and sellers who collectively stabilised new practices of online shopping. From experimenting with escrow payments to refining seller reputations, users provided the density of activity that allowed Alibaba to scale (Shen, 2019b). This was a case of "collective accomplishment": the convergence of state frameworks, corporate strategy, and above all, grassroots adoption.

The question remains whether Western companies recognised the value of localisation and conceptually understood the importance of adaptive innovation to their model of technology development. Building an ecosystem that works within a society requires a better understanding of the real trends of imitative and innovative transformation. It departs from a single idea or model and opens up new evolutionary pathways with diverse trends and models.

E-commerce may be seen as a profit-making commercial machine, or observers might assume that China could not innovate. In conventional conceptual categories, innovation belongs to the elite of society with high education and purely technical elements involved. However, what Shen and Naughton (2013) call a "visible hand", a blend of market responsiveness and infrastructural coordination, often guided subtly but steadily by state policy frameworks—plays a crucial role.

In sum, Taobao's story is more than a tale of market competition; it is a case of ecosystem innovation shaped by the specificities of Chinese society, economy, and governance. It exemplifies the kind of "mass and momentum" required to displace entrenched global players and shows how technological imitation, when adapted and recontextualised, becomes a potent form of innovation (Shen, 2019b). This case encourages us to rethink conventional binaries between innovation and imitation and to recognise the transformative potential of adaptive socio-technical systems.

6.4 Shanzhai Mobile: The Rebel Phones That Democratised Luxury

When Apple launched the iPhone in 2007, it quickly became a global icon of modernity and status. In China, where Western lifestyles were increasingly aspirational, especially among youth, the iPhone symbolised more than just technology; it represented global belonging (Wallis, 2013). This intense desire created strong market demand among consumers who sought access to global technological culture.

However, the iPhone's high price made it unattainable for many. By 2008, official sales channels were absent in China, as Apple delayed its market entry. This gap led to a booming grey market, with iPhones smuggled in and resold at prices ranging from 5,000 to 8,000 RMB, equivalent to two to three months' salary for the average urban worker (Tse et al., 2009). Despite the cost, demand persisted, further intensifying the device's allure.

Enter the *shanzhai* phones. The term *shanzhai* (mountain stronghold 山寨) originates from Chinese folklore, describing rebel hideouts that challenged imperial authority. Central to this mythos is the idea of "robbing the rich to help the poor" (*jiefu jipín* 劫富济贫) (Keane & Zhao, 2012, p. 10). The term carried connotations of resistance, redistribution, and grassroots ingenuity. By evoking this cultural lineage, *shanzhai* phones were not simply viewed as counterfeit products; they became, for many, a legitimate way to level the playing field. Manufacturers did not shy away from imitation, sometimes even highlighting the similarities as a selling point. Their aim was unapologetic—make desirable technologies accessible to ordinary people, bypassing the exclusivity imposed by global tech giants.

By 2008, thousands of nimble manufacturers in Shenzhen were producing iPhone lookalikes, complete with adjusted branding like "Aple" or "iPone" or apples with no bite (Lin, 2011). Priced between 300 to 800 RMB, these devices offered an affordable alternative for workers, students, and rural migrants who could not afford the original. The *shanzhai* phones became symbols of inclusion, allowing users to partake in the global tech culture.

The *shanzhai* phenomenon was not confined to China. During Barack Obama's 2008 US presidential campaign, *shanzhai* phone makers capitalised on his global appeal. In Kenya and other parts of Africa, they sold "Obama" phones, devices bearing Obama's face and the slogan "Yes We Can" (Wallis, 2013). These phones resonated with consumers in emerging markets who identified with Obama's message of change and inclusion. The "Obama" phones sold briskly in Kenya, combining novelty, affordability, and cultural relevance.

As the *shanzhai* phenomenon gained momentum, it quickly outgrew simple mimicry. While the early wave of devices focused on cloning the iPhone's physical form—its sleek aluminium body, single-button interface, and iconic logo—*shanzhai* firms began to focus on adapting functionalities to the needs of Chinese users. This is where the ingenuity of the *shanzhai* model began to shine.

Storage

One of the most striking examples was storage. At the time, Apple's iPhones offered fixed internal memory, typically 16GB or 32GB, with no option for expansion. To upgrade to higher capacity models, users had to pay significantly more. For most Chinese consumers, this was prohibitively expensive (Tse et al., 2009). With online entertainment content booming—music, literature, and videos—storage usage increased dramatically. *Shanzhai* phones started to offer models that came with microSD slots, allowing users to start with modest internal storage and expand it over time. A 64GB card could be purchased for just 50 RMB, and for 100 RMB, users could upgrade to 128GB, enough to carry hundreds of music albums, entire film collections, and offline apps.

Removable Battery

Battery design was another area where *shanzhai* phones diverged from their high-end counterparts. As Apple moved towards sealed, non-removable batteries, requiring customers to pay substantial fees for replacements, *shanzhai* phones kept things open and practical (Lin, 2011). Removable batteries meant users could swap out a dead battery in seconds, without tools or technicians. Some even came bundled with a second battery for an extra 20 – 50 RMB. In a time before power banks were common and in regions where power cuts were frequent, this was a game-changing feature. It was not about being "cheap"; it was about being usable. For people whose jobs required a mobile phone to be constantly on, battery capacity was essential.

Dual SIM Slots

Just as crucial was the inclusion of dual SIM slots, a design feature that became a hallmark of Chinese mobile phone culture (Oreglia, 2013). In a country where telecom carriers offered regionally segmented services, and where many consumers used one number for personal life and another for work, having two SIMs in a single device was more than a convenience, it was a necessity. For people like me, who visit China occasionally, having a Chinese SIM card is crucial, allowing friends and family to contact me when I am in China, while keeping my home number active for receiving messages.

The customisation did not stop there. Some *shanzhai* models featured oversized speakers tailored to public environments or communal music-sharing cultures. I saw people doing morning exercises in the park using mobile phones to play accompaniment music. Others came preloaded with apps or features designed specifically for local interests, TV tuners, karaoke apps, or locally popular games (Keane & Zhao, 2012). While global brands pursued uniformity and polished minimalism, *shanzhai* phones embraced modularity, variety, and responsiveness to the ground-level needs of consumers.

The *shanzhai* story shows most clearly the creative agency of the masses. What global firms dismissed as piracy or counterfeiting was in fact an iterative process of experimentation by small firms and users (Lin, 2011). By buying, modifying, and spreading *shanzhai* products, millions of consumers sustained an alternative ecosystem, one that democratised access to smartphones. Here, critical mass was both material (cheap phones in circulation) and cultural (a shared ethos of playful adaptation and inclusion) (Shen, 2019b).

What is more, many of these producers made no effort to hide their intentions. Rather than pretending to be Apple, they openly acknowledged their derivative origins while touting added features as improvements. Some advertised, "Not iPhone, better than iPhone."[14] (Varsity, 2010). It was imitation not as deception, but as adaptation. The "copy" became a canvas for creativity, one that prioritised local needs over global prestige.

6.5 Discussion: Rethinking Imitative Innovation from the Ground Up

The three preceding case studies, Kelon's potato-washing washing machine, Alibaba's transformation of e-commerce infrastructure, and the *shanzhai* phone movement, highlight a pattern of innovation that emerges not from elite R&D labs or patent portfolios, but from everyday practices in a transforming society. These cases illustrate a model of innovation that is responsive rather than revolutionary, grounded in social participation, technical improvisation, and institutional learning. In each case, the role of the masses was decisive. Farmers redefined washing machines, small traders reshaped e-commerce, and consumers embraced *shanzhai* phones. These were not isolated anecdotes but examples of how innovation depends on participation at scale (Shen, 2019b). Without critical mass, no adaptation, however clever, becomes infrastructure. With it, even imitative beginnings can mature into new socio-technical systems.

---

14 This slogan was reported in the November 2010 issue of Varsity, the student publication of the Chinese University of Hong Kong (Issue 117).

Rather than measuring innovation solely by novelty or intellectual property, this chapter proposes a broader framework that centres the dynamics of adaptation, inclusion, and reflexivity. We explore four interwoven dimensions of this alternative innovation ecology:

- **Affordable engineering**, where cost-conscious design extends access through pragmatism and compatibility
- **Adaptive product innovation**, where imitation becomes a method of localised reconfiguration
- **A participatory ethos of innovation**, where platforms and small enterprises democratise learning and invention
- **The learning state**, whose regulatory and infrastructural responses co-evolve with the society it governs

Together, these dimensions offer a reframing of innovation, not as a singular breakthrough, but as a distributed process of transformation deeply entangled with social, cultural, and political realities (Barad, 2007).

6.5.1 Affordable Engineering

Affordability is not simply a financial concern; it is a foundational design principle, especially in developing countries like China. In these contexts, the majority of consumers are highly price-sensitive. A product that is unaffordable to most is not merely exclusive; it is irrelevant. For many Chinese manufacturers, particularly during the 2000s and early 2010s, the goal was not to design the most advanced product but to design one that most people could actually use (Zeschky et al., 2011). To produce something affordable was not a strategic branding decision; it was the only realistic way to survive in the market.

Yet, this form of "affordable engineering" was rarely the result of long-term strategic planning. Unlike multinational corporations that aimed to impress through signature designs, novel features, or tightly controlled ecosystems, Chinese firms operated with a more pragmatic ethos. Their innovations, adapters, converters, modular parts, dual-SIM options, and removable batteries, were incremental, utilitarian, and driven by the concrete constraints of production and use (Breznitz & Murphree, 2011). They were not seeking to lead the market through differentiation, but to remain useful and usable in environments marked by infrastructure limitations, fragmented services, and tight budgets.

This ethos reflects more than market pragmatism; it resonates with a cultural sensibility rooted in the Confucian tradition of the Doctrine of the Mean (*zhongyong zhidao* 中庸之道). Innovation, in this worldview, is not about standing out or disrupting; it is about fitting in, balancing, and adapting (Xiao, 2005). The popular saying “the gun always aims at the bird that sticks its head out” (*qiang da chutou niao* 枪打出头鸟) captures the aversion to conspicuousness and the preference for incremental, harmonious change. In this light, making a device compatible with existing products, rather than forcing users to switch ecosystems, is not a lack of originality, but a form of social responsibility and practical wisdom.

Gabriel Tarde’s theory of imitation offers a powerful lens to understand this. For Tarde, societies evolve through repetition with variation, through the diffusion and reconfiguration of practices rather than isolated moments of invention (Tarde, 1903). From this perspective, China’s affordable engineering is not second-rate innovation but social innovation: a distributed, collective process of making technologies workable, desirable, and liveable within local constraints.

This helps explain why Chinese firms focused less on proprietary standards and more on interoperability. Apple designed its devices to bind users to specific components, Lightning cables, sealed batteries, fixed storage. In contrast, *shanzhai* phones adopted open configurations: users could swap SIMs, upgrade memory, replace batteries, and adapt devices to different power sources (Lin, 2011). The guiding principle was not ownership or control; it was flexibility and repairability. These features not only reduced production and purchase costs; they also lowered lifetime usage costs, making technology truly accessible.

In sum, affordable engineering in the Chinese context should not be dismissed as low-end manufacturing. It reflects a different orientation towards innovation, not as a race to be first, but as a craft of fitting technology into the social and material fabric of everyday life.

6.5.2 Adaptive Product Innovation

One of the distinctive features of *shanzhai* was its underlying principle. Like many successful Chinese companies, learning was not only for copying but for adapting to Chinese reality. Xiaomi CEO, Lei Jun, often referenced the concept of “standing on the shoulders of giants”, acknowledging the foundation laid by predecessors while striving to innovate and adapt (Greeven & Wei, 2018, p. 78).

“Copying is not the endpoint but a starting point.” This idea captures the evolution of innovation in China not as a straight line from imitation to originality, but as a layered process of learning, adaptation, and contextualisation (Ernst & Kim, 2002). Rather than seeking to disrupt existing systems with a radically new product, Chinese innovators often began with what already worked and then reshaped it to suit specific environmental, economic, and cultural conditions.

Alibaba exemplifies this adaptive logic. While its early platform bore superficial resemblance to existing e-commerce models, what emerged was not a clone of Amazon or eBay but something far more systemic: an entire digital ecosystem designed around the complexities of Chinese business and infrastructure (Shen, 2016). This platform brought together a diverse network of stakeholders, buyers, sellers, logistics providers, manufacturers, and regulators, into a space of dynamic interaction and mutual adjustment. The innovation was not located in any single technology or feature, but in the orchestration of interdependencies that transformed how value was created, exchanged, and trusted.

Though our case focused on the platform's formative years, Alibaba's later developments powerfully underscore this transformation. The launch of MyBank, which offers micro-loans to small enterprises based on digital transaction histories, demonstrates how embedded data infrastructures can extend financial inclusion (Kshetri, 2016). The distributed architecture of Alibaba Cloud, developed to manage the overwhelming surge of transactions during the November 11 shopping festival, illustrates how technical challenges generated solutions that now support not just commerce but public administration and scientific research. These are not peripheral innovations; they represent structural reconfigurations of finance, governance, and social life.

Such examples point to a broader shift: the platform model in China enabled mass participation in innovation, not just from engineers or entrepreneurs, but from users, vendors, and civil servants (Shen, 2019b). Feedback from millions of users shaped design updates; small merchants adapted services in real time based on platform data; entire logistics chains were reorganised around digital coordination. Here, innovation was not confined to the R&D lab; it became a social process, distributed across everyday actors engaged in iterative, small-scale experimentation.

This model again resonates with Tarde's insight: innovation as collective imitation with variation (Tarde, 1903). Alibaba did not invent online shopping, digital payment, or trust mechanisms, but it reconfigured them through ongoing, localised adaptation. In this process, its platform itself functioned as what Michel Callon calls an *interessement device*, a material and institutional arrangement that recruits and aligns heterogeneous actors into a stabilising network (Callon, 1986, p. 211). By embedding technical functions (like payment verification, logistics tracking, and reputation scores) into its core infrastructure, Alibaba did not just facilitate transactions; it constructed relations. These non-human actors, algorithms, data flows, user interfaces, played an active role in shaping how people interacted, trusted, and transacted.

What emerged was not a fixed network but a self-transforming ecosystem, one that continues to evolve as new participants, technologies, and regulations enter the fold. China's e-commerce infrastructure thus operates not only as a service platform but as a social-technical engine of change (Castells, 2009). It enables mass participation in innovation and steadily remakes the society it connects, through financial inclusion, digital literacy, and the routinisation of trust in digital environments. Here, imitation is not backwardness but a catalyst, a way of entering the conversation by reframing it in one's own terms.

6.5.3 A Participatory Ethos of Innovation

Innovation in reform-era China has been marked by a striking contrast: an abundance of activity from below, but without the ideological force or coherence once associated with state-led "mass-line" movements (Young, 1980). While the term "mass-line" evokes Maoist efforts to mobilise the people, it is inseparable from the tragic excesses of campaigns like the Cultural Revolution, when empowering the masses without a framework for critical knowledge led to widespread suffering, especially for intellectuals. The idea of participation was noble in theory, but disastrous in a society where education was limited and populism unchecked.

In contrast, the post-1978 reform era fostered a more pragmatic, dispersed, and diverse form of mass participation, not guided by ideology, but by material needs, individual ambitions, and a willingness to experiment (Breznitz & Murphree, 2011). What emerged was initially top-down mobilisation of the masses, followed by a bottom-up surge of activity that, despite lacking coherence or strategic design, reshaped the country's innovation landscape.

The most successful and orderly transformation started with digital commerce and its support for small businesses and manufacturing. During the early 2000s, it was not unusual to see imitation products of a new gadget from New York appear in a Chinese market the next day. These imitations varied wildly in quality: some were crude copies, symptomatic of scientific illiteracy or short-term profiteering, while others, crafted by skilled engineers, were arguably over-engineered, blending precision with surplus creativity (Keane & Zhao, 2012). The diversity was immense, reflecting the fact that the "masses" in China were never homogeneous. Some entrepreneurs were driven purely by survival, others by dreams that had been suppressed under earlier regimes. But across this spectrum, a shared trait was visible: extreme dedication and hard work, what Churchill once described as "blood, toil, tears, and sweat."

Digital platforms such as Alibaba became the first infrastructures to give form and visibility to this participatory energy. More than just online marketplaces, these platforms educated the population, teaching millions how to search, compare, transact, negotiate, and build reputations in real time (Shen, 2016). They turned sellers into service providers, customers into co-designers, and transactions into forms of mutual learning. In this sense, platforms like Taobao and Alipay functioned as civilising devices, introducing new economic and technical literacies to a population that had only recently emerged from subsistence conditions.

Crucially, these systems fostered innovation not by privileging the exceptional few, but by scaling the contributions of the many. The rapid feedback loops between users and producers, the hyper-adaptable logistics networks, and the data-informed refinements to services and design created an environment where innovation was iterative, collective, and self-organising (Baldwin & von Hippel, 2011). Innovation was not something you waited for; it was something you participated in.

This participatory structure echoes what Barad, drawing from agential realism, would frame as a material-discursive entanglement: where ontology (who gets to act), ethics (who is affected), and epistemology (how we know) are co-constituted (Barad, 2007, p. 185). China's digital ecosystems created new ontological categories, of the rural tech entrepreneur, the gig logistician, the local brand innovator, and embedded ethical challenges into daily technical decisions. Imitation, in this context, became an epistemological method: a way of learning by doing, copying, failing, and refining.

In 2008, I attended a workshop organised by the Chinese Economic Association, where Cambridge professor Peter Nolan gave a keynote speech. He declared that China had little chance of competing with established multinational enterprises, due to the rigid management of large state-owned firms and the inexperience of private ones (Nolan, 2012). His pessimistic forecast brought one young Chinese student to tears. Yet what followed painted a different picture. Over the next two decades, Chinese firms demonstrated a remarkable ability to span the full spectrum of consumer demand, from the cheapest, most basic goods to sophisticated, premium designs. Unlike dominant Western firms that focus on signature, cutting-edge products, China's strength lay in range, responsiveness, and inclusion. In today's increasingly polarised world, this is not a weakness but a strategic depth.

In this light, even the lowest-quality *shanzhai* product had a function, not just economic, but educational. It lowered barriers to entry, invited critique, and created space for differentiation (Keane & Zhao, 2012). Where outsiders might have seen chaos or greed, many inside China found hope, possibility, and the gradual emergence of standards through shared experience. The platform was not a solution to innovation; it was the condition for its emergence.

6.5.4 The Learning State

The role of the state in China's innovation trajectory is often mischaracterised, either framed as an authoritarian puppet master orchestrating top-down modernisation or dismissed as a rigid, bureaucratic obstacle to entrepreneurial energy. Neither captures the more nuanced dynamic that has unfolded over the past four decades: the emergence of a learning state, a state that governs by listening, adjusts by observing, and intervenes not through rigid control but through reflexive adaptation (Shen & Naughton, 2013).

In the early reform period, the state's actions were not guided by strategic foresight so much as by pragmatic experimentation. Regulatory grey zones were tolerated; *shanzhai* manufacturers were largely left alone; pilot zones were rolled out not because outcomes were known in advance, but because they offered sites for learning (Heilmann, 2008). Policy-making was observational, not purely instructional. The explosion of small enterprises, grey markets, and imitative products offered more than administrative challenges; they offered real-time social data about what worked, what failed, and what demanded recalibration.

This adaptive mode of governance was evident in how authorities approached *shanzhai* phones. Rather than cracking down indiscriminately, the state allowed this informal sector to grow, absorbing demand unmet by global brands. Over time, enforcement and regulation evolved, counterfeiting was curbed, quality standards rose, and new domestic brands emerged (Keane & Zhao, 2012). But these shifts did not reflect a grand design; they reflected a learning curve, where the state responded not just to economic pressures but to the creative improvisations of society itself.

Infrastructure was another key domain of state learning. Investments in broadband expansion, rural electrification, and digital payments were not launched in anticipation of innovation; they followed it (Hong, 2017). Once platforms like Alibaba and WeChat began transforming how Chinese citizens interacted with markets, the state responded, not by nationalising them, but by supporting their scaling while slowly formalising their operating environment. In many ways, these platforms began to function as quasi-public infrastructures, facilitating trust, identity, commerce, and education.

A telling comparative case helps illustrate this learning orientation. In the early 2000s in the UK, telecom providers routinely sold phones locked to their networks, effectively trapping customers unless they bought a new device or paid unlocking fees. In contrast, mobile phone retail in China operated through large, open market floors where consumers could browse, test, and compare models across brands and price points. This environment fostered not only consumer empowerment but technical literacy. When I once asked a representative from a Chinese telecom company in 2009 why they did not follow the UK model, the answer was clear: while some firms were interested in lock-in strategies, government regulators prohibited them, stating that telecom providers should "concentrate on providing better services," not restricting market choice.

Such decisions reflect a governing logic not of dominance but of facilitation. The learning state did not always anticipate change, but it knew how to keep pace with it. Policies were reactive as much as proactive; enforcement was selective, often experimental (Heilmann, 2008). The result was not a neatly planned innovation system, but a flexible, evolving socio-technical assemblage that permitted surprise, failure, and adjustment.

Here, the state's role aligns with what Karen Barad, through agential realism, might describe as a co-constitution of agency, not a separate authority acting upon society, but an actor entangled within it (Barad, 2007, p. 185). In China, this meant responding to new ontologies: the rise of the rural entrepreneur, the micro-lender, the app-based logistician. Governance, in this sense, became a kind of innovation in itself: experimental, distributed, and deeply interdependent with the social transformations it was meant to steer.

6.6 Conclusion: Innovation Beyond the Canon

The cases and arguments explored in this chapter point to a different epistemology of innovation, one that emerges not from institutional blueprints or breakthrough inventions, but from pragmatism, participation, and learning. Chinese innovation during the reform era was not driven by a grand national strategy nor a single visionary firm, but by millions of everyday actors responding to shifting constraints with whatever tools, knowledge, and aspirations they had. It was messy, uneven, and often contradictory. But from this disorder came resilience and creativity.

Affordable engineering showed how making technology usable for the majority is itself a form of design intelligence (Zeschky et al., 2011). Adaptive product innovation revealed how imitation, when grounded in context, becomes a platform for reconfiguration and co-creation (Ernst & Kim, 2002). The participatory ethos reflected a social logic of inclusion, not through slogans, but through infrastructures that allowed people to test, fail, learn, and try again (Shen, 2019b). Behind all of this, the state functioned not as a static enforcer, but as a learning actor, shaping and being shaped by the experiments unfolding across society (Shen & Naughton, 2013).

What emerges from these case studies is a challenge to conventional innovation paradigms that privilege breakthrough moments, individual genius, and institutional R&D. Instead, we see innovation as a fundamentally social process, distributed across millions of participants, embedded in everyday practices, and sustained through collective learning. This perspective shifts our attention from the exceptional to the ordinary, from the laboratory to the marketplace, from invention to adaptation.

The washing machine that washes potatoes demonstrates that innovation often begins with users, not designers. Rural farmers did not wait for manufacturers to understand their needs; they improvised solutions and manufacturers learned to follow. This pattern of user-driven innovation challenges the linear model where companies create products that consumers passively adopt (von Hippel, 2005). Instead, we see a recursive relationship where use shapes design, which enables new uses, which drives further adaptation.

Alibaba's platform evolution illustrates how imitation can become a generative strategy rather than a deficit. By starting with eBay's model but adapting it to Chinese conditions, Alibaba created something qualitatively different, not just an e-commerce platform, but a digital ecosystem that reshaped finance, logistics, and social interaction. This suggests that in a connected world, the capacity to adapt and integrate may be more valuable than the ability to invent from scratch.

The *shanzhai* phone phenomenon reveals how copying can democratise access to technological capabilities. By making smartphones affordable and customisable, *shanzhai* manufacturers did not just create cheaper products; they created new user populations and new forms of digital participation. The modifications they introduced, dual SIM slots, removable batteries, expandable storage, later influenced mainstream manufacturers, showing how marginal innovations can reshape industry standards.

A central insight running through all three cases is the importance of critical mass in innovation systems. Kelon's potato-washing machine succeeded not because of its technical sophistication, but because it resonated with millions of rural users who provided the market scale necessary for commercial viability. Alibaba displaced eBay not through superior technology alone, but by mobilising a critical mass of Chinese users who collectively stabilised new practices of digital commerce. *Shanzhai* phones thrived because they created an alternative ecosystem supported by millions of consumers who valued accessibility over prestige.

This highlights a crucial but often overlooked dimension of innovation: that breakthrough technologies require social infrastructures to become viable systems. Without mass adoption, even clever adaptations remain curiosities. With it, incremental improvements can accumulate into transformative change. This suggests that innovation policy should focus not only on supporting inventors and entrepreneurs, but also on creating conditions for mass participation and collective learning.

These insights have broader implications for how we understand innovation in an interconnected world. If innovation increasingly depends on the ability to adapt, integrate, and scale rather than to invent from scratch, then the geographic and institutional distribution of innovative capacity may be shifting. Countries and regions that excel at affordable engineering, adaptive product development, and participatory innovation may gain advantages over those that focus exclusively on frontier research and breakthrough technologies.

This is not to diminish the importance of basic research or radical innovation, but to recognise that different forms of innovation may be becoming more significant in a globally connected economy. The capacity to notice emerging user needs, adapt existing technologies to new contexts, and mobilise mass participation may be as valuable as the ability to create entirely new scientific knowledge.

For developing countries, this suggests alternative pathways to technological capability that do not require replicating the institutional structures of advanced economies. Instead of focusing exclusively on building world-class universities and R&D centres, they might also invest in creating conditions for widespread experimentation, user-driven innovation, and adaptive product development.

The cases examined in this chapter come primarily from China's reform era, when regulatory environments were relatively permissive and global integration was accelerating. Whether similar patterns of imitative innovation can emerge under different conditions, tighter intellectual property enforcement, slower economic growth, or more restrictive regulatory frameworks, remains an open question.

Moreover, the environmental and social costs of the mass participation model described here deserve critical examination. The rapid proliferation of cheap electronics and disposable goods has contributed to significant environmental challenges. The labour conditions in many of the factories producing affordable innovations often fall short of international standards. A complete assessment of imitative innovation must grapple with these externalities, not just celebrate the democratisation of technological access.

Future research might explore how the principles of affordable engineering, adaptive innovation, and participatory development could be applied to address pressing global challenges like climate change, public health, and social inequality. Can the same distributed, experimental approach that characterised China's consumer electronics sector be channelled towards developing sustainable technologies and inclusive innovations?

Ultimately, this chapter argues for understanding innovation as a fundamentally social process rather than a technical one. Technologies succeed or fail not based on their intrinsic properties alone, but on their ability to become embedded in social practices, to mobilise collective participation, and to evolve through use. This perspective emphasises the agency of ordinary users, the importance of context and adaptation, and the value of inclusive participation in technological development.

What China's trajectory offers, then, is not a model to be copied, but a provocation to rethink what innovation is, where it comes from, and who gets to be part of it. To innovate is not only to invent the new, but to remake the familiar, materially, socially, and ethically, in response to the world as it is. In recognising the innovative potential within imitation, we open space for more democratic, participatory, and inclusive forms of technological development.

The future of global innovation may depend less on protecting intellectual property and more on fostering the conditions for collective creativity, adaptive learning, and mass participation in technological development. In this light, the washing machine that washes potatoes becomes not an anomaly to be explained away, but a glimpse of innovation's democratic potential. What appears absurd to the canonical lens becomes, under a different frame, a powerful symbol of how innovation truly unfolds, messy, situated, and collective.

7 Enter the Laboratory: The Dynamic Evolution of China's Digital Cultural Industries

Preamble

My project on intellectual property (IP) in cultural industries paralleled China's own passage from unregulated creativity to highly competitive platform consolidation, showing how both researcher and country grappled with the contradictions of protection and participation.

Between 2015 and 2017, I led a research project titled *"Convergence or differentiation in IP protection? A case study of emerging models for digital film, music and e-fiction production and distribution in China."* The project explored the transformation of China's digital cultural industries, with a particular focus on intellectual property protections in online music, literature, and film. My interest in intellectual property, which began with the study of Linux and open-source software (see Chapter 4), had by then deepened. From a developing-country perspective, I saw the urgency of IP reform; from a Science and Technology Studies (STS) standpoint, I sensed the deeper problem of an economic-legal framework that treats all technologies as abstract, disembedded entities.

When I embarked on the project, I hoped it would provide insights into the practical world of a latecomer country which, lacking its own traditions of intellectual property, had been pressed to imitate IP practices under top-down pressure from both its government and international economic sanctions. Personal experience reminded me that culture and creativity resist such rigid frameworks. People rarely fall in love with a piece of music upon first hearing, and creative products are extraordinarily complex and dynamic, defying uniform rules. Growing up in China, I knew how songs once used for propaganda were still sung decades later at reunions with classmates or old friends, not just because everyone remembered the lyrics, but because these songs carried the weight of shared memory.

In the field, I was struck by the reality that the absence of strict IP enforcement, particularly in the early stages of reform, had allowed creativity to bloom in unanticipated ways (see Section 7.2). Weak legal frameworks coincided with explosive innovation. Yet as our research deepened, a more complicated picture emerged. The very companies that had flourished in this unregulated space, Baidu, Alibaba, and Tencent, eventually turned IP law into a competitive weapon (see Section 7.3). Protection became less about fostering creativity than about de-

https://doi.org/10.1515/9783110757576-013

fending territory and stifling rivals. The outcomes grew polarised, and government intervention was sometimes needed to rein in costly platform rivalries.

This contradiction compelled me to rethink the standard narratives around IP. It was not simply a balance between protection and creativity. IP appeared instead as a dynamic, strategic tool, one that evolved with markets and power structures, and whose impacts were always contextually bound (see Section 7.4).

As I was not a specialist in cultural sectors or IP law, we formed an interdisciplinary team and conducted fieldwork across Beijing, Shanghai, Guangzhou, and Shenzhen. We carried out 59 semi-structured interviews with 73 respondents, including platform executives, content creators, and users (Shen et al., 2019a), and collected extensive secondary data and policy documents.

Our analytical framework drew from Science and Technology Studies (STS), particularly the socio-technical systems perspective. Innovation emerged not through the planful intervention of the state or media corporation but through an evolving co-produced process involving businesses, the state, creators and citizen-users, with outcomes that reconfigured the digital ecology itself (see Section 7.5). Cultural products are too heterogeneous and dynamic for simple rules or models to apply.

This realisation also planted a seed for me, to appreciate later how data-driven infrastructures might offer new possibilities for visibility and traceability (see Chapter 8). My intermittent engagement with IP across different fields deepened my understanding of the role for STS: its interdisciplinary orientation makes it uniquely able to capture the complexity of a field where commercial interests, cultural practices, and state strategies are deeply entangled.

7.1 From Mass-Line to Mass Platforms: Historical Context

Under the socialist regime, China's cultural production operated on fundamentally different principles from those in the West. Books were extremely cheap, music was freely available, and films could be viewed at minimal cost. Creators of these works, writers, musicians, filmmakers, were employed by the state. Their task was not to generate profit but to produce art that reflected and uplifted the lives of ordinary people. Cultural work was directed by ideological priorities: certain themes were encouraged and celebrated, while others were suppressed. This system functioned as a top-down model, with clear political boundaries and moral expectations embedded in cultural expression (Shen et al., 2019a).

A pivotal moment in this model was Mao Zedong's 1942 "Talks at the Yan'an Forum on Literature and Art," where he articulated the enduring principle that art should serve the workers, peasants, and soldiers (Mao, 1942, p. 3). According to Mao, artists should "go into the midst of the masses" to observe, experience, and study their lives (Mao, 1942, p. 12). This foundational idea, that literature and art must reflect and serve the people, was reaffirmed in the All-China Congresses of Literary and Arts Workers (CLAW) in 1949, 1953, and 1960. These gatherings institutionalised what became known as the mass line in cultural work.

Two key strategies underpinned this approach: professional artists were commissioned to create content for the masses, and the masses themselves were encouraged and trained to become cultural producers. However, despite sustained promotion, the mass line remained more of an ideological aspiration than a lived reality. Creative production was highly centralised, and grassroots participation was limited by structural hierarchies and ideological gatekeeping.

During the Great Leap Forward (1958–1962), the campaign for mass participation intensified. Art schools were required to recruit heavily from proletarian backgrounds, workers, peasants, and soldiers, reflecting the ideal of bottom-up creativity. Yet even then, outputs were filtered through narrow political narratives. Over time, the definition of "the masses" expanded, but mass art became increasingly a vehicle for mobilisation and propaganda rather than a platform for diverse or spontaneous expression.

Growing up during the 1960s and 1970s, I remember how deeply this policy shaped everyday life. Schools regularly held cultural variety shows with performances of poetry recitations, singing, and dance. Competitions were organised at district or city levels. During the Cultural Revolution (*wenhua dageming* 文化大革命), everyone, including janitors at my school, participated in daily morning drills, singing revolutionary songs broadcast over loudspeakers and marching in formation. The most iconic cultural products of this time were the Eight Model Plays (*yangban xi* 样板戏), which became fixtures in our lives. We all memorised their songs and lines. As young girls imitating the ballet scenes, we would ruin our shoes by trying to stand en pointe, dreaming of that same grace. These works were far more than entertainment; they were instruments of political education and moral instruction.

In the reform era, the mass line remained part of official rhetoric, but its execution shifted. The state continued to promote "mass art" (*qunzhong wenyi* 群众文艺) as a form of cultural participation, though with increasing professionalisation and decreasing direct political control. Despite this evolution, the promise of bottom-up cultural creativity remained largely unrealised.

It was not until the digital revolution that this ideal began to be fulfilled in a more substantive way. With the rise of internet platforms and mobile technology, ordinary people gained unprecedented access to tools for content creation and distribution (Shen et al., 2019a). Platforms like QQ Music, iQIYI, and China Literature enabled individuals not only to consume but also to actively participate in cultural production, writing, remixing, performing, commenting, and sharing. These platforms introduced new logics: user engagement, data monetisation, and, crucially, intellectual property regulation. While IP had been virtually absent during socialism, it became a central mechanism through which cultural content was owned, managed, and monetised.

Initially, IP was adopted largely in response to international trade pressures (Street et al., 2015). Over time, however, Chinese firms began to reinterpret and localise it, not just as a legal framework, but as a tool for platform differentiation, content control, and strategic competition. Just as significantly, users themselves became active agents in this ecosystem. Prosumers, simultaneously producers and consumers, generated, circulated, and monetised content, making platforms deeply dependent on mass participation.

What unfolded was a cultural environment that was chaotic, experimental, and unexpectedly fertile. Platforms competed intensely for user attention, constantly copying features from one another and learning from global models (Tang & Lyons, 2017). They were not just building platforms; they were assembling ecosystems in real time, through adaptation, improvisation, and user-driven feedback. In this sense, the digital revolution finally realised what socialist cultural policy had long aspired to: a mass cultural system, dynamic and multidirectional, where the people were no longer passive recipients but co-creators.

Mass participation extended beyond cultural sectors; it interacted with digital internet technology development in other areas. Participation in online activities transformed multiple service platforms into social and technical spaces for digital literacy and diverse experimental projects, providing pathways to build infrastructures for educational communication, negotiation and interaction.

7.2 The Digital Transition and the Hundred Flowers Blooming

The early 2000s marked a transformative juncture in China's cultural landscape. This was not a linear march towards modernisation or market reform, but a period of vibrant experimentation, an era some came to describe as a digital "hundred flowers blooming" (Shen et al., 2019a). Animated by expanding internet access and emerging digital technologies, it ushered in a wave of grassroots expression that reshaped the contours of cultural participation and created a messy, generative commons of innovation.

This phase stood in stark contrast to the centrally controlled cultural production of the socialist era, where the state determined themes and works were distributed as ideological instruments. In the new digital landscape, cultural products no longer flowed solely from the top down. Instead, they were uploaded, remixed, and reimagined from the bottom up. As internet infrastructure expanded and the friction of distribution fell, anyone with a modest connection could become a creator. Piracy was widespread, yet so was experimentation and creativity.

Following China's accession to the World Trade Organisation (WTO) in 2001, new intellectual property laws were swiftly introduced to align with international standards (Liu, 2010; Shen, 2015). However, enforcement lagged and public understanding remained limited. This legal ambiguity inadvertently opened a space for platforms and users to collectively explore new cultural practices. Rather than lawlessness, this was a window for exploratory adaptation, an environment where digital content could circulate widely, unencumbered by rigid rules.

7.2.1 Network Music and Grassroots Creativity

One early and vivid example of this grassroots creativity was the rise of "network music." In 2001, an untrained singer named Xue Cun released the song "Northeast People Are Living Lei Feng" (Shen et al., 2019a, p. 237). Carried by email chains and online forums, the song's humour and regional pride resonated deeply with internet users. Soon, user-generated Flash animations[15] transformed it into a viral multimedia work. Xue's breakout success bypassed traditional gatekeepers, demonstrating the internet's capacity to host new, amateur-driven cultural voices.

Alongside this, a constellation of online music services sprang up, some launched by small startups, others by search engines like Baidu. These platforms allowed users to upload, download, stream, and collect music with minimal restriction. Baidu's MP3 search engine, introduced in 2002, indexed thousands of unauthorised tracks (Dong & Jayakar, 2013). Despite multiple lawsuits, courts ruled in Baidu's favour under "safe harbour" provisions, as long as it did not host the files directly. In this legal grey area, a participatory culture of remixing and sharing blossomed.

This explosion of network music reflected not just technological change, but shifts in cultural behaviour. Musicians wrote background scores for online games, blended folk melodies with electronic beats, and experimented with cross-genre innovation. Platforms adapted Western models but adjusted to a context where cultural goods had traditionally been public or low-cost. While monetisation was elusive (aside from ringtones), the groundwork was being laid for a new digital cultural economy (Liu, 2010).

15 A 2D digital animation technique from Adobe Flash, formerly Macromedia Flash.

7.2.2 Online Literature and Participatory Platforms

Literature followed a parallel path. Online storytelling, initially informal and posted on forums, evolved into a large-scale sector. At the centre was Qidian.com (起点中文网), launched in 2002 and later absorbed into Tencent's broader entertainment ecosystem (Shen et al., 2019b). Qidian introduced a flexible business model: initial chapters of serialised fiction were free, with micro-payments required to access ongoing content. This freemium approach reshaped reading habits and introduced new user expectations.

The platform lowered barriers to entry for writers. Submissions of just 3,000 words could earn a writing column after editorial approval. Over time, authors could qualify for contracts offering revenue sharing, virtual currency tipping, and opportunities for adaptation into print, film, or games, laying the foundation for the "Super IP" model that would later define Tencent's cultural strategy.

Crucially, Qidian was more than a content repository; it was a participatory space. Readers rated chapters, tipped authors, posted feedback, and even influenced plot directions. Writers, in turn, accessed dashboards that tracked reader behaviour, guiding decisions on pacing, genre, and character development. This was not a coercive structure, but a responsive ecosystem where stories evolved through interaction between creators, readers, and platform algorithms.

This participatory logic extended to gendered spaces. In 2009, Qidian launched Qidian MM (起点女生网), a dedicated platform for female readers. Genres such as romance, time-travel, and domestic drama flourished, and serials like *Startling by Each Step* (*Bubu jingxin* 步步惊心) gained large followings and multiplatform adaptations. These platforms opened new space for female writers and readerships long overlooked in conventional publishing.

7.2.3 Expanding Digital Inclusion

By 2017, digital platforms had reached beyond youth audiences to include elderly users and migrant workers. According to Tang's (2024) PhD study, Tencent's WeSing Karaoke app tailored its design to elderly users by incorporating large fonts and simple navigation, often becoming their primary digital entertainment tool. Initially unfamiliar with karaoke, many users became active participants through social introductions. They spent hours recording and perfecting performances, managing profiles, and engaging with nostalgic repertoires like red songs, military ballads, and folk music. For many, this was more than entertainment, it offered mental, social, and physical benefits, fostering community and well-being.

During the same period, a wave of migrant songs went viral on short video platforms. These were often raw, heartfelt, and authored by workers themselves. One poignant lyric captured the emotional tension between economic survival and personal relationships: "If I pick up the bricks, I have no hands to hold you; if I put them down, I have no money to support you" (*wo ban qi le zhuantou jiu mei shou bao ni, wo fang xia le zhuantou jiu mei qian yang ni* 我搬起了砖头就没手抱你，我放下了砖头就没钱养你).[16] These songs travelled through informal networks, gaining resonance through their honesty and cultural specificity. They reflected lives not typically included in formal cultural production, yet here they shaped and led online discourse.

Unlike many societies where digital technologies primarily serve the young or urban elites, China's platforms, motivated initially by inclusive policy but realised through design innovation and mobile ubiquity, extended access to the broad population. This widespread adoption enabled a cultural transformation, giving marginalised communities tools for expression and inclusion.

7.2.4 A Formative Era

In sum, the "hundred flowers blooming" phase was more than a fleeting moment of digital chaos. It was a formative era in which new infrastructure emerged through experimentation, informal participation, and bottom-up innovation. Rather than flowing from policy or pre-designed strategies, this transformation was authored by countless users navigating the digital world, learning, contributing, and reshaping culture along the way. The groundwork laid here made way for the consolidation and strategic competition that would define the next stage, led by the internet giants Baidu, Alibaba, Tencent, and NetEase (Wang, 2017).

7.3 Copyright Enforcement and Market Restructuring (c.2011–2015)

7.3.1 From Piracy to Enforcement: A Paradigm Shift

In the early 2000s, China's digital landscape was characterised by a proliferation of online services and a surge in amateur creativity. This era, often described as "a hundred flowers blooming," was facilitated by a relatively liberal environment

16 卢文韬 Lu Wentao's《搬砖》(Brick Moving), the album was official released on 27–03–2021.

and rapid digital advancements. However, it was also marked by widespread piracy and weak enforcement of intellectual property rights (Liu, 2010; Priest, 2014). Unlicensed content was freely distributed online, inhibiting innovation and undermining the health of creative industries.

A notable example was Baidu's MP3 search service, which provided users with easy access to a vast selection of unlicensed music, dominating the market share (Dong & Jayakar, 2013). Despite facing multiple lawsuits from organisations like the International Federation of the Phonographic Industry (IFPI) and major record labels, Baidu often prevailed in court, benefiting from the "safe harbour" rule that absolved search engines of liability if they did not store infringing content on their servers.

7.3.2 Turning Point: Legal Settlements and Policy Reforms

A significant shift occurred in 2011 when Baidu reached an out-of-court settlement with major Western record labels, including Universal Music Group, Warner Music Group, and Sony BMG (Dong & Jayakar, 2013). As part of this agreement, Baidu licensed over 500,000 songs for an estimated RMB 37 million (USD $5.7 million). This move was influenced by a combination of factors: increasing international pressure on China to comply with WTO rules, tightening domestic internet regulations, and a strategic shift in Baidu's business model amid growing competition.

This settlement marked a critical moment, signalling a broader transformation in China's approach to IP enforcement (Street et al., 2015). The realisation among industry players that copyright could serve as a competitive tool led to a re-evaluation of business strategies across the digital cultural sector.

7.3.3 Institutionalising IP Enforcement

The momentum continued with the third revision of China's Copyright Law in 2012 and the establishment of specialised Intellectual Property Courts in Beijing, Shanghai, and Guangzhou in 2014 (Shen et al., 2019a). These developments institutionalised IP enforcement, compelling internet platforms to acquire licences for content and implement pre-upload reviews to prevent copyright infringements.

In July 2015, the National Copyright Administration issued a directive requiring all online music service platforms to remove unauthorised music by 31 October 2015. This directive, part of the broader "Sword Net Campaign (" *(jianwang xingdong* 剑网行动), aimed to strengthen copyright enforcement and promote the healthy development of the digital music industry.

7.3.4 Market Restructuring and Industry Consolidation

The stringent enforcement of IP rights led to a rapid restructuring of the digital cultural market. Small and medium-sized enterprises (SMEs), which had thrived in the earlier liberal environment, struggled to afford the high costs of licensing content (Shen et al., 2019a). The financial burden, coupled with the continued prevalence of piracy, made it challenging for these companies to sustain their operations, leading to a wave of mergers and acquisitions.

In contrast, the BAT (Baidu, Alibaba, and Tencent) internet giants, with their substantial financial resources, were strategically positioned to capitalise on the new landscape. They acquired smaller startups, expanded their content libraries, and solidified their dominance in the digital cultural sector. This consolidation marked a shift from a fragmented market to one dominated by a few powerful players, aligning with the state's objectives of promoting a more structured and controlled digital environment.

The period between 2011 and 2015 was transformative for China's digital cultural industries. The shift from a permissive environment to one characterised by stringent IP enforcement reshaped the market dynamics, leading to industry consolidation and the rise of dominant platforms. This evolution reflects a broader strategy by the Chinese state to balance innovation with control, fostering a digital ecosystem that supports both economic growth and regulatory oversight.

7.4 The Rise of BAT and Cross-Platform Innovation (2015 – 2018)

7.4.1 Emergence of BAT as Cultural Industry Architects

The period following the crackdown on piracy and the enforcement of licensing regulations saw the dramatic rise of China's three internet giants, Baidu, Alibaba, and Tencent (collectively known as BAT), as the dominant architects of China's new digital cultural infrastructure (Shen et al., 2019a). These companies did not simply step into a vacuum left by weakened traditional intermediaries; they fundamentally reshaped how culture was produced, distributed, and monetised by integrating their core businesses with content-driven strategies.

Having amassed large user bases through their respective strengths, search (Baidu), e-commerce (Alibaba), and social media/gaming (Tencent), each firm began to invest heavily in cultural sectors, including music, literature, film, games, and online performance. These investments were not driven by a short-term vision for profit, but rather a long-term strategic objective: to attract users into their ecosystems by embedding cultural services as value-adding layers across their multi-service platforms.

7.4.2 Cross-Platform Integration: Cultural Infrastructure at Scale

The strategic direction of BAT was characterised by deep cross-platform integration. Rather than treating cultural content as a stand-alone product, these companies embedded it within larger service frameworks that spanned everything from payments and logistics to messaging and gaming (Tang & Lyons, 2017). For instance:

- **Tencent**, via China Literature and Tencent Music Entertainment Group, developed an end-to-end cultural value chain encompassing online literature, music, video, and games. Popular literary IPs could be developed into TV dramas, games, or merchandise. Tencent Video further extended this loop, often securing exclusive streaming rights for adapted works. As one of its product managers told us in 2016, "Music isn't about profit yet, it's about stickiness" (Shen et al., 2019a, p. 237).
- **Alibaba**, which entered later through acquisitions like Xiami Music and Youku Tudou, leveraged its data from e-commerce to inform content production and marketing. Its strategy was focused on building a unified content and commerce ecosystem, where cultural content could drive merchandise sales and vice versa. Music and literature services were allowed to grow without the expectation of short-term profit. An Ali music manager interviewed in 2016 stated: "We did not make a profit for many years at the start of the platform for e-commerce business; it was the future that our CEO, Ma Yun, foresaw. Ali music is still young. We may follow the same line as we did before. We are not under any pressure from the top to make a profit. We are now concentrating on creating service platforms for people to come to us" (Shen et al., 2019a, p. 242).
- **Baidu**, after its decline in music streaming, shifted focus to artificial intelligence (AI) and cloud services but still maintained strategic stakes in encyclopaedias, video streaming, short videos, forums, and news aggregation. iQIYI remained its most prominent cultural asset, with growing ambitions to compete globally in the streaming market. At the time of our interviews

in 2016, it had crossed 50 million subscribers and was testing original content as a differentiator.

This model allowed BAT to capture value across multiple points, advertising, subscriptions, e-commerce transactions, tipping and gifting systems, and virtual currency exchanges. More importantly, it enabled them to subsidise loss-making cultural services (e.g., music) with revenues from more profitable segments.

7.4.3 Discovery-Driven Innovation and Experimental Platforms

The post-2015 period was marked by intense experimentation, what Shen et al. (2022) describe as "discovery-driven innovation." Unlike Western companies, which often refine business models before scaling, Chinese platforms frequently launched incomplete or unstable models and refined them in real time based on user behaviour and competitive responses (McGrath, 2010).

Tencent's **"Musician Plan,"** for instance, aimed to attract grassroots creators by offering royalty shares, promotional support, and offline concert opportunities. While it faced mixed responses from creators regarding payouts, the plan was instrumental in surfacing new voices and testing monetisation structures such as virtual gifts, karaoke add-ons, and fan membership tiers.

Alibaba's integration of content with commerce led to novel combinations such as selling fan merchandise directly through streaming apps or bundling music access with delivery subscriptions. These were not planned from the outset, but emerged as platforms iterated based on user data and partner input.

What united these initiatives was a willingness to experiment and to tolerate failure, as long as the larger ecosystem benefited. The tolerance for losses in cultural services was part of a broader strategy: build platform stickiness and gather behavioural data.

7.4.4 Fan Economy and Super IP: Monetising Attention

As user engagement became the central metric of value, BAT invested heavily in monetising attention via the "fan economy" (Liang & Shen, 2016). This involved structuring cultural content and platform features to amplify fan participation: livestream interactions, fan voting systems, online fan clubs, and tipping/gifting functions became standard across platforms.

Parallel to this was the evolution of the "Super IP" strategy. Originating from the online literature sector, this model involved leveraging a popular IP across multiple formats: web novels → TV series → mobile games → merchandise. *The Tale of Zhenhuan* (*Zhenhuan zhuan* 甄嬛传) and *Hua Qiangu* (*Hua qiangu* 花千骨) exemplified this strategy, with massive fan engagement across platforms driving monetisation at each stage.

This industrial-scale coordination was made possible only by the comprehensive data infrastructures BAT had built. Algorithms tracked user preferences, informed acquisition decisions, and optimised distribution, blurring the line between cultural production and consumption analytics.

7.4.5 Platform Regulation and the Return of the State

However, BAT's rapid ascent and aggressive competition, particularly in the form of exclusive licensing wars, prompted concern from regulators. In response to the monopolistic behaviour and rising licensing costs, the state began to enforce collaboration and create an environment for firms to operate under "controlled competition" (Shen et al., 2019a). This included policy actions mandating the sub-licensing of exclusive content, such as the 2016 directive by the National Copyright Administration, as well as investigations into anti-competitive practices.

This marked a subtle but significant evolution in state intervention. The state was no longer directly dictating content, as in the Maoist period, but was now moderating platform behaviour through flexible tools, copyright law revisions, administrative orders, anti-monopoly probes, and guidance campaigns like Sword Net.

This environment of "controlled competition" enabled platforms to innovate, scale, and compete, but only within boundaries aligned with the state's broader cultural and social objectives: keeping content affordable, discouraging exclusive lock-ins, and supporting regulated IP protection.

7.5 Challenges and Complexities in the Platform Era

As China's digital cultural industries matured in the 2010s, the early promise of grassroots digital creativity began to give way to new forms of complexity, stratification, and institutional friction. With BAT, Baidu, Alibaba, Tencent, and later NetEase consolidating control over the infrastructure, frictions emerged across every layer of the system (Shen et al., 2019a). These challenges were no longer about access or innovation alone but about the very architecture of cultural participation under platform capitalism. The ecosystem remained experimental, but the risks and tensions became increasingly visible, spanning legal, creative, economic, and regulatory dimensions.

7.5.1 Persistent Piracy and Weak Enforcement at the Margins

Despite major advances in legal frameworks and the formalisation of copyright regimes, piracy persisted as a structural vulnerability. In online literature, this took the form of extensive re-posting of serialised fiction on mirror sites, cloud services, and bulletin board system (BBS) platforms (Shen et al., 2019b, p. 12). In 2015, pirated literature was estimated to cause losses of 7.7 billion yuan (about USD 1.18 billion) in subscription revenue. Notably, 64.3% of traffic to pirated works came from BBS platforms (Shen et al., 2019b, p. 12).

The cultural logic of piracy had deep roots. Many readers, especially outside major cities, were accustomed to downloading content onto local devices, a habit shaped by high mobile data costs and uneven connectivity. Where platforms refused to offer downloads, often to preserve control and traceability, unauthorised versions filled the gap. Some users defended these practices with a quasi-utopian ethos: "all knowledge should be shared," scanning printed books for online distribution.

Interestingly, many authors shared this ambivalence. Several expressed a pragmatic view that wider distribution, even via piracy, could raise visibility and improve their chances of adaptation into games or films. Some internet companies echoed this stance. For them, piracy was less a threat than a sign of market demand, one that might be captured downstream through monetisation of derivative rights.

In film and television, piracy evolved with technology. The case of TVpad, a set-top box that preloaded or streamed unauthorised content from Chinese and global broadcasters, underscored this challenge. Though eventually banned and sued, its popularity revealed a persistent consumer appetite for unregulated access.

Legal enforcement struggled to keep pace. Even after China's 2012 Copyright Law revision and the establishment of specialised IP courts in 2014, enforcement remained weak. Our sources at Beijing IP Court described growing case volumes and increasingly complex infringement patterns, particularly in the online information sector. (personal communication, 8 July 2016). Courts were also criticised for awarding relatively low damages. A legal team from a major internet company recounted that pursuing litigation generated "a large quantity of paperwork" for "far too little" compensation to justify the effort, discouraging enforcement against small-scale or diffuse violations (personal communication, 15 June 2016).

The emergence of "writing tools" in literature production added another layer. These tools often generated formulaic plots or recycled popular phrases, resulting in what editors described as "many similar and nonsensical works." (personal communication, 22 June 2016). Such content blurred the line between homage and plagiarism, complicating the work of moderators, legal teams, and courts.

7.5.2 Creative Fragmentation and Content Homogenisation

Beyond legal friction, platforms introduced new creative tensions driven by over-efficiency rather than scarcity. On literature platforms like Qidian, authors began to shape their writing in response to statistical dashboards showing drop-off points, keyword trends, and genre popularity (Shen et al., 2019b). This fostered reliance on proven tropes, romance arcs, reincarnation, cultivation, and cliffhanger devices designed to retain attention.

This dynamic aligned production with market feedback but constrained narrative innovation. As one editor observed, authors were "optimising for data, not story." This was not imposed coercively but encouraged through infrastructure, rankings, reader feedback, and algorithmic visibility. A co-evolution emerged between what platforms rewarded and what writers produced.

The tendency towards sameness was intensified by multi-platform publication. Writers often posted identical works across several sites, weakening platform loyalty and complicating exclusivity contracts. Some platforms responded by enforcing stricter controls or promoting signed authors more visibly, but these strategies highlighted a deeper structural tension between openness and differentiation.

Whilst platform infrastructures expanded access to content creation, they also narrowed the distribution of rewards. A handful of blockbuster hits drew widespread attention and adaptation opportunities, whilst the vast majority of works circulated in niche or semi-visible spaces, contributing to a landscape of creative fragmentation.

7.5.3 Power Asymmetries in Contracts and Payments

As participation increased, platforms formalised content monetisation through contractual agreements. For a small subset of top creators, this yielded income and recognition. But for most, especially newcomers or those without ties to agencies or state-backed institutions, terms were less favourable.

Contracts often required creators to transfer derivative rights, including film, game, and merchandise adaptations, to the platform. Whilst this enabled cross-sector deployment within companies like Tencent, it also stripped creators of control over their own futures. Writers could earn through tipping, virtual currencies like Qidian Yuan, or minor subscription shares, but payouts were unpredictable and often modest.

Many interviewees noted the imbalance. Some described relying on day jobs for income; others viewed digital creation as a secondary pursuit (personal communication, June 2016). Meanwhile, platforms initiated bidding wars to secure exclusivity, offering signing bonuses and guaranteed royalties to top talent. This dynamic inflated IP licensing values, especially for properties with cross-media potential.

At both ends, pressure mounted. Creators needed constant output to maintain visibility, whilst platforms raced to recoup costs through IP expansion and derivative monetisation. The logic mirrored global platform capitalism, but in China, it was amplified by ecosystem integration, linking fiction to games, merchandise, and film within unified corporate networks.

7.5.4 Regulatory Friction and Soft Censorship

China's cultural regulation is often misunderstood as uniformly repressive. In practice, it operates through layered moderation, infrastructural embedding, and subtle constraint (Shen et al., 2019a). As platforms scaled, content moderation became routinised. Systems of keyword filtering, pre-upload review, and editorial oversight were built into technical frameworks.

The complexity of the Chinese language made automation particularly fraught. One editor shared a vivid example in our 2016 interviews: the idiom "as harmonious as water and milk" (*shui ru jiaorong* 水乳交融) was flagged for containing the character breast), resulting in the entire phrase appearing as "□□□□" blank squares. The algorithm did not just obscure the single character; it blanked out all four, undermining the meaning entirely. Editors noted how such cases discouraged literary experimentation and produced a chilling effect. Even innocuous phrases could trigger warnings due to resemblance to banned content.

To mitigate this, Qidian introduced tools like the "Writing Cat" app to help authors pre-screen their text. Yet the broader outcome was a regime of soft censorship, less overt repression than a system of anticipatory self-restraint shaped by algorithmic friction.

Sectoral differences persisted. In film, the New Film Law (2017) required official approval for foreign festival participation, signalling increased oversight in global arenas. On user-driven platforms like Bilibili, content faced community guidelines and formal reviews, though enforcement thresholds were often opaque.

In every case, moderation introduced hidden costs: for platforms, which had to invest in staff and AI tools; for creators, who learnt to self-censor; and for audiences, who encountered curated and constrained cultural landscapes.

7.5.5 Monetisation Uncertainty and Cross-Subsidisation Limits

At scale, the core economic question shifted to sustainability. Music, in particular, struggled to turn a profit (Shen et al., 2019a). A Baidu strategy manager stated bluntly in our 2016 interviews: "It's burning money for strategic gain." (personal communication, 18 May 2016). Music was not expected to generate revenue, it was a hook to retain users and stimulate engagement across platforms.

Alibaba echoed this view. Their investment in Ali music was framed as infrastructure-building, not an immediate return. Cross-subsidisation was key: music drew users who might later spend on e-commerce, games, or video services. This bundling worked for BAT giants but created entry barriers for smaller firms.

Freemium models dominated, free basic access with VIP tiers offering high sound quality, early release, or exclusive extras. Yet margins were thin. Virtual gifts, engagement points, and fan rewards brought modest returns. As losses accumulated, smaller platforms folded or were acquired, further centralising the market and narrowing cultural diversity.

7.5.6 Weaponising IP: The Bidding War for Exclusive Content

The most acute manifestation of these dynamics occurred during the music licensing wars of 2014–2016 (Tang & Lyons, 2017). Tencent struck exclusive deals with Sony and Warner; Alibaba responded with BMG and Universal. Music rights became strategic assets. Platforms sued rivals for unauthorised distribution. The goal was not cultural enrichment, but user lock-in.

Public backlash followed, especially as users lost access to beloved content. Regulators intervened. Officials called for content sharing and warned against monopolistic practices. Sub-licensing deals were eventually reached, though not all players, like NetEase, were immediately included.

By 2019, the antitrust bureau opened an investigation into Tencent Music, later suspended. The episode encapsulated a recurring cycle: innovation pushing boundaries, backlash triggering recalibration. Platform expansion, it seemed, always met a threshold where policy reasserted itself.

7.5.7 The Friction Beneath the Flow

These overlapping tensions, legal, creative, economic, and regulatory, revealed the deeper structure of China's digital platform culture. Far from a seamless progression, the story is one of frictions negotiated in real time: piracy coexisting with regulation; creative experimentation tempered by homogenising algorithms; soft censorship shaping expression; and monopolistic instincts moderated by state intervention.

The process remained deeply experimental, marked not only by bold innovation, but also by missteps, recalibrations, and unintended consequences. This frictional terrain would shape the insights gathered in the final analysis of the chapter.

7.6 Analysis: Reimagining the Mass-Line Through Digital Platforms

7.6.1 From Revolutionary Slogans to Platform Reality

The dream of mass participation has long held sway in Chinese governance traditions, particularly at the core of Mao's regime. Perhaps it was grounded in Confucian ideas of governance aimed at accomplishing a harmonious social order in Chinese society. Later, it was reframed through the Communist Party's mass-line doctrine. In Maoist ideology, the mass-line was framed as a core principle: the idea that policies should emerge from the masses and return to them in refined form (Mao, 1942). Yet in practice, campaigns like Three-Anti and Five-Anti (*sanfan, wufan* 三反，五反), the Great Leap Forward (*dayuejin* 大跃进), and the Cultural Revolution (*wenhua dageming* 文化大革命) led not to empowerment, but disruption. The masses were mobilised, their participation was heavily orchestrated, but the outcomes were often at a primitive level.

It was the digital age that made the mass-line dream come true. Digital and internet technologies introduced new tools that made mass involvement not only feasible but also orderly and productive, without depending solely on top-down government detailed and planned activities. Rather, it was the digital revolution, particularly the growth of internet platforms, that made true mass participation in culture possible (Shen et al., 2019a). Unlike the ideological mass-line, digital participation emerged through practical, low-cost experimentation. With the proliferation of online platforms in the early 2000s, hundreds of small services enabled users to create, upload, remix, and share content. This was the real "mass-line" : bottom-up, voluntary, and diverse.

Platforms like Qidian in literature and early music-sharing websites hosted amateur voices long before monetisation or regulation caught up. Internet users became creators, critics, and curators, roles previously reserved for elite intermediaries in publishing houses, studios, or state bodies. As platforms matured, especially under BAT (Baidu, Alibaba, Tencent), they structured these flows into scalable services, adding layers of professionalisation, data analytics, and monetisation, but preserving the participatory logic at the core.

In contrast to Western models, where major record labels, film studios, or publishers long dominated gatekeeping, even in the digital age, China's model allowed for broad-based cultural engagement. Spotify, for instance, emerged as a sleek streaming solution, but its licensing deals were tightly negotiated with the same large Western labels that have structured the industry for decades (Prey, 2020). In China, however, cultural content originated from a far wider user base and was incubated through a mix of market trial and institutional improvisation.

One of the most profound outcomes of China's digital cultural transformation has contributed to building a digital online ecosystem for the mass participation of the whole population, not only in cultural life but also in other aspects, long a pillar of Chinese political discourse but never fully realised in practice. The digital era has enabled a more fluid, decentralised, and participatory realisation of the mass-line through internet platforms.

This transformation can be understood through the lens of Karen Barad's theory of socio-technical entanglement and intra-action (Barad, 2007, p. 33). Barad argues that interaction is always performative: it does not just reflect relationships but enacts them. In the context of China's digital cultural ecology, platforms are not neutral intermediaries; they are performative infrastructures. They shape and are shaped by citizens in Chinese society, creating a dynamic space where participation is not only possible but constitutive of the system itself.

Platforms did not simply deliver content; in practice, they enabled interaction, expression, and experimentation. Citizens engaged with culture not just as consumers, but as critics, curators, and increasingly, as creators. In this sense, the digital space functioned as a vast co-learning ecosystem. Every playlist curated, every novel serialised, every comment or virtual gift contributed to an emergent cultural commons. This process aligns with Barad's notion of social-technical entanglement and performativity: the interaction between users, platforms, and content was itself formative, shaping not just what people consumed, but how they thought, responded, and participated (Barad, 2007, p. 185).

What made this mass participation even more distinctive was the social bonding it fostered. Digital communities began to form around shared interests, habits, and sensibilities. A widely used internet phrase, "sharing the same rotten taste" (*chouwei xiangtou* 臭味相投), became a humorous way to describe the pleasure of discovering like-minded peers in digital spaces. These online affinities were not just about shared fandom, but about co-producing value: communities of taste often determined what content rose in popularity, giving ordinary users a role in setting cultural agendas. Parallel developments in music services echoed this dynamic: users built fan circles, shared playlists, and exchanged commentary in ways that mirrored and reinforced the participatory culture in online literature.

In this entangled environment, platforms like Qidian (literature), Xiami (music), and Bilibili (video) also became powerful educational spaces. Users are not passive consumers; they are cultural actors continuously learning through participation. Writers respond to real-time reader feedback, musicians tweak their styles based on platform data, and fan communities generate spin-off content. Algorithms and dashboards serve not just as sorting tools but as pedagogical devices, guiding user attention, suggesting trends, and structuring creative choices.

This mass participation is performative in Barad's sense: it enacts a cultural system where boundaries between producer and consumer, amateur and professional, teacher and learner blur. The internet, in this view, becomes a large-scale socio-technical learning environment. Cultural production is embedded in everyday digital life, and participation becomes a mode of ongoing education.

Furthermore, this mode of learning is inherently distributed. Readers learn to discern plot dynamics and narrative conventions; musicians learn engagement strategies and genre appeal; even platform operators learn from user behaviour to adjust algorithms and interfaces. The architecture of these platforms, ranking systems, comment sections, tipping mechanisms, creates feedback loops that enable iterative learning. These loops substitute the rigid central planning of earlier cultural policies with a flexible, emergent order.

7.6.2 The State's Evolving Role: From Command to Coordination

For much of the 20th century, the Chinese state was both producer and censor of cultural content. Post-reform, it began to relinquish direct control, but not its interest in cultural coherence. The internet posed a new challenge: how to allow freedom without losing oversight?

Early on, the state's posture was one of deliberate latency (Shen et al., 2019a). During the explosive growth of digital cultural industries in the 2000s, the government adopted a "wait and see" approach. Rather than setting strict parameters from the outset, it observed how platforms evolved and intervened only when necessary, such as through campaigns like Sword Net when piracy became untenable.

Over time, this matured into a model of sophisticated interventionism. The state no longer tried to micromanage every cultural product, but instead used key levers, like IP reform, platform accountability, and algorithm transparency, to shape behaviour from a distance. For example, the state intervened whilst observing the bidding war for exclusive content (see Section 7.5.6). Importantly, this model acknowledged that platforms could be allies in governance: incentivised to moderate content, protect minors, or promote "positive energy" (*zheng nengliang* 正能量) messaging. Without the platforms, it would be difficult for the government to reach out to people in society.

Comparatively, Western digital cultures operate under different governance dynamics. Regulation typically comes from independent bodies, courts, or transnational agreements, and is often reactive. In the US or Europe, platforms like Spotify or Netflix are private entities focused primarily on commercial outcomes. Whilst they may respond to public pressure or court rulings, they rarely function as intermediaries of national cultural policy.

China's approach blurs these lines. Through its relationship with platforms, the state is able to both encourage innovation and enforce norms. It uses IP law not just to protect rights holders, but to shape market structure. It balances the desire for vibrant creativity with ideological boundaries and public accessibility. This coordination model reflects not a retreat from control, but a reconfiguration of it, less visible, but still potent.

7.6.3 New Business Logics and IP Flexibility: Enabling the Prosumers

One of the most consequential developments has been the adaptation of intellectual property frameworks to suit platform-based business models (Shen & Zhan, 2020). Initially seen as a Western import poorly suited to China's cultural traditions, IP has been transformed into a flexible tool that serves multiple goals: platform growth, creator monetisation, user engagement, and regulatory governance.

Unlike the Western model, where IP is tightly held by a few conglomerates (e.g., Universal, Warner, Sony), China's platform-based model allows for a continuum of rights arrangements. Creators can upload freely, sign exclusive contracts, or licence partially. Platforms offer granular monetisation options: reader tips, micro-payments, reward systems, and promotional services.

Take Spotify as an example. It is a technologically sophisticated platform, but it mainly streams content already owned or controlled by big labels (Prey, 2020). Artists are paid per stream, often meagrely, based on complex licensing deals negotiated at the top. The average creator on Spotify has little direct control or engagement with the audience.

In contrast, platforms like Qidian, Tencent Music, or Bilibili provide creators with dashboards, real-time feedback, and direct payment structures (Shen et al., 2019a). Writers adjust stories in response to reader comments. Musicians host live streams with tipping systems. This not only democratises access but enables a new class of prosumers, users who also produce.

Prosumers may be students writing fan fiction, retirees singing folk songs, or niche genre writers building small but loyal followings. Some transition into full-time careers; others remain part-time but vital contributors. The platform infrastructures support this with tiered access, recognition systems, and pathways to professionalisation (Tang, 2024).

Meanwhile, for users, low-cost access is preserved. Freemium models ensure basic content is available to all, whilst VIP tiers, early access, or bonus features create revenue streams. This dual approach, monetisation with accessibility, satisfies both market and state. Platforms earn enough to sustain operations; the public enjoys cultural enrichment at little or no cost; and the state maintains stability and ideological oversight.

To achieve this balance, platforms have adopted tiered service models that strategically differentiate between user segments. For instance, in the music sector, listeners can access a broad catalogue of songs for free, albeit with lower sound quality or delayed release compared to premium users. Similarly, in online literature, readers can access early chapters at no cost, but must pay small fees to unlock newer or VIP content. This design reflects a careful calibration: monetising engagement without excluding large swaths of the population.

In effect, users are invited to choose the trade-offs they are comfortable with, between cost and immediacy, quality and convenience. Such flexibility has allowed the platforms to cultivate loyalty among both paying and non-paying users, expand their base, and maintain compliance with the state's long-standing cultural policy principle: to ensure broad public access to cultural content.

Importantly, this system offers low-cost or even free access to culture. Users who are willing to accept delayed access, lower-quality audio, or partial content can still participate fully in the cultural life of the platform. This affordability democratises access and ensures that cultural engagement is not a privilege but a public good, aligning closely with the socialist ideals that originally motivated the mass-line.

In sum, the platform-based cultural ecosystem achieves what earlier ideological campaigns could not: a functioning, inclusive, and self-sustaining version of mass participation. Through performative intra-action, it turns cultural life into an everyday educational experience for millions, making the mass-line not just an aspiration, but a living, evolving practice.

In contrast to China's platform-driven realisation of the mass-line, Western digital cultural industries, exemplified by companies like Spotify, YouTube, and Amazon, operate on different logics of participation, monetisation, and cultural learning. These platforms also enable user engagement and creative expression but do so within ecosystems shaped by more entrenched intellectual property regimes, established intermediaries (like major music labels and publishers), and market-centric business strategies (Srnicek, 2017).

Take Spotify, for example. Whilst it offers a vast library of content and facilitates user-generated playlists and algorithmic discovery, its core architecture revolves around professionally licensed content and a subscription model that privileges paying users. Independent artists can upload music through aggregators, but they often find themselves navigating opaque royalty systems and struggling for visibility without label backing. The feedback loop between creator and audience exists but is weaker and less dynamic than in China's platforms like Xiami or NetEase Cloud Music, where user comments, bullet screens, and virtual gifting form direct and continuous engagement mechanisms.

YouTube represents a more participatory model but still retains the asymmetry between creators and platforms. Whilst it has enabled countless amateur creators to gain visibility and even income, its monetisation model (primarily advertising-based) is centralised, and algorithmic visibility is tightly controlled by opaque platform logic (van Dijck et al., 2018). Content moderation and copyright enforcement on YouTube also reflect a heavy-handed, often punitive approach rather than a negotiated learning process.

In contrast, China's cultural platforms are structured as co-learning systems. They do not merely deliver content but organise participation as a formative process, where users, creators, and platforms adapt together. The Chinese model is distinguished by:

- **Infrastructural Flexibility:** Platforms function as modular ecosystems where creators can start small and scale gradually, with different tiers of contracts, access, and remuneration.
- **Data-Driven Pedagogy:** Real-time analytics are democratised to inform creative and consumption choices, fostering a kind of embedded media literacy.
- **Monetisation for the Long Tail:** Even occasional or niche creators can earn through tipping, subscriptions, or secondary adaptations, something Western models struggle to offer at scale.

- **Low-Barrier Access:** Free or low-cost models with delayed or lower-quality access ensure mass participation, unlike subscription walls that dominate Western services.

These differences do not necessarily position one system as superior. Rather, they reflect distinct socio-political and economic trajectories. The Chinese model, rooted in an evolving interpretation of the mass-line, has aligned digital infrastructure with state developmental goals, public access principles, and dynamic market experimentation. The Western model, by contrast, is anchored in established commercial norms, stronger individual property rights, and a more rigid producer-consumer division.

By reframing digital culture as a performative, educational, and inclusive system, China's model offers a unique configuration of participatory governance, platform capitalism, and cultural citizenship, highlighting an alternative path to media modernity.

7.6.4 Reflections on the Mass-Line Ecosystem

The dream of mass participation has long shaped Chinese governance. From Confucian ideals of cultivating individual virtue to produce a harmonious society, to Mao Zedong's mass-line slogan "from the masses, to the masses," this principle has been ever-present but seldom realised without difficulties. Many likened Chinese society in the pre-liberation era to a plate of loose sand (*yipan sansa* 一盘散沙): scattered, disorganised, and difficult to mobilise unless coherently guided. And yet, earlier attempts, including Confucianism in Chinese history and Mao's regime in contemporary China, resulted either in collectivism built on repression of individual development or produced chaos and fear in society rather than flourishing.

My childhood experience used to compel me to suspect that the promise of mobilising an entire population to elevate collective life, culturally and socially, was distant. It was only decades later, during my fieldwork in China from 2015 to 2017, that I began to see this promise come alive, not through slogans, but through digital infrastructure.

I remember sitting in the Beijing University Law Library in June 2016, ordering a simple lunch via mobile phone apps, and having it delivered on time. I could summon a ride with Didi, Chinese Uber, and track the car's approach in real time on my mobile screen. Shared bikes, though occasionally chaotic, filled the streets, linking last-mile transport to metro stations. Even as a foreigner with limited access to Alipay and WeChat Pay, I could glimpse how these platforms had changed everyday life. Shopping online was no longer a novelty; it was second nature.

And perhaps most significantly, people from every background were participating in culture: writing, remixing, singing, commenting, gifting. Migrant workers were sharing heartfelt songs (see Section 7.2.3), which did not come from state directives or major studios. They came from ordinary lives, and they went viral, striking chords across class lines.

This is the mass-line reimagined. Not as ideological mobilisation, but as participatory infrastructure. The digital revolution, particularly mobile internet and platforms, created the conditions for meaningful, scalable, and diverse cultural involvement. Platforms like Qidian for literature, Xiami and NetEase for music, and Bilibili for video, hosted an explosion of user-generated content. Unlike the top-down variety shows of my youth, these new expressions were voluntary, interactive, and adaptive.

Karen Barad's theory of intra-action is useful here (Barad, 2007, p. 33). She argues that social-technical entanglement is performative: it does not just reflect relationships but enacts them. Platforms are not passive transmitters. They provide the space and environment where citizens and technologies co-construct meanings. In this light, every playlist, every serialised novel, every fan edit or virtual gift becomes a contribution to a living cultural system, one that teaches as it evolves.

This co-learning environment blurs traditional boundaries: between producers and consumers, professionals and amateurs, teachers and learners. Algorithms suggest what to watch, but also respond to what is watched. Writers and musicians adjust their work in real-time based on user feedback. Users train their own sensibilities through repeated engagement. This is not education by curriculum; it is cultural formation through doing, experiencing, and iterating.

Communities of taste formed not just around classics or official content, but around idiosyncrasies and affinities. A popular internet phrase, "sharing the same rotten taste" (*chouwei xiangtou* 臭味相投), captures this beautifully. Users built micro-communities not just to consume, but to elevate, amplify, and celebrate what might otherwise remain niche. This social bonding, once an abstract aspiration of socialist policy, now had digital architecture.

7.7 Conclusion

China's digital transformation reveals an experimentalist trajectory, shaped not just by technological advancement but by deeply entangled social processes. At the heart of this evolution is a distinctive platform ecology, one that operates through ongoing interactions between the state, major internet firms, and users themselves. Borrowing from Callon (1986), we may understand these platforms as *interessement devices:* tools not only for coordination, but also for knowledge creation and meaning-making. They help articulate shared interests, stabilise relations, and generate new ways of knowing and organising social life.

This ecology has emerged through navigating crises, embracing contradiction, and fostering adaptive learning. While unresolved tensions remain, particularly around regulation, inequality, and global positioning, the system continues to evolve, offering glimpses of alternative futures. The vibrant cultural activities that populate these platforms are not marginal or decorative; they express everyday creativity and collective energy. They are both reflections of contemporary life and reservoirs of potential for future modernity.

At the same time, this raises critical questions for global governance, especially regarding intellectual property regimes. Can Western models of IP protection, long structured around exclusion and ownership, be reimagined to support broader societal development? Can they adapt to a world where innovation is increasingly collaborative, embedded, and culturally grounded? If so, perhaps the prosperity of digital modernity might be more equitably shared, not only within China, but across the world.

As the ancient Greek philosopher Protagoras argued, "Man is the measure of all things"—or in contemporary terms, humanity is the measure of all things. In this platform era, we are witnessing a measure-in-practice: a reworking of participation, policy, and public life through everyday digital experiences.

As I described in the preamble, my childhood memory of imitating ballet from a model play now takes on new meaning. It was not simply mimicry, but a form of participation constrained by the technologies and politics of its time. Today's digital platforms offer a different kind of stage—one where millions can perform, create, and connect. Not perfectly, not without friction, but with possibilities that earlier generations could only imagine.

And that, I believe, is a revolution worth studying, and remembering.

8 Dataveillance: Visibility and Traceability

Preamble

The COVID-19 case study brought me to a new frontier: the recognition that data-driven infrastructures not only govern crises but also reconfigure the very conditions of social life. Theoretically, it brought me to appreciate the philosophical and methodological frameworks of monadology proposed by Gabriel Tarde and further developed in Latour's interpretations—though I reinterpret monads concretely as traceable units whose histories and relations can be followed through data infrastructures. It also drew me back to traditional Chinese ideas of people-centred relational governance (*renzhi* 人治) and the governance of relationships (*guanxi* 关系) rooted in Confucian thought. Over more than four decades of reform, China has learned from Western legal principles and institutional mechanisms, while also grappling with Western democratic ideals in theory. Many contemporary studies remain harshly critical of China's reliance on *renzhi* or *guanxi*-based governance, calling for a wholesale shift to Western-style legal frameworks.

From an STS perspective, however, my long-standing reflections on the mass line and on intellectual property protection (see Chapters 2, 4, and 7) helped me to see new possibilities in the rise of digital, data-driven technologies. Datafication, data capture, and auditing make governance newly visible and traceable. For a developing country that has been imitating Western market-economic mechanisms for only a few decades, the mixed outcomes of these digital transformations, their negative and positive forces alike, demand careful, detailed study (see Sections 8.2 and 8.3).

My more recent entry into artificial intelligence (AI) ethics research is only a starting point. My understanding is still evolving, but these explorations have given me hopeful expectations for China's current efforts to build socio-technical infrastructures and to accelerate the broader project of human development (*ren de suzhi de tigao* 人的素质的提高). The case of the Health QR Code and wider practices of dataveillance (see Section 8.2) became for me not just an empirical study of governance under crisis, but also a philosophical and ethical inquiry into how collective selves may emerge through infrastructures of visibility and traceability.

https://doi.org/10.1515/9783110757576-014

8.1 The Context: The Crumbling Moral Landscape in Post-Reform China

China's economic reforms of the 1980s and 1990s ushered in what was widely described as an "economic miracle." Yet beneath the surface of this growth lay a terrain of dislocation and moral unease. The 1990s witnessed growing debates about a "moral crisis" and "spiritual vacuum" as state socialism gave way to market socialism (Wang, 2008).

While the reforms achieved remarkable poverty reduction, they simultaneously intensified income inequality, reflected in a Gini coefficient exceeding 0.45, similar to that of several Latin American economies (Naughton, 2007, p. 212).

Corruption, amplified by decentralised power and dual-track pricing, became endemic. Intellectual debates mirrored this fragmentation, some hailed Westernisation as progress, while others lamented the erosion of socialist egalitarian values.

By the late 1990s, personal identity was no longer tied to work unit (*danwei* 单位) affiliation but to individual ID cards. Housing, medical care, and personnel dossiers were privatised. Structural individualisation transformed citizens into what some scholars termed the "uncivil individual": a rights-bearing but duty-thin self, focused on personal gain rather than collective obligation (Yan, 2009).

Earlier socialist structures had imposed conformity but also embedded individuals in visible moral infrastructures. When these collapsed, economic success became the new ethical benchmark. Market logic supplanted solidarity, trust, and even shame.

8.1.1 The Melamine Milk Scandal: When Imitation Turned Toxic

The 2008 melamine milk scandal exemplified how bottom-up imitation could turn corrosive. Initially a small number of infant illnesses in Hebei, it spiralled into a national crisis: over 290,000 infants were affected, six died (BBC, 2009). The culprit was melamine, fraudulently added to diluted milk to inflate protein readings.

In the early 2000s, the slogan "raising cows brings wealth" (*yangniu zhifu* 养牛致富) swept across rural China. Farmers, traders, and local officials rushed to imitate modern agribusiness models. But this "dairy gold rush" invited deception: ordinary cows painted to resemble Holsteins, reconstituted milk powders sold as fresh milk, and finally melamine itself, a chemical stand-in for nutrition.

The scandal was more than regulatory failure. It was a systemic expression of the imitation paradox: diverse grassroots-level imitations, while enabling millions to seize new opportunities, also carried a darker side of moral decline. Once milk moved from relational trust within socialist supply chains to technical metrics, fat content, protein levels, nitrogen ratios, quality became detached from responsibility. What had been a relationally governed good was reduced to manipulable data points.

8.1.2 Urban Disembedding: From Neighbourhoods to Nodes

Urban China experienced a parallel breakdown of moral infrastructures. By the mid-2000s, more than 250 million people had joined the world's largest human migration (Chan, 2010, p. 355). Migrants became the backbone of city economies, working in construction, services, and care, but lived on the margins, excluded from social protections under the household registration (*hukou* 户口) system.

Cities strained under the influx. Migrants and locals occupied separate social worlds, often divided by suspicion and discrimination. I recall this shift in my family's neighbourhood in the late 1990s: petty theft surged, and households installed iron gates and metal bars on balconies. When our family's bicycles disappeared, relatives shrugged with resignation: "So many migrants here now, and they're not paid fairly." There was neither outrage nor police report, only a recognition that economic unfairness was unravelling moral expectations.

This everyday resignation marked a deeper transformation. Neighbourhood accountability, once rooted in shared routines and tacit moral surveillance, gave way to anonymity. Apartment blocks prioritised privacy over collectivity; gated compounds replaced alleyway familiarity; surveillance cameras substituted for neighbourly watchfulness.

Here too, the imitation paradox was visible. Migrants and locals alike imitated survival strategies in the city, locking doors, fencing balconies, seeking new ways to get by. Yet the negative side was a fraying of moral fabric: suspicion replaced solidarity, empathy coexisted with blame, and ontological insecurity (Giddens, 1991) became an everyday condition.

8.1.3 From Moral Repair to Data Infrastructure

By the 2010s, these twin breakdowns, in rural food systems and urban neighbourhoods, generated public demand for more reliable mechanisms of coordination. Tech giants such as Alibaba and Tencent stepped into the void. Alipay and WeChat became not only platforms for commerce but infrastructures of trust: embedding ID verification, transaction histories, and behavioural scoring. Reviews, ratings, and digital records substituted for missing moral cues.

The state soon integrated these digital systems into governance. The rise of the Social Credit System after 2014 cannot be read solely as a top-down imposition (Creemers, 2018). It was also a response to fragmentation and distrust, a way to simulate presence and accountability where older socialist infrastructures had collapsed. In this sense, data-driven governance became a new moral infrastructure: a digital remedy to the cracks left by bottom-up imitation, moral decline, and the erosion of everyday trust.

The moral fragmentation of the reform era left China struggling to build reliable systems of coordination. Efforts to standardise data infrastructures across the country had long stalled in bureaucratic silos and competing institutional interests. The COVID-19 pandemic abruptly altered this trajectory. In the urgency of crisis, every individual, institution, and platform became part of a new type of mass movement. The rapid rollout of Health QR codes and mobile-enabled contact tracing demonstrated that wide participation was possible: citizens, local administrations, and digital platforms worked together to protect lives. Crucially, this was not only a technical achievement but also a relational one. The pandemic reminded people that every individual's behaviour mattered, and that collective safety depended on mutual acknowledgement and cooperation. Unlike earlier episodes of blind imitation or Mao-era mass campaigns, this was a consciously active mobilisation in which people became collectively accountable. What emerged was an improvised yet functioning dataveillance infrastructure, one that re-embedded the relational element of society through digital means.

8.2 Dataveillance: COVID Health QR Code and Beyond

8.2.1 Lockdown in DSL: An Ethnographic Study

Between 16 February and 28 May 2020, I conducted a virtual ethnographic study of Dong-shan-long (DSL), the neighbourhood in Hangzhou that has been my family's residence for over three decades. Normally I visited at least once a year, but during COVID-19 I was thousands of miles away in Edinburgh. Paradoxically, the very digital infrastructures that became central to China's pandemic response also made this ethnography possible. Mobile networks, social media platforms, and real-time data transmission enabled me to remain in close contact with family, classmates, and neighbours in DSL, observing their experiences almost as they unfolded.

WeChat was my daily field site. More than a messaging app, it was a social infrastructure: facilitating gossip, organising neighbourhood errands, relaying official notices, and processing payments. Through dozens of group chats, screenshots, photos, and video clips, I followed how residents adapted to sudden restrictions and new digital requirements. On my own phone in Edinburgh, I installed the Hangzhou Health QR code app, enabling me to see my personal code colour, explore service menus, and in a small way inhabit the digital world my relatives were navigating.

When the nationwide lockdown rippled outward from Wuhan in late January 2020, everyday rhythms in DSL came to an abrupt halt. Side gates were sealed with tape, steel fences locked, and only one gate set up with a checkpoint guarded 24 hours a day, seven days a week. DSL, covering 0.8 square kilometres, is home to over 7,000 residents living in 92 apartment blocks interspersed with green courtyards. Daily needs are met by a cluster of shops, markets, banks, and small services: hairdressers, laundries, and bicycle repairs.

One of the most symbolic closures was the small gate connecting DSL directly to the Hangzhou Botanic Garden's bamboo grove. This had long been a cherished pathway: residents strolled through for morning tai-chi, evening walks, or to sit quietly among the bamboo. During lockdown, the gate was firmly shut with a large lock hanging there.

The layered administration of Hangzhou shaped this response. DSL is one of ten small districts within the Lingyin street district, itself one of nine street districts in West Lake district, one of Hangzhou's nine urban districts. This nested structure meant that lockdown directives filtered down from multiple levels of authority, but implementation happened on the ground in DSL itself, through local officials, security guards, and volunteers improvising rules at the gate.

For residents, the experience was disorienting. Long-familiar paths to shops or parks were suddenly blocked. Yet, interestingly, people in the same neighbourhood began to recognise one another across queues at checkpoints. The pandemic turned DSL into both a bounded field of surveillance and negotiation, and a renewed relational community where mobility, trust, and safety were redefined daily.

8.2.2 From Paper Pass to Health QR Code

At the outset of lockdown, mobility in DSL was tightly rationed. Each household was told to stay home, with only one member allowed out every two days for "essential shopping." To enforce this, the neighbourhood administration issued small paper booklets, just 8 × 6 cm, bearing the household's name, address, and an official red stamp. Each outing was recorded by ticking a dated box.

At checkpoints, these passes were inspected and stamped again, alongside the obligatory temperature check. For a brief period, this simple paper device became the key to mobility, a token of permission in a world suddenly governed by scarcity and risk.

But the flaws became obvious almost immediately. People misplaced their passes, creating embarrassing scenes at gates when they could not re-enter their own homes. Some tried to "borrow" others' passes, bending rules to make extra trips. Most fundamentally, the paper pass represented only the risk level at the moment it was issued; it could not be updated to reflect changing health or exposure. To compensate, local officials resorted to door-to-door visits, an exhausting and ultimately unsustainable practice. It was clear that such a system could not support the transition from full lockdown towards reopening.

The first breakthrough came in Yuhang district, the most populous part of Hangzhou and also the hardest hit by COVID-19 cases. Conveniently, it was also home to Alibaba's headquarters. In early February, district officials, working with IT specialists, developed an electronic pass within 12 hours. Known as the "Yuhang Green QR Code," it was tested and launched on 6 February 2020. Its functionality was limited—updates were not automatic—but the proof of concept was enough.

Within days, Hangzhou's municipal government scaled up the experiment. Partnering with Alibaba's Ant Financial, it launched the Hangzhou Health QR Code on Alipay on 11 February 2020. This was a decisive moment. The app drew on Alipay's existing infrastructure—powerful cloud computing, cross-platform data integration, and secure identity verificationto create a city-wide tool for contact tracing and risk management.

At first, the requirement was limited: only those entering Hangzhou from outside were instructed to download the app. Yet almost immediately, its adoption spread far beyond official mandate. Businesses, transport operators, residential communities, and individual citizens embraced it as a way to secure both order and reassurance. Within days, the Health QR Code became the de facto passport for daily life.

The logic was simple but powerful. After registering basic information and answering a short health questionnaire, residents received a code in one of three colours:

- **Green:** low risk, free to move.
- **Yellow:** restricted mobility, seven-day home observation.
- **Red:** full quarantine, fourteen days.

Obtaining a code took less than two minutes, yet its impact was profound. People could no longer simply *be* residents or citizens; they had to be visible as data. Their colour determined whether they could board a bus, enter a shop, or pass through a neighbourhood gate.

In principle, the system should have updated automatically with new data. In practice, this depended on the integration of information from a dizzying array of sources: healthcare providers, transport operators, residential registries, and more. China's medical system alone spans small neighbourhood clinics, municipal hospitals, provincial centres, and specialised institutions, each with its own data practices. Even within the same sector, formats varied, and bureaucratic silos complicated integration. Lockdown thus required not just technical design but sustained collaboration between actors: engineers at Ant Financial, multi-layered administrations, medical institutions, and millions of ordinary users.

Users themselves played a critical role. They had to enter data accurately, refresh their codes, and sometimes correct errors. Many phoned hotlines or reported problems to local officials, effectively co-producing the system's reliability. The Health QR Code was therefore not a finished artefact handed down from above but a performative device, continuously shaped by interactions between technology, institutions, and citizens.

The choice of Alipay as the host platform was decisive. By 2020, more than 700 million people used Alipay for payments, shopping, transport, and services (Ant Group, 2020). The platform had evolved since its launch in 2003 from a PC-based payment tool with clunky security checks into a seamless mobile app trusted for everyday transactions. By building on this established infrastructure, the Health QR Code leveraged existing user habits and institutional trust. It also tapped into Alipay's vast data ecosystem: Sesame Credit, ride-hailing, bike-sharing, healthcare, and education, all potential streams for cross-checking and enriching information.

Thus, the Health QR Code was not simply a replacement for a fragile paper pass. It was the crystallisation of an emerging data infrastructure of visibility and traceability, transforming every resident's mobility into a calculable, monitorable, and governable activity. In the process, it redefined what it meant to be a safe, responsible member of the community.

8.2.3 Local Administration and the Information Platform Under Pressure

The Hangzhou Health QR system scaled with extraordinary speed. On its first day of launch, 700,000 people registered; by noon of the second day, the number had surpassed 7 million (Hangzhou Municipal Government, 2020). Almost overnight, risk was categorised: 6.7 million green, 198,800 yellow, and 316,300 red. These colour codes translated abstract data into everyday consequences, whether one could shop, commute, or even step outside.

Yet the scale of uptake exposed the fragility of the system. Errors abounded. Families that shared one phone found their records tangled. Elderly residents who entered details incorrectly were flagged as yellow. Some withheld information, fearing the stigma of being marked red. Others discovered that their codes mysteriously changed overnight. As with any new system opened to millions at once, technical glitches became social crises.

The usual channel for complaint, the Mayor's hotline, was quickly overwhelmed. In response, Hangzhou's municipal government set up a dedicated emergency workforce on the day of the app's launch. An online re-application channel followed, where users could contest their code. Within eight hours, 29,000 people had reapplied (Hangzhou Daily, 2020). Many of these cases cascaded down to the grassroots level, where neighbourhoods like DSL bore the responsibility for resolving them one by one.

In DSL, officials suddenly found themselves adjudicating digital anomalies. They checked residents' situations, issued temporary paper slips when phones failed, and reassured anxious families. They also had to address practical gaps: children and senior citizens without smartphones, residents who lost their devices mid-journey, or people stranded across district borders with codes unrecognised on the other side. Each case required both administrative judgement and moral reasoning.

At the same time, lockdown meant that staying home could only succeed if services came to residents. Multi-layered administrations collaborated to ensure that medicine, food, and official information reached people without exposing them to cross-district risks. Increasingly, the Health QR Code app became the portal where these services were aggregated.

Built on Alipay, the interface soon expanded far beyond risk codes. Icons linked residents to a growing ecosystem: ordering medicine for delivery, pre-booking facemasks, checking local infection maps, arranging hospital appointments, even booking special trains for migrant workers' return to factories. There were also channels for reporting price-gouging, accessing psychological counselling, and dispelling rumours. By late spring 2020, the Health QR Code had become not just a pass but an entire information platform of governance, visible to every user in the palm of their hand.

For residents of DSL, these services became essential. My relatives described how they checked the "self-inspection" map each morning to see whether any confirmed cases appeared nearby. Knowing that DSL itself had none gave them the confidence to walk outdoors, exercise, and maintain some semblance of normality. In this way, the QR code mediated not only surveillance but reassurance: it transformed invisible risks into visible data points, grounding people's decisions about safety in the midst of uncertainty.

8.2.4 The Central Government: Unified or Distributed?

On 16 February 2020, the central government called for the creation of a unified national health code (People's Daily, 2020). Yet, despite this top-down directive, a single national system never materialised. Instead, hundreds of variants persisted, developed by different provinces, cities, and even districts. Shanghai residents used *Suishenma*; those in Suzhou, *Suzhou Code*; Wuhan had its own; and in Hubei province some travellers carried five or six codes on their phones to move across jurisdictions.

What emerged was a patchwork that the centre tolerated, so long as colour codes were mutually recognised across borders. This compromise reflected a pragmatic balance: Beijing coordinated interoperability, but allowed local administrations to preserve their own systems. For local officials, tailoring rules to their constituents was essential: an elderly population might require stricter gatekeeping; industrial districts might loosen restrictions to enable factories to restart. Standardisation gave way to negotiated diversity.

In this environment, checkpoints became crucial interaction interfaces. Whether at the gates of residential compounds, office towers, bus stations, or supermarkets, the QR code had to be shown, inspected, and verified. These eclectic points became the everyday sites where "technology met the social." Here, codes were not simply scanned but interpreted, performed, and contested.

For some, especially those who relied on speed, couriers, commuters, small traders, checkpoints were a source of frustration. Delays, malfunctioning phones, or mistrust of non-local accents made life difficult. Yet even the most impatient courier might admit, at another moment, that the system helped keep the community safe. This duality, frustration and reassurance, was part of the everyday negotiation of the Health QR system.

The meaning of a code at any given checkpoint depended on a web of factors:
- The governing body's interpretation of lockdown rules
- The design and speed of the app
- The computational capacity of the system
- The inspector's understanding of the technology
- The social relationship between guard and resident
- The tacit agreements between local officials and their constituents

In other words, the Health QR system was not fixed but situated and performative. It operated less as a single "state surveillance machine" and more as what Michel Callon might call an *interessement device*, a tool that enrolled diverse actors (officials, citizens, tech companies, and inspectors) into a shared network of pandemic governance (Callon, 1986, p. 211). Decisions about whether to enforce rules strictly or flexibly, accepting a screenshot versus demanding a live scan, waving through a neighbour versus interrogating a courier, could only be made through ongoing negotiation.

The system's success depended on mass enrolment. Millions had to scan, refresh, and comply, day after day. This constant participation drew citizens into new relations of mutual visibility: residents came to appreciate not only their immediate peers, but also strangers whose behaviours (mask-wearing, scanning, isolating) shaped the safety of the collective. Migrants, once marginal and often invisible, suddenly became indispensable as delivery workers, cleaners, and carers. Their problems, lack of recognised codes, difficulties in quarantine, were pushed to the fore, and local administrations were forced to respond.

Over time, the central government's ambition for a fully unified system gave way to an appreciation of distributed governance. Diversity was not weakness but resilience: different localities adapted to their circumstances, while coordination across jurisdictions ensured the system held together. The Health QR Code thus revealed a distinctive feature of China's dataveillance: not a monolithic structure, but a flexible, layered assemblage where central and local authorities adjusted their roles in practice.

8.2.5 Checkpoints: The Interactive Theatre of the Neighbourhood

The introduction of Health QR Codes made the checkpoint the everyday stage where technology and society met. In DSL, as in countless other neighbourhoods, the gate became a site of performance, negotiation, and sometimes confrontation.

Inequalities and scrutiny

Not all residents experienced the checkpoint equally. Long-term neighbours, whose faces were familiar to guards, often passed with ease. Migrants and new arrivals faced closer scrutiny, as did couriers rushing in and out. For them, the checkpoint was not simply a matter of scanning a code but of navigating suspicion and unequal treatment.

Technical glitches and social drama

Peak hours often brought queues. Some residents prepared their QR codes in advance, phones charged and screens ready; others fumbled with frozen apps or forgotten devices, holding everyone else up. Occasionally, a code that was green in the morning turned yellow or red by afternoon due to system updates. Couriers, whose livelihoods depended on speed, were hit hardest. One complained to my relatives in March 2020: "My mobile often fails me; sometimes it only shows half the code after minutes of waiting". Another felt mistrusted because of his non-Hangzhou accent.

The social gaze and restraint

Yet the checkpoint was not only a site of tension. It was also a space of visibility. Under the combined gaze of surveillance cameras and their peers queuing behind them, both guards and residents learned restraint. Checkers and officials, conscious that their behaviour was being recorded and observed by neighbours, curbed the temptation to overuse their discretionary power. Residents, too, moderated their conduct, preparing codes in advance, keeping tempers in check, mindful of the long line waiting behind them. This everyday mutual gaze created a subtle form of accountability, reinforcing order without requiring formal sanctions.

Some other districts experimented with facial-recognition gates, reducing screening times to around ten seconds. But DSL did not see this as a priority. Such technology required costly investment from the district, while DSL relied instead on a combination of human judgement, peer visibility, and camera oversight, slower, but effective enough for a community where 60–70 % of residents were retired elders who valued caution over speed.

Improvisations and workarounds

Residents also developed collective solutions. Sympathising with couriers, many helped collect deliveries directly at the gate. Before long, the rundown post office inside DSL was repurposed as a delivery depot, where parcels were dropped in bulk and collected later at residents' convenience. What began as a pandemic improvisation became a lasting service, continuing well after lockdown ended.

The long gaze of surveillance

Even after restrictions eased, the checkpoint left visible traces. When I returned to DSL in June 2023, cameras still gazed down at the gates, including the side entrance to the Botanic Garden bamboo grove. More cameras had been added across the neighbourhood. On my morning runs, I was struck by another change: buses and cars now routinely stopped at zebra crossings, a sharp break from past experience. My family attributed this to fines triggered by traffic cameras, but also to new habits formed under constant surveillance: "Drivers have now got used to that," they said. On one occasion, when tourist crowds jammed the crossing, I saw police install mobile traffic lights, perhaps another extension of the surveillance assemblage.

Checkpoint as theatre

The DSL gate thus embodied the contradictions of pandemic governance. It was at once a site of frustration and reassurance, inequality and solidarity, surveillance and improvisation. More than a technical apparatus, it was an interactive theatre where residents, guards, officials, and technologies enacted the meaning of "lockdown." Every queue, quarrel, and workaround was part of the daily performance of safety, trust, and collective life under dataveillance.

8.2.6 The Lesson Beyond COVID

After the acute phase of the pandemic (2020–2022), many liberal democracies dismantled or paused contact-tracing apps and deleted much of the accumulated data. China followed a different path: rather than abandoning these tools, it has continued to cultivate data-driven technologies as part of longer-term governance and social infrastructure. Conversations I had with colleagues, neighbours and acquaintances between 2020 and 2023 captured this ambivalence. Many people said they felt safer under dataveillance; others remained uneasy.

A striking comment came from a middle-aged woman I sat next to on a flight to Beijing in June 2023: "We are now naked," she said, meaning constantly visible. Then she added, "I have nothing to hide... but if I am wronged, I hope the digital evidence can help me." That tension, visibility as both exposure and protection, recurs in many people's reflections.

On my resumed visit in 2023, the legacy of pandemic dataveillance was obvious. Cameras still watched the gates of DSL; I was asked for my passport in many places; friends joked, "You're certainly being watched." I did not feel anxious. More salient to me was a pragmatic hope: that dataveillance might recognise my individual circumstances rather than stereotyping me as a "foreigner," and that it might make bureaucratic interactions (access to information, services, or travel) less fraught than before.

I also remember a more melancholy experience from before COVID-19, when my sister and I tried to trace lost relatives through local archives and administrative records, and found little. That absence made me reflect on another side of data: if records existed, could they help preserve memory, accountability and social recognition? If people know their actions leave traces that can be reviewed, might that encourage greater care for the collective?

These reflections point to a central paradox. Dataveillance can constrain crime, reduce fraud, and make service delivery more precise. It can also normalise constant visibility, entrench inequalities, and create new forms of exclusion if data systems are poorly designed or unfairly enforced. In China, where mobile phone Subscriber Identity Module (SIM) cards and many digital services are strongly linked to identity, the infrastructure of visibility has practical benefits, but it also raises urgent ethical and governance questions.

In short: the Health QR Code experiment did more than contain a virus. It re-embedded a form of collective responsibility, visible, traceable, and digitally mediated, into everyday life. What remains is to learn how to govern these systems so that they support civic possibility rather than merely extend surveillance. The next section turns to that task: what did authorities, communities, and platforms learn from the crisis, and how might these lessons shape a more accountable, participatory form of data governance?

8.3 Learning from Crisis and Scaffolding the Collective Self

8.3.1 From Moral Decline to Civic Awakening

As discussed in Section 8.1, the reform era's dismantling of collective infrastructures created a condition of ontological insecurity. By the late 1990s, China's reforms had delivered extraordinary economic growth, yet prosperity was accompanied by profound fractures. The erosion of collective infrastructures was felt not only in material terms but also as a moral unravelling. Public discourse was filled with laments about a "moral crisis" and a "spiritual vacuum." Scandals seemed to confirm these anxieties: melamine-tainted milk, counterfeit medicines, gutter oil recycled into cooking, rampant pyramid schemes, and online fraud. Trust became fragile: residents doubted the safety of what they ate, migrants were eyed with suspicion in cities, and rumours often carried more weight than official announcements.

The COVID-19 pandemic disrupted this trajectory in an unexpected way. Suddenly, every individual's behaviour, whether wearing a mask, scanning a QR code, or staying indoors, was visibly consequential for collective survival. The Health QR Code condensed epidemiological uncertainty into a simple set of colours: green for mobility, yellow for caution, red for quarantine. Unlike the blind imitations and opportunistic shortcuts that had fuelled so many reform-era scandals, participation in this system was conscious and collective. Citizens, digital platforms, and local administrations all had to enrol themselves into a shared project of protection.

For the first time in decades, ordinary people were reminded that their choices mattered not just for themselves or their families, but for neighbours, colleagues, and strangers. As the World Health Organization (WHO) observed during the pandemic, "in our interdependent world no one is safe until everyone is safe"

(WHO, 2020, para. 1). The Health QR Code made this interdependence tangible: each scan, each colour change, linked the fate of one individual to the wellbeing of many.

This global reminder of relational responsibility resonates strongly with long-standing Chinese traditions. Confucian ethics (Shen & Gao, 2025) emphasises that morality is never abstract but always situated within relationships, between parent and child, ruler and subject, neighbour and neighbour. Daoist thought, too, sees harmony as emerging from responsiveness to the flows of circumstance rather than from rigid control. In this light, the pandemic was not only a health crisis but also a moment in which infrastructures of visibility reawakened the relational dimensions of civic life.

8.3.2 Experimental Infrastructures of Crisis

When the Health QR Code was launched in Hangzhou in February 2020, it was less a finished product than a bold experiment. As described in Section 8.2.2, the first electronic pass in Yuhang district, developed within 12 hours, proved the concept. Hangzhou's municipal team then scaled it onto Alipay's vast platform, leveraging its computational power, data integration, and existing user base. Within weeks, variants appeared across the country. By spring 2020, hundreds of health codes coexisted: some mounted on Alibaba's systems, others on Tencent's, still others built on local infrastructures.

Rather than imposing uniformity, the central government tolerated this diversity, stepping in only to coordinate interoperability across jurisdictions. A green code in Hangzhou had to be recognised in Shanghai; a red code in Wuhan had to be honoured in Guangzhou. Standardisation was partial, negotiated through practice rather than decree.

In this way, the pandemic revealed a distinctive mode of governance: not the execution of a fixed blueprint, but what might be called crisis experimentalism. Systems were tested in real time, scaled through feedback, and stabilised by collective improvisation. The QR code's legitimacy did not stem from its technical perfection, it was full of flaws, but from its responsiveness and the willingness of citizens, officials, and platforms to adjust together.

For residents, this experimentalism was not abstract. It was lived daily: queues at checkpoints, colour codes refreshed anxiously, screenshots shared in WeChat groups, neighbours helping elders navigate apps. Infrastructures were not static tools but evolving devices of coordination, teaching people how to act responsibly in conditions of radical uncertainty.

8.3.3 Crisis-Embedded Governance as Ethical Learning

The Health QR Code was not only a technical device for contact tracing; it quickly became a medium for teaching people how to live responsibly during a crisis. In design terms, its colour signals functioned as cues for ethical orientation. A green code reassured residents that they could travel freely. A yellow code prompted self-restraint: a week of rest, limited movement, avoidance of gatherings. A red code carried a heavy demand: strict quarantine, protecting the community by removing oneself from circulation.

For residents, these signals condensed the uncertainties of epidemiology into everyday practice. People did not have to interpret complex data about viral transmission. Instead, they acted on the visible, colour-coded logic of risk. In this way, the infrastructure itself became a pedagogical tool: shaping routines, reinforcing norms, and cultivating awareness that one's personal behaviour mattered for the wellbeing of others.

Learning, however, was not passive. People interpreted, contested, and sometimes resisted. Families checked each other's statuses in WeChat groups; neighbours reminded one another of restrictions; residents with wrongly classified codes called hotlines, appealed to local officials, or found temporary workarounds. Guards at checkpoints exercised discretion, sometimes enforcing rules rigidly, sometimes applying them flexibly to accommodate urgent needs. Each decision became a lesson in balancing safety, empathy, and practicality.

Officials and engineers also learned. Every misclassification generated feedback; every breakdown required adjustment. Citizens revealed loopholes, screenshots used in place of live codes, phones borrowed between family members, that forced designers to strengthen verification mechanisms. The system evolved through this recursive loop of use, error, and correction. Governance was not the unilateral imposition of rules but a process of learning by doing, shared across multiple levels of society.

This recursive adaptation gave the Health QR Code a form of legitimacy that pure coercion could not. People complied not only because they were compelled, but because they saw the system respond, improving, correcting, and accommodating. In this sense, pandemic governance was not just administrative but pedagogical: it cultivated civic reflexivity by embedding ethical lessons in the very tools people used to move, shop, and interact.

These improvisations and adjustments point to a wider insight: infrastructures like the Health QR Code did not merely constrain behaviour; they also scaffolded new capacities for civic responsibility. In education, scaffolding refers to temporary supports that enable learners to achieve tasks they could not accomplish alone (Wood et al., 1976). In a similar way, the QR system provided supports, colour signals, shared protocols, visible reminders, that helped residents act responsibly under uncertain conditions. The system did not dictate morality; it offered cues and frameworks through which people learned to practice it together. In this sense, crisis governance functioned as an improvised civic classroom, cultivating habits of care and restraint that might otherwise have been absent.

8.3.4 From Data to Ethical Affordances

Digital infrastructures do more than regulate; they structure possibilities for action. In design and Science and Technology Studies (STS), these are called affordances: features that guide practice, frame choices, and create conditions for learning (Gibson, 1979). During the pandemic, the Health QR Code offered precisely such affordances. It made the invisible visible, transforming abstract risks of viral transmission into actionable signals.

For most residents, the QR code was not experienced as a faceless technology of surveillance but as a practical orientation device. A green code meant one could visit shops, take the bus, or see family. A yellow code urged caution, seven days of rest, postponing travel, checking in with neighbours. A red code demanded self-quarantine, reminding residents that their individual presence could endanger others. Each colour condensed uncertainty into responsibility, turning data into ethical cues.

This reframes the familiar metaphor of the panopticon. In Foucault's account, the panopticon disciplines by rendering subjects visible to an unseen authority, producing obedience through internalised fear (Foucault, 1977). The Health QR Code worked differently. Visibility was distributed and relational: neighbourhood committees, employers, family members, and even peers in WeChat groups could see, discuss, and interpret QR statuses. Surveillance here was not only top-down but horizontal, enacted through daily interactions.

People monitored themselves as much as they were monitored. They routinely checked their own codes, shared screenshots, and demanded corrections when errors occurred. Parents reminded children to refresh apps; friends urged one another to stay home if a code turned yellow. The infrastructure became part of social habitus, a routine practice.

From a Chinese philosophical perspective, this resonates with deep traditions. In Confucian ethics, moral rightness (*yi* 义) is situational and relational: one acts appropriately within roles and relationships, not in isolation. A sudden code change became a moment to ask: *Whom have I been near? What responsibilities do I owe to my family, neighbours, community?* Daoist thought, meanwhile, speaks of non-coercive responsiveness (*wu wei* 无为). The QR code nudged behaviour without explicit compulsion, encouraging people to adapt fluidly to circumstances.

In this way, data traces acted less as cages than as mirrors. They reflected back to individuals their entanglement in collective life. A shift in colour did not simply impose a restriction; it revealed a relational truth—that personal mobility is never only personal, but bound up with others' safety.

Yet these affordances were ambivalent. They enabled ethical reflection, but also risked reinforcing inequalities. Migrants, couriers, and digitally marginalised groups were more likely to face misclassification or heightened scrutiny. Elderly residents without smartphones sometimes found themselves excluded altogether. The same infrastructure that scaffolded responsibility for some could stigmatise or penalise others.

The challenge, then, is to recognise digital systems not only as technical substrates but as ethical infrastructures, media through which responsibility is elicited, contested, and distributed. Their significance lies less in whether they surveil than in how they configure relations of care, trust, and accountability.

8.3.5 Towards a Collective Self

The pandemic brought into sharp relief what Chinese reform-era transformations had obscured: the interdependence of individual and collective life. Every scan of a Health QR Code, every change of colour status, tied personal conduct to communal safety. A trip to the market, a visit to a friend, even a casual bus ride suddenly carried visible ethical weight. The infrastructure made it impossible to imagine the self as detached; responsibility was continuously refracted through the presence of others.

This stood in stark contrast to the decades of moral decline that preceded it. Scandals such as melamine-tainted milk, rampant fraud, and reckless speculation had exemplified a society where blind imitation and opportunism often overwhelmed accountability. During COVID-19, by contrast, the collective dimension of life was rediscovered, not through abstract moral preaching but through the very infrastructures that structured daily action.

Historically, Chinese intellectuals had grappled with this tension. Sun Yat-sen famously lamented that the Chinese people were like "a sheet of loose sand," lacking cohesion (Sun, 1924, p. 56). Lu Xun critiqued the "onlooker mentality," where people observed others' suffering with detachment rather than acting in solidarity (Lu, 1918). The Health QR Code experiment suggested a different trajectory: a fragile but real sense of collective self, where individuals experienced themselves as parts of an assemblage bound by visibility, risk, and shared accountability.

This rediscovery was both practical and symbolic. Practically, mass enrolment in QR infrastructures normalised everyday coordination: residents complied with restrictions not only because of state enforcement but also because their peers and neighbours were doing the same. Symbolically, the codes served as reminders that the wellbeing of the collective depended on the behaviour of each. In this sense, the pandemic functioned as a civic pedagogy: teaching that "to protect oneself is to protect others, and to protect others is to protect oneself" (People's Daily, 2020).

Yet this collective self was uneven and contested. Migrants without stable registrations, couriers under constant suspicion, and elderly citizens without smartphones were often marginalised. For them, visibility could mean exclusion or discrimination rather than recognition. Their struggles highlighted that the collective self was not an accomplished fact but an ongoing project, contingent on how infrastructures are designed and how inclusively they operate.

In STS terms, each citizen became a monad in the sense I develop in this book: a traceable unit whose relations, familial, occupational, digital, bureaucratic, passed (Tarde, 1903; Latour, 2005). The pandemic did not create these relations but made them newly traceable. Infrastructures of dataveillance acted as prisms, refracting connections that had always existed but were often hidden. Through them, the Chinese self was repositioned: less an isolated unit than a node within a dense web of mutual obligations.

The lesson of this moment lies not in the perfection of technology but in the possibility of civic imagination. The Health QR Code, for all its flaws and exclusions, demonstrated that a society long described as fragmented and distrustful could rediscover relational responsibility when infrastructures made interdependence unavoidable. In doing so, it offered a glimpse of how the "collective self" might be scaffolded, not as a utopian ideal, but as a fragile achievement sustained through everyday practices of visibility, negotiation, and care.

8.3.6 Conclusion: From Survival to Cultivation

The infrastructures born of crisis were initially designed as tools of survival. They restricted movement, minimised contagion, and enabled officials to manage risks at an unprecedented scale. Yet as they were enacted in neighbourhoods like DSL, they became more than defensive barriers. They served as ethical laboratories, scaffolding new habits of responsibility, cooperation, and civic awareness.

This shift was subtle but significant. Residents did not simply endure surveillance; they participated in it, contested its errors, and adapted to its cues. Guards learned discretion; officials balanced rules with empathy; engineers refined algorithms through feedback. The Health QR Code was never a finished technology imposed from above, but a constantly evolving assemblage shaped through collective practice.

In this process, society rediscovered that personal conduct is inseparable from collective wellbeing. The pandemic made visible what reform-era moral decline had obscured: that trust, accountability, and care are not luxuries but necessities. The Health QR Code reminded citizens daily that their actions mattered, not only for themselves but for strangers standing beside them in queues, for neighbours in their compounds, for couriers delivering their parcels.

At the same time, the exclusions and inequalities that accompanied this rediscovery, digital divides, migrant marginalisation, discretionary bias, showed how fragile and uneven the scaffolding of a collective self can be. The challenge going forward is whether infrastructures of visibility can evolve beyond emergency tools into durable platforms for civic cultivation.

This opens onto the central theoretical questions taken up in the next section. How should we understand dataveillance when it is not only coercive but also participatory and pedagogical? What does it mean to rethink the panopticon in relational rather than unilateral terms? Can infrastructures act as affordances for ethical reflection and collective selfhood, rather than simply instruments of control? And what insights might concepts like monads and governing by affordance bring to our understanding of China's distinctive path of digital governance?

What this illustrates is a mode of governing by affordance. Instead of compelling action through explicit commands or penalties, the QR code structured the field of possible behaviours. Its colours signalled when to move, when to pause, when to withdraw. Its interface allowed residents to check themselves, correct errors, and confirm safety with others. These features did not operate as rigid controls but as affordances, subtle prompts that channelled conduct while leaving space for discretion and reflexivity. This style of governance relied less on surveillance as domination and more on design as participation, where infrastructures quietly shaped what felt reasonable, safe, and responsible to do.

The answers lie not in declaring success or failure, but in recognising that crises reveal the conditions of possibility. COVID-19 transformed dataveillance from a distant concept into an everyday reality, and in doing so, illuminated the paradoxes of moral decline and civic possibility. The theoretical task now is to make sense of these paradoxes, an undertaking to which the next section turns.

In this sense, the Health QR Code was not simply a device of control but a form of scaffolding through affordances, an improvised infrastructure that supported civic responsibility by shaping how people could see, act, and relate to one another.

8.4 Discussion: Reassembling Dataveillance

The preceding sections suggested that governance-through-affordance should be seen as a tentative and revisable scaffold: a fragile infrastructure that supported civic responsibility during the pandemic but remained uneven and provisional. This section takes that observation further. Rather than treating dataveillance as a monolithic system of control, it discusses how such scaffolds are co-produced, how they operate through affordances rather than commands, and how they may foster the fragile emergence of a collective self. By rethinking panopticism, monads, and the ethics of visibility, we can better understand both the possibilities and the limitations of these experimental infrastructures.

8.4.1 Rethinking Dataveillance: Mobile-Enabled Surveillance as Socio-Technical Practice

The term *dataveillance* was coined by Roger Clarke in 1988 to describe the systematic use of personal data in monitoring behaviour (Clarke, 1988, p. 499). In Euro-American debates it has often been imagined through dystopian lenses: Orwell's *Big Brother*, the Snowden revelations of state overreach, or *Black Mirror*'s portrayal of digital life as a panoptic nightmare. These imaginaries emphasise asymmetry, an all-seeing eye watching passive subjects from above.

China's Health QR Code system complicates this picture. Here, surveillance was not only vertical but mobile-enabled and participatory. Every individual carried the device of visibility in their pocket. Instead of a hidden sovereign gaze, there was a distributed, everyday performance: residents refreshing codes, presenting screens at checkpoints, negotiating errors with officials. The QR code was thus less a static surveillance mechanism than an epidemic device, a socio-technical apparatus that translated viral risk into legible colours and actionable routines.

What made this significant was not only enforcement but learning. Citizens acquired epidemiological knowledge through the process: they came to understand that contact histories mattered, that mobility patterns shaped risk, that infection was not an abstract threat but a condition mediated by their own actions. Green, yellow, and red codes condensed complex epidemiological processes into visible cues that could be interpreted, contested, or resisted. In this sense, mobile-enabled surveillance worked pedagogically, teaching society how contagion spread and why collective discipline was necessary.

This pedagogical role also shaped resistance. As the Delta and Omicron variants emerged, many citizens realised that the virus could no longer be contained by mobility controls alone. They also learned to see the temporal gap between exposure and infection: a red code did not mean someone was ill, only that they had been in contact with a potential case. To be sent to quarantine on this basis was increasingly perceived as a precautionary measure that carried risks of its own. The very visibility that had supported compliance during the first waves, daily reminders of risk, collective vigilance, now fed disillusionment when "dynamic zero-COVID" policies dragged on. Residents who had learned to read codes and maps began to question their proportionality; the infrastructural pedagogy that once legitimised restrictions now eroded their credibility.

The QR system thus exemplifies dataveillance as socio-technical practice. It did not simply impose visibility from above but enacted it through interaction: officials, platforms, and citizens co-produced an epidemic device whose authority depended on responsiveness and adaptation. Its legitimacy was performative, sustained by feedback loops and everyday negotiation. And when those loops broke down under Omicron, legitimacy faltered.

In short, mobile-enabled surveillance during COVID-19 was not only about control; it was also about making risks knowable, behaviour traceable, and responsibility tangible. It scaffolded civic participation in public health while simultaneously teaching the limits of governance by data alone.

8.4.2 The Digital Panopticon: Visibility, Reflexivity, and Governance

The metaphor of the *panopticon*, first elaborated by Jeremy Bentham and famously theorised by Michel Foucault (1977), has long served as a dominant lens through which surveillance is understood: a centralised structure enabling the few to watch the many, conditioning behaviour through the internalisation of visibility. In the digital age, this metaphor has been widely extended to describe the logics of platform-based monitoring, algorithmic oversight, and data capitalism (Lyon, 2018). Yet, as China's pandemic response illustrates, the digital panopticon is more than a metaphor, it is a complex and shifting mode of governance that blurs the boundaries between observation, participation, and self-regulation.

The Health QR Code exemplifies this shift. Its success relied not only on hierarchical surveillance but also on horizontal legibility, making individuals visible to neighbourhood committees, workplaces, schools, and even family members. Rather than being an invisible gaze from a central tower, the system functioned as a distributed matrix of mutual watching and data-based coordination. Visibility here was layered: individuals were rendered legible not only to the state, but to multiple social intermediaries embedded in daily life. The digital panopticon thus operated less as a unidirectional gaze and more as a field of relational visibility.

One illustrative example of this visibility regime is the deployment of large digital screens at pedestrian crossings in several Chinese cities, which publicly displayed images and partial identification details of individuals caught jaywalking (The Guardian, 2018). The actions would show on the screen to the offenders themselves and the facial recognition system would automatically capture an offender's face and link to the identity and the history of behaviours when needed. This was not just deterrence through surveillance; it was surveillance through public exposure. The goal was not only to discipline but to instil reflexive self-monitoring through real-time visibility.

These screen-based interventions reveal a distinct modality of digital panopticism, public, performative, and hyper-local. They extend Foucault's model by rendering the act of watching visible itself, turning the gaze into a shared mechanism to activate the individual self's collective conscience. Yet this also raised discomfort as mentioned earlier. Moreover, digital surveillance under crisis conditions provoked new forms of reflexivity. Individuals routinely checked their own QR status, verified health reports of others, and engaged in behaviours shaped by algorithmic judgements. This self-monitoring was not purely coerced. It was tied to practical benefits, access to space, services, and social belonging, and became a routinised part of everyday life. In this sense, the digital panopticon functioned as both infrastructure and habitus: an embedded system that shaped action not through repression but through affective and logistical entanglement.

However, this reflexive surveillance was not without friction. Errors in QR code classification, inaccessible interfaces for elderly populations, and conflicting policies across regions all exposed the fragility of this visibility regime. The system's authority rested not on its perfection, but on its perceived responsiveness. Individuals did not simply obey the system—they engaged with it, contested it, sought redress, and sometimes circumvented it. As a result, the digital panopticon was always under negotiation.

China's experience thus challenges the idea that digital surveillance produces docile subjects through omniscient oversight. Instead, it reveals a more complex dynamic: surveillance as socio-technical performance, where visibility, legitimacy, and functionality are continually co-constructed. In the context of crisis governance, visibility does not signify total control—it becomes a resource, a risk, and a site of politics.

Crucially, the digital panopticon intersects with the infrastructural turn in governance. In China, QR codes, AI-assisted policing, and data integration platforms are not simply tools of control; they are efforts to build coherence across fragmented bureaucratic regimes. Surveillance becomes infrastructural not just in function, but in aspiration: a means of producing order in a society marked by complexity, mobility, and contingency.

This reconfiguration of visibility invites us to rethink the panopticon not as a static architecture but as a mode of relational governance. Digital technologies do not simply watch—they mediate, translate, and reconfigure social relations. And in doing so, they reveal how contemporary governance is enacted not only through coercion, but through infrastructural visibility and reflexive engagement.

8.4.3 The Collective Self: Data, Responsibility, and Relational Governance

Surveillance studies in Western contexts often assume the primacy of the individual as the unit of analysis—an atomised, rights-bearing subject whose autonomy is threatened by intrusive systems. But this liberal individualist imaginary sits uneasily with the normative logics underpinning Chinese governance, where identity and responsibility are fundamentally relational. To understand China's data-intensive governance, especially during the pandemic, we must instead attend to the emergence of a *collective self:* a subject constituted through entangled social relations, communal obligations, and data-mediated interdependence.

The Health QR Code system exemplifies this shift. Unlike privacy-centric models that emphasise data minimisation, China's system was premised on *data legibility:* making individuals visible to others within nested collectivities—households, work units, neighbourhoods, and cities. This visibility was not merely for state surveillance; it enabled mutual care, risk coordination, and social regulation at multiple scales. Neighbours checked on each other's statuses, shared updates in WeChat groups, and collectively adjusted behaviours based on changing QR colours. The self here was never isolated, it was embedded, situated, and co-constituted.

This collectivist orientation reflects deeper traditions. In Confucian ethics, the self is defined through roles and relationships, between parent and child, ruler and subject, friend and friend. Responsibility (*ze* 责) is not an individual burden but a distributed obligation across relational networks. During the pandemic, this ethical grammar translated into governance forms that emphasised communal risk, shared responsibility, and coordinated response.

Importantly, this was not simply a return to collectivism as a state ideology. Rather, it was a reconfiguration through digital infrastructures that made the collective visible, actionable, and accountable. For instance, during lockdowns, QR systems and online maps allowed residents to monitor the infection status of their residential compounds. Communities organised services like group food orders and medicine delivery based on collective data, transforming neighbourhoods into functional nodes of care and control.

Yet this collectivisation also introduced tensions. Individuals could be locked down, denied entry, or stigmatised due to the health status of someone in their building. The algorithmic aggregation of risk often treated the collective as an epidemiological unit, overriding individual variation. This raised new ethical questions: What rights does an individual have when subsumed into a collective risk profile? Who decides how risk is calculated, and how collective responsibility is assigned?

Moreover, the collective self was not homogenous. Migrant workers, elderly populations, and digitally marginalised groups experienced QR-based governance differently. Their reduced access to platforms, inconsistent policy enforcement, and limited recourse revealed the fragility of digital collectivism. As some neighbourhoods relaxed QR checks, others like DSL (Dong-shan-long) continued rigorous enforcement, especially for high-risk groups. These divergences suggest that the collective self is always situated, structured by geography, class, age, and infrastructural unevenness.

Nevertheless, the notion of a collective self helps us grasp how governance under crisis functions not through abstract norms or static laws, but through embedded practices that link data, identity, and moral responsibility. It reveals a shift from surveillance as extraction to surveillance as *coordination*—an attempt to enact order not by monitoring isolated individuals, but by producing collective coherence through technological mediation.

In this way, the collective self challenges liberal imaginaries of autonomy and offers an alternative lens for analysing surveillance: not as a violation of privacy, but as a mode of relational governance that mobilises shared visibility for both control and care. This reframing is crucial for understanding China's evolving data regimes, and for rethinking the ethical and political implications of digital governance in other emerging contexts.

8.4.4 Monadology and Digital Social Science: From Relational Subjects to Embedded Governance

The emergence of the collective self in China's data governance signals a profound ontological shift: from individualistic subjects governed through abstract norms, to relational actors constituted within dynamic socio-technical contexts. To make sense of this reorientation, I draw on Gabriel Tarde's concept of monads, but reinterpret it in a more concrete, empirically tractable way.

In this book, I understand monads as **traceable units:** entities—whether persons, firms, or countries—whose histories and relations can be followed like footprints across sand or threads in a fabric. A monad is not an abstract category but a unit that leaves traces, connects, and becomes meaningful through its path. This differs fundamentally from Western traditions of horizontal generalisation, which categorise societies by static labels. For example, defining a society simply through ideological categories obscures its actual historical trajectory and relational patterns. Similarly, whilst consumers may compare firms horizontally in a marketplace, our deepest commitments often emerge from long vertical ties built up over time—brand loyalty, platform dependency, accumulated data relationships.

This granular and relational visibility is what dataveillance infrastructures make newly possible. The Health QR Code, for instance, did not merely identify "a person" but operationalised a person-as-traceable-unit: linked to places visited, contacts made, declarations given, and risks accumulated over time. Each citizen's data profile became not an isolated record, but a situated account of collective entanglements—household registration, employment affiliations, mobility patterns, and communal obligations, all rendered visible and auditable.

This trace-based perspective has profound implications for governance. Rather than governing through horizontal categories (citizens, migrants, workers), data systems govern through vertical histories—what this specific individual has done, where they have been, whom they have encountered. Bruno Latour's *Reassembling the Social* (2005) develops this relational ontology, arguing that actors are defined by the networks they trace and retrace: a subject is not a node but a bundle of translations, a carrier of associations (Latour, 2005, p. 128).

Yet, this vision also foregrounds the crucial role of *intellectual and educated individuals* capable of reading, interpreting, and negotiating these entanglements. In a society increasingly mediated by data, those who can critically inhabit their own monadic positions, understanding the metrics, meanings, and moral implications of their digital traces, are better placed to shape the direction of governance. These individuals do not merely obey or resist; they curate, reflect, and sometimes recalibrate the networks in which they are embedded.

Thus, data governance becomes a form of *reflexive social science*, not only in the academic sense but as a mode of life. Citizens learn to interpret heat maps, QR statuses, and algorithmic classifications as they navigate urban spaces. Bureaucrats adapt policies in real time, based on data flows and citizen feedback. Even platform engineers become attuned to emergent social frictions, tweaking interfaces and functionalities in response. In this landscape, governing is not just about rules but about *learning by doing and performative understanding*, a continual experimentalism that blurs the line between science, politics, and ethics.

This leads us directly to the next subsection: governing by affordance. If monads are embedded, reflexive actors navigating complex networks, then governance must accommodate such navigation. It must create conditions for action without overdetermination, what STS might call *infrastructures of affordance*. These infrastructures do not coerce or prescribe; they guide, nudge, and invite participation. In China's pandemic response, we see how such affordances emerged not just from design, but from practice, co-produced by users, regulators, and systems in flux.

What we witness, then, is a movement from *surveillance as control* to *governance as coordination*; from *citizens as subjects* to *monads as relational actors*; from *top-down enforcement* to *performative alignment*. In this evolving regime of embedded crisis governance, surveillance becomes both a tool and a mirror, revealing not just how we are governed, but how we govern ourselves together.

8.4.5 Governing by Affordance: Experimentalism and the Politics of Learning

These digital affordances, colour signals, app interfaces, checkpoint routines, did not simply dictate behaviour but offered cues through which people oriented themselves in relation to others. They made visible the ethical stakes of everyday life, turning mobility into a matter of responsibility. Yet it is important to stress that such affordances were never complete or unproblematic. They worked unevenly, sometimes scaffolding civic reflexivity, at other times excluding or frustrating those less digitally equipped.

It is against this backdrop that we can speak of the fragile emergence of a collective self. Not a settled reality, but a precarious achievement sustained by infrastructures of visibility and the willingness of diverse actors to interpret and respond to them.

The evolving contours of China's data-driven governance signal not only a shift in institutional technique but also a transformation in political ontology. Surveillance is no longer strictly top-down, nor are infrastructures merely instruments of enforcement. Rather, what is emerging is a form of *governing by affordance:* a mode of rule that works through enabling conditions, adaptive feedback loops, and the cultivation of participation, not through command but through coordination.

The concept of *affordance*, rooted in ecological psychology (Gibson, 1979) and widely adopted in Social Shaping of Technology (SST) and Human-Computer Interaction (HCI), refers to the possibilities for action that an environment or object provides to a user. In governance contexts, this means that digital systems, platforms, algorithms, apps, do not simply dictate behaviour; they shape it by making certain actions more intuitive, desirable, or legitimate than others. Health QR Codes, for example, do not *force* individuals to move or stay still, but by signalling risk and authorising mobility, they channel choices and facilitate coordination across systems.

In China, this governance-through-affordance has unfolded as a distributed, situated, and highly responsive architecture. Local officials interpreted central guidelines flexibly. Citizens engaged with interfaces daily, reporting errors and demanding clarity. Tech firms iterated design based on real-time friction. What held these disparate actors together was not a rigid law or ideology, but a *performative convergence* around functionality, legitimacy, and shared stakes in managing uncertainty.

This is what we might call an *experimentalist politics*, a regime of rule premised not on blueprint designs but on *learning by doing*. Governance here is iterative and reflexive: small-scale trials, feedback mechanisms, and situational problem-solving take precedence over universal principles or static protocols. The launch of the Health QR Code, its rapid local iterations, the subsequent need for national standards, and the eventual deactivation of the system all reflect this logic of experimentation under conditions of crisis.

Importantly, experimentalism in China is not anarchic. It operates within bounded parameters: the state retains oversight, and red lines remain. But within these constraints, considerable room exists for local innovation, public contestation, and infrastructural negotiation. This reflects a broader principle in Chinese governance, the legacy of "crossing the river by feeling the stones" (*mozhe shitou guohe* 摸着石头过河), now reconfigured in the digital age.

Governing by affordance is also a governance of *crisis*, where crisis is not simply a rupture to be overcome but a condition of risks and opportunities to be inhabited. Under crisis, infrastructures are deployed not merely to stabilise order, but to *generate knowledge:* about actors, responses, contexts, and limits. Surveillance systems become epistemic devices, not just disciplinary ones. They co-produce publics, institutional learning, and political adaptability.

Yet this affordance-oriented governance raises questions: Who controls the design of affordances? Whose actions are made possible, and whose are excluded? Affordances, after all, are not neutral; they encode assumptions, biases, and institutional interests. An interface that works for the digitally literate may exclude the elderly; a heat map that visualises "risk" may stigmatise communities. Thus, the politics of affordance must be analysed not only in terms of utility but also in terms of *justice*.

China's pandemic governance offers a vivid empirical case, but the implications are broader. As more governments and platforms experiment with data infrastructures to manage crises, climate, migration, health, security, the question of *how* to govern adaptively, ethically, and inclusively becomes pressing. Affordance is one answer, but only if paired with transparency, accountability, and participatory reflexivity.

In conclusion, governing by affordance reframes the relationship between state, technology, and society. It displaces static models of rule and opens up space for negotiated, embedded, and reflexive governance. In the context of China, it reveals a mode of experimental statecraft that is neither purely authoritarian nor fully open, but something more complex: a system of co-produced control, mediated through platforms, shaped by crisis, and oriented towards continual adaptation.

8.4.6 Synthesis: Reassembling Governance Through Crisis

Across the sections of this chapter, we have examined how China's pandemic-era dataveillance infrastructures, particularly mobile-enabled surveillance platforms, have redefined the architectures and ontologies of governance. Far from fitting the mould of static authoritarian control, these systems reflect a dynamic and experimental form of statecraft grounded in participatory surveillance, contextual ethics, and socio-technical co-production.

We began by reframing *dataveillance* not simply as a tool of observation but as a relational and performative apparatus. Drawing on Roger Clarke's foundational concept, we argued that mobile-enabled systems such as Health QR Codes exemplify how surveillance can be reconfigured into a participatory infrastructure, shaped not only by state imperatives but also by user agency, platform design, and contextual negotiation.

In tracing the shift from legacy models of surveillance to mobile interfaces, we explored how asymmetrical surveillance models are giving way to distributed regimes of visibility, where legitimacy depends on responsiveness and the ability to accommodate exceptions. This led us to articulate the idea of dataveillance as co-production: an ongoing interplay of infrastructures, users, and institutional actors that constitutes governance as a shared, if unevenly distributed, endeavour.

Building on this, we explored the formation of a collective self—a relational subjectivity emergent from digital traceability and patterned interactions. In contrast to the liberal individualism underpinning Western data governance models, China's platforms constitute individuals as nodes within interdependent matrices of responsibility and risk. This ontological configuration aligns with the relational ethics discussed in earlier chapters and anticipates the shift from governance *of* individuals to governance *through* relational enactments.

We then turned to monadology and digital social science, using insights from Gabriel Tarde and Bruno Latour to theorise the interface between individual and collective agency. By reinterpreting Tarde's monads as traceable units,entities rendered visible through their accumulated relations and historical paths—we gain analytical purchase on how dataveillance operates not through static categories but through dynamic, granular tracking of situated actors. This frames governance as not merely an exercise of power, but a form of ontological composition: a process of assembling, contesting, and recalibrating the social through data.

Finally, we introduced the concept of governing by affordance, highlighting the experimentalist and adaptive dimensions of China's digital governance. Through feedback loops, user interactions, and platform affordances, the state learns and adapts, not always smoothly, but often effectively. This mode of governance, rooted in *embedded crisis*, eschews universal rules in favour of contingent coordination, revealing an emergent politics of learning-by-doing.

Together, these threads illuminate a distinctive trajectory in Chinese governance: one that is neither wholly top-down nor bottom-up, but organised through recursive alignment across platforms, publics, and policy domains. This experimental mode does not dissolve power asymmetries or political constraints. Yet it reconfigures them, offering a model of governance that is flexible, participatory, and deeply contingent upon the affordances of socio-technical infrastructures.

These insights set the stage for a broader theoretical synthesis. What does it mean to govern in a world shaped by platform logic, data flows, and ongoing crisis? How do experimental governance and infrastructural politics reshape the relationship between state, society, and technology, not just in China, but globally?

As this chapter has shown, these socio-technical experiments illustrate a broader mode of governance under *continuous crisis*, a recursive, participatory, and infrastructural adaptation to uncertainty. In doing so, they foreshadow a new phase of digital modernity, in which China's recursive governance cycles lay the foundations for what Chapter 9 will describe as a potential *digital enlightenment*, a post-Western configuration of socio-technical order built on traceability, collective selfhood, and infrastructural world-making.

9 The Conclusion: Cross-Case Analyses and Reflections

Preamble

Looking back across the chapters of this book, I see how my own research journey has unfolded in parallel with China's trajectory of technological transformation. From my early fieldwork on digital switches in the 1990s, through explorations of open-source software, standards, platforms, cultural industries, and finally the Health QR Code, each stage of inquiry echoed the dilemmas and paradoxes China was facing in real time. Both my research and China's development moved from questions of imitation and catch-up to challenges of innovation, governance, and ethics. In coming to appreciate Tarde's monadology, I have found a lens that makes sense of this shared path: a way of recognising how mass and diverse technologies, like the people who use them, require infrastructures of visibility and traceability to become governable and to foster a collective self.

9.1 At the Crossroads of Science and Technology Development

Imitation has been more than the defining force of China's science and technology development; it is also a constitutive force of modernity itself (Tarde, 1903). From state-led technology transfer projects in telecommunications to the grassroots vitality of the *shanzhai* spirit and the experimentation with data-driven governance, China's modernisation has unfolded through the paradoxes of imitation: at once dependent and creative, coerced and chosen, disciplined and unruly. As argued in Chapter 1, imitation is never a neutral act of copying (Latour, 2005). It is always embedded in social contexts, entangled with politics, and infused with contradiction, coercion, creativity, constraint, and possibility (Bijker, Hughes, & Pinch, 2012). To understand China's path is therefore to understand how imitation has been evaluated, managed, and reimagined, not only as a tool for catching up, but as a generative condition of technological and social life in the modern world.

The driving questions of this book turn on this problem of imitation. How do imitation, innovation, and governance intertwine in China's science and technology trajectory? At the international level, the Chinese state actively pursued catch-up through selective imitation of Western technologies, while simultaneously

https://doi.org/10.1515/9783110757576-015

being compelled to implement a globally aligned intellectual property protection regime that contradicted China's own historical view of knowledge as a shared social resource (Alford, 1995). At the domestic level, top-down technology transfer projects built the infrastructures of modernisation, while bottom-up practices, grassroots piracy, market-driven adaptation, and fashion-inspired consumption, pushed in more unruly directions (Keane, 2007). Between these poles of state strategy and mass practice, imitation became the arena where order was negotiated, contested, and reinvented.

In drawing these cases together, I also return to my own intellectual journey. What began in fieldwork and case studies of imitation has, over the years, been shaped by the frustrations of observing both Chinese and Western modes of governance. These reflections have led me to value the resources of monadology and relational governance, especially as mass and diverse technologies demand infrastructures of visibility and traceability. Chapter 9 is thus not only a conclusion to the empirical studies but also a return to the philosophical questions that have accompanied me throughout this work.

The cases explored in this book illustrate how these dynamics unfolded across multiple sites over time. The System-12 technology transfer project in telecommunications (Chapter 3) exemplified the state's commitment to selective imitation of advanced systems. By securing a joint venture to acquire, produce, and embed the ITT/Alcatel System-12 public digital switching system, Chinese authorities sought not merely to import hardware but to absorb the organisational and technical knowledge accompanying it. Yet the process exposed the limitations of wholesale technology transfer: gaps in software design, mismatches in quality standards, and difficulties retaining trained engineers revealed how deeply technology is embedded in social and institutional environments (Shen, 1999). Ironically, the project helped rescue a struggling European technology by giving it a second life in China, while also teaching Chinese engineers that imitation inevitably carries blind spots and dependencies. This was the paradox of empowerment through infrastructural leapfrogging, despite dependence on systems never fully their own.

A similar contradiction surfaced in the domain of intellectual property (Chapter 4). Compelled by international institutions, the state established a legal framework that often clashed with domestic realities and cultural understandings of knowledge as a collective good (Drahos & Braithwaite, 2002; Sell, 2003). Grassroots actors widely copied software, producing what appeared to be chaos, yet the unintended outcome was the establishment of de facto standards that cemented Microsoft's dominance in the Chinese market (Shen, 2005). In a paradoxical twist, piracy, nominally a threat to Western firms, became a business tool for them, even as the state cracked down on practices many citizens considered legitimate. Imitation here was doubly charged: coerced from above in compliance with Western IP protection regimes, and generative from below as a mass practice that reshaped the market on its own terms.

A third variation emerged in the case of TD-SCDMA (Chapter 5), China's attempt to develop a domestic 3G telecommunications standard. This was not simply a pre-planned top-down directive but a collaborative effort involving research institutions, state agencies, telecom operators, and foreign firms (Naughton, 2007). The project drew heavily on technologies that originated in the West but recombined and reoriented them for China's market conditions and industrial base. Its eventual adoption was controversial, criticised as inefficient by some, praised as strategic by others, but its deeper significance lay in demonstrating that imitation could be scaled and institutionalised as a collective process. It was not that China had definitively caught up, once and for all, but that imitation could be orchestrated across diverse actors to generate momentum and mobilise resources, even amid geopolitical resistance.

At the grassroots, the *shanzhai* culture (Chapter 6) offered yet another form of imitation. Emerging in mobile phones and consumer electronics, *shanzhai* enterprises thrived on rapid adaptation, low-cost production, and creative recombination of designs (Keane, 2007). Dismissed as counterfeiters, they nonetheless responded with agility to the diverse demands of China's fragmented consumer base, rural and urban, rich and poor, young and old. Unlike Western models oriented towards homogeneous markets of affluent consumers, *shanzhai* producers leveraged social diversity as a source of innovation. Their imitative practices destabilised the boundary between piracy and creativity, showing how copying could become a mode of responsiveness and inclusion. If System-12 illustrated the state's ambitions and limits, *shanzhai* illustrated the vitality of bottom-up improvisation. Both demonstrate that imitation cannot be reduced to a single logic: it is at once regulated and unruly, disciplined and playful, derivative and inventive.

The rise of internet platforms (Chapter 7) extended these dynamics into the digital realm. Companies such as Alibaba, Tencent, and Baidu began by imitating successful foreign models but quickly moved beyond them through relentless adaptation to local conditions (Shen, 2019). Their ecosystems thrived not only due to corporate strategy but because they mobilised participation from millions of users. Every repost, remix, and reconfiguration was a small act of imitation that collectively steered technological evolution in ways that neither firms nor the state could fully control (Ong & Collier, 2005). Mass participation thus became a form of governance. Yet as platforms grew in power, they altered the balance between state, market, and society, compelling the state to reassert authority (Roberts, 2018). Imitation here was both grassroots creativity and a structural challenge to political order.

Most recently, the pandemic response (Chapter 8) revealed how digital, data-driven technologies transformed imitation into a mode of governance. Apps for health codes, contact tracing, and movement restrictions were initially imitative of tools developed elsewhere but quickly became embedded in a uniquely Chinese system of participatory surveillance (Cong, 2021; Shen, 2020). Citizens imitated one another in adopting these technologies, creating a feedback loop in which compliance became a social norm. At the same time, the system exposed new risks of exclusion, inequality, and overreach (Lyon, 2018). Yet it also demonstrated how data could be mobilised for rapid crisis management, governance by affordance as a practical reality. Digital imitation enabled resilience and solidarity but also entrenched new forms of control and dependency.

Taken together, these cases reveal imitation's dual character as both trap and resource. It is a trap when it locks China into dependency on foreign technologies or externally imposed intellectual property regimes. It is a resource when it enables China to set new standards, mobilise mass creativity, or experiment with governance. It is a trap when it represents coerced compliance with global rules, yet a resource when appropriated and reoriented to local needs. This paradox, imitation as constraint and possibility, subordination and creativity, runs through all the stories in this book.

The larger stakes go beyond China alone. If imitation is not a transitional stage to be outgrown but a constitutive force of technological modernity (Tarde, 1903), then the key question is not whether to imitate, but how to govern imitation. Should it be bound by rigid intellectual property regimes that privilege accumulation, or guided towards more collaborative and socially generative ends? Should it be treated as dependency, or as a creative practice that produces new hybrids and possibilities? These are not only Chinese questions; they are global ones.

This chapter takes up these themes in turn. It examines how imitation's paradoxes have been navigated in China's experience, what they reveal about the inseparability of the technical and the social, how tradition and pragmatism have shaped responses to modern challenges, and what new forms of governance are emerging in the age of digital and data-driven technologies. It then extends the analysis outward, considering what lessons China's trajectory may offer other developing countries, before concluding with a provocation: that imitation is not a mere stage of backwardness, but the very condition through which science and technology circulate, transform, and define modern life.

9.2 The Paradoxes of Imitation

If there is one concept that runs like a red thread through this book, it is imitation. As Gabriel Tarde argued, "imitation is not secondary or derivative but the fundamental process through which societies live and change" (Tarde, 1903, p. 74). Individual choices gain meaning only when they are repeated, circulated, and sedimented into norms, standards, and institutions. Imitation links the personal to the collective: it is where freedom meets discipline, creativity meets conformity, and the unruly spark of desire meets the heavy hand of governance (Borch & Stäheli, 2009).

Tarde did not, however, work out in detail the diverse forms and outcomes of imitation. Passive and unconscious copying may lead to very different results from active and deliberate imitation (Deleuze, 1994). Traditions and cultures, the sediment of past imitative acts, continue to shape how imitation unfolds in the present and even how it projects into the future. China's trajectory in science and technology provides rich empirical ground to extend Tarde's insights: it shows how deliberate, strategic imitation can coexist with unconscious, everyday mimicry, and how governance must grapple with both.

China's trajectory illustrates this paradox vividly. As Chapter 1 foreshadowed, imitation is never a neutral act of copying. It is always entangled with politics and culture, and always poised between coercion and creativity (Latour, 2005). To imitate is to improvise as much as to replicate, to navigate contradictions rather than escape them.

At the level of the state, imitation appeared as deliberate strategy. The System-12 transfer project epitomised this effort: selective borrowing of Western telecommunications promised national advancement but imported not only hardware and software, but also assumptions about labour discipline, software design, and quality control that clashed with Chinese realities (Shen, 1999). Chinese engineers often resolved hidden blind spots and software design flaws, and through the joint venture, Chinese and foreign partners together managed mismatched quality control practices. Engineers trained on the new system frequently left for higher-paying jobs, leaving state-owned firms struggling to retain capacity. Meanwhile, parallel adaptations, such as the domestically developed HJD-04, revealed how imitation was always refracted through the multiple vested interests of actors. The outcome was neither pure success nor pure failure but a hybrid formation that revealed both the empowerment and dependency inherent in imitation.

At the grassroots, desires animated another paradox. Piracy was not simply lawlessness, but a way to participate in modern life (Shen, 2005). Copying Microsoft operating systems and Office suites was a demand for inclusion in global culture, an everyday improvisation that produced new standards even as it defied international law. What international regimes condemned as disorder was, for ordinary users, a form of belonging. Here, imitation was simultaneously resistance and compliance, subversion and consolidation.

The *shanzhai* spirit pushed the paradox further. Small manufacturers imitated global designs but reworked them to meet the diverse needs of Chinese consumers: rural families wanting dual-SIM phones, students seeking prestige knock-offs, professionals experimenting with hybrids (Keane, 2007). Their improvisations blurred the line between piracy and innovation, creating a vibrant ecosystem that state enforcement could never fully suppress. *Shanzhai* revealed imitation not as failure but as responsiveness, copying as a form of participation in a fragmented, dynamic society.

The platform economy amplified these dynamics. Alibaba, Tencent, and others began with imitative models, but their success depended on the everyday acts of millions of users: reposts, remixes, clicks, each shaping technological evolution (Shen, 2019). Imitation here was not imposed but emergent, a form of mass participation that both empowered and destabilised. The state responded by reasserting control but never fully contained the unruly energy of the crowd (Roberts, 2018).

The pandemic crystallised imitation's paradox in governance itself. Citizens adopted health codes and tracing apps partly out of desire for safety and mobility, and partly because others were doing the same (Cong, 2021). What began as voluntary uptake quickly hardened into obligation: without a green code, access to everyday life was denied. Compliance was at once solidarity and surveillance, participation and exclusion. Imitation thus blurred the line between empowerment and control, showing how governance increasingly unfolds through the circulation of imitative practices.

Across these cases, the paradox is unmistakable. Imitation is never just copying. It is the medium through which desire becomes order, improvisation becomes discipline, and mass practices reshape state strategies. It is both unruly creativity and institutional standardisation, both resistance to authority and its reinforcement.

This insight challenges dominant narratives. Western observers often dismiss imitation as backwardness, a temporary stage on the way to true innovation (Chang, 2002). But China's experience suggests the opposite: imitation is permanent and constitutive. It is how technologies circulate and embed themselves socially; it is how governance adapts to crises and mass participation. The question is therefore not whether imitation should exist, but how it should be governed. Can it be channelled towards creativity rather than dependency, collaboration rather than exclusion?

As Chapter 1 suggested, the people remain central to this dilemma. It is through their desires, improvisations, and imitative practices that technologies acquire life, and it is through their collective uptake that governance finds both its strength and its limits. The paradox of imitation, then, is not simply a puzzle of technology policy; it is a window onto the inseparability of the technical and the social, the theme to which we now turn.

9.3 The Inseparability of Technical and Social

The cases traced in this book underscore a central lesson: technology never travels alone (Latour, 2005). Every act of transfer, adaptation, or imitation is inherently social, interwoven with values, norms, and institutions (Bijker et al., 2012). To describe China's development merely as technical catch-up would obscure its deeper trajectory. As Chapter 1 proposed, China's rise is a process of socio-technical becoming: an improvisation where machines and infrastructures are inseparable from the social orders that give them shape (Callon, 1986).

Consider the System-12 transfer project. Officially a technical initiative to modernise China's telecommunications, it quickly revealed that technical systems come embedded with social assumptions. The imported infrastructure presumed disciplined labour routines, stable careers, and strict quality control. In contrast, Chinese engineers switched jobs, workers improvised under precarious conditions, and ministries pursued divergent priorities. To imitate System-12 meant not merely replicating software or hardware but experimenting with new forms of organisation, training, and professional commitment. This echoes Chapter 1's classroom vignettes, where knowledge acquisition was inseparable from social relations: technical knowledge lives in and through practice.

Conflicts over intellectual property revealed similar entanglements. Software may be reducible to code, but copying it was interpreted differently depending on cultural and institutional contexts (Alford, 1995). International institutions defined piracy as violation; Chinese users often saw it as a means of participating in global modernity (Shen, 2005). Installing a Microsoft Office suite was less about theft and more about inclusion. The fact that piracy helped solidify Microsoft's dominance in China was not an aberration but an outcome of the complex interplay of desire, legality, and infrastructural reach.

Similar issues came to the fore in China's attempts to create a domestic 3G standard (TD-SCDMA). Its trajectory and eventual outcomes were shaped less by spectral efficiency or chipset design than by the alignments and misalignments of ministries, firms, and researchers (Shen, 2013). Whilst technically ambitious as a homegrown 3G standard, its development was shaped not just by engineering choices but by bureaucratic alignments, industrial policy, and inter-ministerial negotiations (Naughton, 2007). Its partial inefficiencies and strategic gains both emerged from its nature as a socially negotiated artefact (DiMaggio & Powell, 1983). Here, technology development became a site of institutional coordination, not merely technical specification.

Grassroots practices make the inseparability even more vivid. The *shanzhai* phone economy did not succeed due to circuitry alone, but because it interpreted and embedded global designs into local lives (Keane, 2007). Whether serving rural families, urban youth, or elderly customers, *shanzhai* enterprises reconfigured technology around lived conditions. Copying here became a form of sociotechnical translation, reworking material forms to respond to diverse, situated needs.

Digital platforms carried this logic forward. Firms like Alibaba and Tencent constructed complex technical infrastructures, but their power lay in engaging millions of users whose reposts, payments, and interactions simultaneously shaped digital architectures and social norms (Shen, 2019). Infrastructure became governance; participation became code. As Ong and Collier (2005) argue, such assemblages blur the boundaries between technical and social systems: rules are no longer just programmed; they are enacted, negotiated, and contested by users in everyday life.

The pandemic response crystallised this dynamic. Health codes were merely software lines, but their adoption relied on collective compliance and normative alignment (Cong, 2021). Citizens mimicked one another's behaviour, establishing a loop in which technology became institution. Voluntary use became mandatory; affordance became obligation. This is not interaction between two realms but their co-production (Barad, 2007): the social made the technical operational, and the technical reshaped the social in turn.

These examples also expose the perception gaps introduced in Chapter 1. Imported technologies carried assumptions mismatched with local realities; piracy was condemned globally but seen as enabling at home; *shanzhai* was reviled by some as counterfeit, revered by others as ingenious (Haraway, 1988). These are not minor discrepancies but central to how technology operates across cultures. Technologies travel with baggage: visions of use, expectations of behaviour, and assumptions about order.

Seen through this lens, the inseparability of the technical and social is not merely an analytical claim but a lived condition. To govern technology is to govern people; to regulate imitation is to shape collective aspiration. Each transfer, imitation, or innovation becomes an experiment in social organisation. This is why China's technological rise, as foreshadowed in Chapter 1, cannot be reduced to state policy or linear progress. It is a form of socio-technical improvisation, a continual negotiation amongst tools, traditions, and the desires of the people.

9.4 Tradition Meets Technology: Historical Trajectory

If imitation in China is always socio-technical, it is also always historical. The paradoxes explored in this book, between dependence and creativity, coercion and agency, discipline and improvisation, cannot be fully understood apart from China's intellectual and cultural traditions (Fairbank & Goldman, 2006). Every moment of technical adaptation has been shaped by long-standing debates on how to reconcile Western science with Chinese ways of life, and every act of imitation has been driven by pragmatic concerns of survival, sovereignty, and renewal.

The late Qing reformist formula 中体西用 (*zhongti xiyong*), "Chinese learning as essence, Western learning for application", offers a succinct expression of this historical tension. It proposed preserving a Chinese moral-philosophical core whilst selectively adopting Western technologies. Such imitation, from the start, was framed not as passive replication but as strategic appropriation. Yet this formulation introduced its own paradox: could one extract application without also importing essence? Could technologies be borrowed without also absorbing the institutions and social orders in which they were embedded?

This dilemma re-emerged in Joseph Needham's enduring question: why did modern science not emerge in China, despite its long history of technical ingenuity (Elman, 2005)? His answer did not point to a lack of creativity but to cultural orientations that emphasised harmony, moral cultivation, and pragmatic flexibility over the pursuit of universal scientific laws. Chinese intellectuals themselves grappled with this question. As recalled in Chapter 1, the students who founded the Science Society of China after returning from the United States did not simply transplant technical expertise (Shen, 1988). They reflected deeply on the social environments that sustained science, writing essays not only on experimentation but on education, culture, and reform. For them, as for the 1980s reformers who debated calls to let the light of science illuminate itself, imitation of Western science was inseparable from imitation of the broader social and cultural frameworks that enabled it.

What emerges is a historical pattern of pragmatism and improvisation. From the self-strengthening movement post-Opium Wars to Maoist mass mobilisation and Deng's market reforms, science and technology were never framed as ends in themselves (Wang, 2008). They were seen as tools to serve urgent national needs: defence, industrialisation, sovereignty, and stability. This utilitarian orientation explains why China's imitative practices have so often been experimental, even improvisational. The Great Leap Forward mobilised vast labour but failed without institutional foundations. The reform era released entrepreneurial energies but also generated stark inequalities. Across these phases, imitation was constantly recalibrated through trial and error, guided by one core question: what works now?

This pragmatism also underlies the cyclical interplay between tradition and modernity. Confucian values, once criticised for suppressing innovation, have been reinterpreted as ethical resources for navigating rapid change (Perry, 2008). Taoist flexibility, once marginalised, is now praised as a philosophy of adaptive governance in uncertain times. Even utilitarianism itself has been reimagined, not as short-term opportunism, but as experimental pragmatism: a flexible orientation towards institutional change responsive to lived realities. In this sense, tradition is not a static heritage but a dynamic resource, reactivated through iterative practices of imitation.

Viewed historically, the persistence of Needham's question is not a sign of lagging modernity but a reminder that China's trajectory is not one of delayed originality. Rather, it represents a distinctive mode of socio-technical formation. Modern science and technology did not originate indigenously, but the very act of imitating them has produced new hybrids, simultaneously traditional and modern, local and global, derivative and inventive.

This trajectory is crucial for understanding the present. As the next section will show, China's digital and data-driven infrastructures are not merely borrowed technologies or instruments of state control. They are embedded in a longer history of pragmatic governance and improvisational problem-solving. Just as the Qing-era dilemma asked how to adopt railways and telegraphs without undermining cultural essence, today the question is how to govern platforms, algorithms, and data systems whilst preserving social cohesion and civic ethics. Imitation, once again, becomes the site where historical traditions and contemporary challenges meet.

9.5 Governance by Affordance and the Monadological Collective

China's historical relationship between imitation and governance reaches new levels of complexity in the digital era (Zuboff, 2019). Earlier episodes of technological transfer, such as the importation of System-12, the enforcement of intellectual property rights, or the development of TD-SCDMA, mostly remained confined to ministries, laboratories, and firms. Today's digital infrastructures permeate everyday life. Platforms mediate commerce, communication, mobility, and even public health. Health codes, scoring systems, and e-governance platforms shape access to services and spaces. These are deeply socio-technical systems: enabling mass participation whilst simultaneously embedding new forms of control (Lyon, 2018).

Digital governance operates through recursive feedback loops (Liang, Das, Kostyuk, & Hussain, 2018). Platforms do more than deliver services; they trace, analyse, and learn from user behaviour. Every click, repost, and purchase generates data that is fed back into algorithms that, in turn, shape the next layer of user interaction. Imitation in this context is no longer limited to firms borrowing designs or governments copying systems. It is enacted by users, millions of times per day, as they mimic, adapt to, and respond to one another within digital architectures. Governance thus emerges not only from top-down command, but from participatory loops that co-produce behavioural norms.

This form of governance extends but also transforms Michel Foucault's panopticon. Traditional surveillance disciplines through visibility; digital governance disciplines through traceability (Creemers, 2018). Citizens are aware that they are being tracked, and this knowledge shapes behaviour. Sometimes this prompts compliance; at other times, performative display or subtle forms of evasion. Surveillance becomes interactive, dependent on the very data subjects generate.

This approach can be termed governance by affordance: a mode of governance that works by shaping the environment in which people act, rather than issuing direct commands (Amoore, 2013). Authorities design digital infrastructures that nudge behaviours through defaults, options, and feedback mechanisms. Local governments test and adjust policies. Citizens learn, adapt, comply, or resist. Governance becomes recursive and experimental, relying on participation and improvisation rather than rigid control.

Yet digital traceability is not only coercive; it can also be constructive (Zeng, 2016). When every imitative act leaves a digital trace, imitation becomes a visible and potentially valued form of participation. Rather than treating imitation as hidden or deviant, digital infrastructures make it possible to track how users adopt, adapt, and circulate practices. In theory, this opens space to recognise thoughtful and responsible imitation as a social contribution. One can imagine a future where trustworthiness is judged not only by originality but also by the ethical quality of imitation: how well users adopt wisely, adapt carefully, and share generously.

What makes China's case distinctive is not only the scale of digital governance but its historical pragmatism. Just as the *zhongti xiyong* formula once justified appropriating Western techniques to preserve Chinese essence, and Maoist campaigns mobilised the masses as instruments of governance, today's digital systems harness mass participation as both input and output. Citizens imitate one another's behaviours. Platforms imitate user patterns through algorithms. The state imitates successful policy experiments across local contexts. Governance becomes an ecology of imitation, improvised yet patterned, coercive yet participatory.

This raises the question: can such hybrid governance transcend traditional binaries? Rather than labelling it authoritarian or liberal, top-down or bottom-up, China's digital governance might be better understood as an ongoing experiment in how to govern imitation itself. It channels desires, norms, and improvisations into patterned behaviours that sustain both social order and state authority. Fraught with contradictions, this experiment also reveals possibilities for hybrid governance that extend beyond China.

Gabriel Tarde's monadology offers a useful framework for understanding this development (Tarde, 1999). For Tarde, every individual is a monad, a distinct centre of perception and desire, yet also a node in vast networks of imitation. Society is not constructed from isolated atoms but from relational entities whose identities emerge through mutual influence and mimicry. In this view, governance is not about controlling discrete subjects but about orchestrating the flows of imitation that bind individuals into collectives. Digital infrastructures, with their capacity to trace, aggregate, and visualise countless acts of imitation, bring Tarde's vision into practical reality. They enable what might be called a monadological collective: a social order constituted through the visibility and traceability of imitative practices.

The provocation here is both analytical and ethical. If imitation can be traced and evaluated, then perhaps governance need not rely solely on coercion or on assumptions of homogeneity. Instead, it could recognise and cultivate diversity, rewarding thoughtful adaptation and generous sharing whilst discouraging blind copying or destructive mimicry. This would require shifting from a model of governance that treats imitation as deviance to one that sees it as a legitimate and necessary form of participation. It would also demand infrastructures of accountability: ensuring that traceability serves ethical ends rather than becoming a tool of arbitrary control.

China's digital governance is far from achieving such ideals. Surveillance has deepened, inequalities persist, and systemic risks abound. Yet the experiments underway, from health codes to platform ecosystems to AI-driven policy coordination, suggest that new possibilities are emerging. Whether these lead towards more inclusive and ethical futures, or towards new forms of domination, remains an open question. What is clear is that imitation, once dismissed as mere backwardness, has become central to how governance itself is conceived and practised in the digital age.

9.6 Lessons for Other Developing Countries

China's experience does not offer a simple blueprint for others to copy, but it does provide critical lessons on navigating the dilemmas of technological development in a world defined by unequal access to science and innovation (Chang, 2002). The paradoxes of imitation, between dependence and creativity, coercion and agency, discipline and improvisation, are not unique to China. They are structural features of modernity. What makes China's case distinctive is the scale at which these tensions have been confronted, the speed of response, and the willingness to experiment across state, market, and society. It is worth noting that the sheer size of China's markets drove foreign firms to accept joint venture and other arrangements that might not be available to smaller nations.

The first lesson is that imitation is never mere copying. As Tarde (1903) argued, it is the fundamental social act that connects individual desire to collective discipline. For developing countries, this implies that imitation must be treated as an embedded social practice, shaped by institutions, cultural values, and perception gaps. Elite-led projects rarely suffice. China's early wave of overseas students brought home knowledge, but without supportive infrastructures and social conditions, their expertise struggled to take root (Shen, 1988). Effective imitation thus requires more than technology transfer; it demands socio-technical embedding, aligning tools with local norms and institutional realities.

A second lesson is that selective imitation can be both empowering and precarious. The System-12 project provided essential infrastructure, but also revealed blind spots in quality standards, training, and institutional fit. Piracy helped expand software access whilst simultaneously entrenching Microsoft's dominance (Shen, 2005). TD-SCDMA showed how imitation could be institutionalised across multiple stakeholders, yet also exposed the frictions arising from fierce competition. For other nations, the lesson is not to replicate outcomes, but to anticipate imitation's inherent tensions. Empowerment and dependency are always entangled; the challenge lies in navigating them rather than avoiding them.

Third, grassroots improvisation matters. The *shanzhai* economy proved that bottom-up imitation can produce highly adaptive responses to consumer diversity. Platforms like Alibaba scaled not only through state support but through the micro-actions of millions of users, reposts, remixes, and transactions that gradually shaped ecosystem logics (Keane, 2007; Shen, 2019). For developing countries, this suggests that creativity is not confined to formal institutions, but extends to the diverse arenas where technologies are implemented and used in everyday economic and social life. Allowing room for unruly, adaptive practices may generate innovation precisely where formal institutions falter. Supporting such practices may require regulatory flexibility and a willingness to tolerate ambiguity.

The pandemic underscored a fourth lesson: digital imitation depends on social trust (Beck, 1992). Health codes and contact tracing apps were effective to the extent that citizens adopted them collectively, transforming compliance into a social norm (Cong, 2021). However, these systems also revealed fractures: exclusion, fatigue, and mistrust. Here, Chapter 1's insight becomes global: governance always rests on social contracts of legitimacy and accountability. Technologies can amplify state capacity, but only when underpinned by collective trust and social alignment.

Ultimately, China's lesson is methodological, not prescriptive. Imitation should not be seen as a one-off act or transitional phase, but as a continuous field of governance. State-led strategies, grassroots participation, and institutional coordination must all be cultivated. But their balance will vary by context. Some countries may imitate China's policies; others may draw on its pragmatism. The key is to treat imitation as a dynamic, negotiated process—, subject to contestation, experimentation, and reconfiguration.

Today's global context makes this task more difficult. Intellectual property regimes are stricter, geopolitical tensions sharper, and global value chains more rigid than during China's rise (Zenglein & Holzmann, 2019). The pragmatic room that once existed for piracy, *shanzhai*, or selective appropriation may now be constrained. All the more reason to understand imitation not as a moral failure, but as a mode of survival and creativity. Developing countries must work within and against existing structures, leveraging their own histories and conditions.

As in the classroom where students approach China and the West from different vantage points, so too must nations recognise and work through perception gaps. Imitation is shaped not only by technical capacity but by cultural interpretations. The task is not to erase those differences, but to activate them, to turn diversity into a resource for innovation, and improvisation into a force for development.

9.7 Towards Hybrid Governance Ecosystems

China's developmental path is not simply about catching up through imitation or asserting autonomy through innovation. It is also a long-running effort to discover workable modes of governance within a vast, diverse, and rapidly evolving society (Wang, 2008). Governance, like technology, is never neutral. It is embedded in cultural traditions, institutional logics, and socio-technical infrastructures. What emerges from China's experience is a continual experiment in hybridisation, the blending of Confucian ethics with Western legal frameworks, of top-down control with bottom-up participation, and of coercion with collaboration.

This hybridity draws on deep intellectual traditions. Confucianism emphasises hierarchy, ritual, and moral authority; Taoism prizes responsiveness, adaptability, and flow (Perry, 2008). Though often treated as oppositional to Western ideals of codified law and individual rights, these traditions have not disappeared. Instead, they have been reinterpreted. Like *shanzhai* culture that reworked global designs to suit local needs, China's governance practices remix inherited frameworks in response to modern challenges.

Modern crises have reinforced this experimental ethos. The failure of the Great Leap Forward, the pragmatism of the reform era, and the institutional improvisations of the digital age all illustrate a governance culture based on trial, adjustment, and responsiveness (Yang, 2003). In the digital domain, this has become what we earlier called governance by affordance: shaping behaviours not through mandates alone but through the structuring of environments, feedback systems, and participatory mechanisms (Amoore, 2013).

Digital infrastructures have further hybridised this model. Platforms like Alibaba and Tencent engage millions of users as both economic actors and governance participants. The state leverages these platforms for taxation, pandemic control, and public service delivery (Roberts, 2018). During the COVID-19 pandemic, the Health QR code system depended not just on state enforcement but also on citizens imitating one another, normalising new behaviours and expectations (Cong, 2021). Governance was not purely coercive or voluntary, but a shifting mix, a dynamic ecosystem in which authority, participation, and infrastructure continually reshaped each other.

Artificial intelligence adds another layer. On the one hand, AI promises predictive coordination, efficiency, and large-scale insight. On the other, it brings opacity, algorithmic bias, and new asymmetries of power (Hilgartner, Prainsack, & Hurlbut, 2017). The Chinese state experiments with these tools in ways that rely on citizen data, platform integration, and behavioural feedback. Governance by AI is not only top-down control; it is a socio-technical arrangement, dependent on how people participate, trust, and respond.

What would such hybrid governance look like beyond China? It would require integrating Western commitments to legal safeguards with China's emphasis on adaptive flexibility. It would treat mass participation not as a threat to order, but as a potential source of resilience and responsiveness. It would need to balance the collective trust that underpins coordination with the scepticism that always accompanies surveillance and control (Wynne, 1992).

In essence, governance must itself become a socio-technical improvisation, an ongoing process of negotiating norms, feedbacks, and institutional forms. This is the crossroads where China now stands, and where others may soon find themselves. One path continues to replicate Western models of property and power, often reproducing global inequalities (Harvey, 2005). The other builds on hybrid practices already visible: digital participation, experimental pragmatism, ethical reinterpretation, to reimagine governance as a dynamic, inclusive process attuned to the complexities of the digital age.

9.8 Concluding Provocations

This book began with a deceptively simple question: how does imitation shape the trajectory of science and technology? As the preceding chapters have shown, the answer is neither linear nor simple. Imitation is not a stage to be transcended nor a relic of backwardness. It is the constitutive condition of technological modernity, the means through which knowledge circulates, transforms, and embeds itself in diverse contexts (Tarde, 1903).

China's trajectory brings this dynamic into sharp relief. From the selective transfer of telecommunications systems to the vitality of *shanzhai* culture, from contested intellectual property regimes to the participatory governance of digital platforms, China's rise has been driven by imitation's paradoxes. Imitation has been a tool of empowerment and a source of dependency, a means of creative reappropriation and of coerced compliance.

The provocation here is not simply to defend imitation but to reframe it. International policy regimes often treat imitation as deviation from a normative path of innovation (Heller & Eisenberg, 1998). Domestic narratives frequently portray it as a ladder to be discarded once originality is achieved. Both views miss the point. Imitation is not the opposite of innovation; it is its condition. It is the space where technologies are socialised, where knowledge acquires meaning, and where governance experiments take form.

China's story also compels a rethinking of the state. Often portrayed as a monolith, the state emerges here as a complex negotiator, at times coercive, at times adaptive, always entangled with grassroots practices (Law, 2004). It imposed strategic transfers, tolerated piracy, absorbed informal innovation, and leveraged digital participation. Governance, in this light, has been less about rigid command than about navigating a fluid ecology of imitative acts.

The contradictions of this approach remain stark. Surveillance has deepened, inequalities persist, and systemic risks abound (Zuboff, 2019). Yet new possibilities have also emerged: collective resilience through participation, innovation from unexpected quarters, and hybrid forms of legitimacy forged in practice rather than decree. These are not flaws to be corrected; they are features of a modernity shaped by entangled technologies, desires, and institutions.

Data-driven and AI technologies add another provocation. If every imitative act can be traced, then perhaps imitation itself could be evaluated ethically: not by whether it is novel, but by whether it is thoughtful, responsible, and generative (Biagioli & Lippman, 2020). Likewise, innovation could be judged not only by its originality, but by how well it enables meaningful imitation, how it invites adaptation, inclusion, and contribution. Traceability, often framed as a coercive force, might instead become a scaffold for ethical reflection: making visible the creativity embedded in repetition and the generosity of sharing.

These reflections also make me reconsider my years of observing governance in Western societies. The tendency to extrapolate from isolated incidents, to condemn all immigration because of the behaviour of a few, to subject black people to disproportionate police checks, or to ban liquids over 100 millilitres worldwide because of one attempted attack, reveals both the strengths and the weaknesses of the Western analytical style. Its strength lies in its clarity, in formulating universal principles that can be systematically applied. But its weakness lies in its tendency to simplify multiplicity into homogeneity, ignoring context and relation.

My journey with Chinese cases has led me to value another orientation. Tarde's monadology, together with Chinese traditions of relational governance, offers a different vantage point: one that accepts multiplicity, seeks traceability, and values visibility over blanket generalisation. In this light, the promise of data-driven infrastructures lies not in their capacity to enforce uniform rules, but in their ability to register differences, to enable more nuanced forms of coordination, and to cultivate a collective self without erasing its diversity.

Placed in historical perspective, these dilemmas echo long-standing questions. From the late Qing reformers to Needham's puzzle over the non-emergence of modern science in China, the challenge has always been how to reconcile local traditions with global epistemologies (Elman, 2005; Kwok, 1965). Today, as China stands at the frontier of AI and platform governance, the question returns in new form: will technologies reinforce national power alone, or might they foster more inclusive, cooperative futures?

This is not a question for China alone. Western traditions often valorise competition, property, and individualism; Chinese traditions foreground pragmatism, ethics, and collective order (Perry, 2008). The future likely demands hybrid ethoses: combining protection of individual dignity with collective coordination, valuing novelty whilst recognising that all innovation rests on imitation.

Against this backdrop, we stand at a global crossroads. One path doubles down on Western frameworks, with their universalist blind spots and systemic exclusions. The other learns from hybrid practices—like those described in this book—to build more inclusive and situated modes of governance. This is not a call to idealise China, but to take seriously the experiments it has undertaken and the questions it poses. The next phase of human development may depend less on technological acceleration than on cultivating ethical and institutional capacities to coordinate across difference. Digital infrastructures make large-scale coordination possible, but without a reimagining of moral and political frameworks, they risk deepening inequality and fragmentation. What is needed is not a digital Enlightenment in the image of Europe's past, but a pluralist ethics for a multiplex world—one that embraces contingency, recognises knowledge as relational, and holds space for multiple trajectories of human flourishing—where imitation becomes not a constraint, but a catalyst for collective creativity.

As in the classroom metaphor revisited throughout this book, students from different worlds encounter the same technologies but bring different assumptions, values, and interpretations. The point is not to erase these gaps but to learn from them. Perception gaps become pedagogical spaces. Difference becomes a resource for creativity.

As Tarde's insights remind us, imitation flows between entities based on perceived differences and desires (Tarde, 1903). Such distinctions are not fixed hierarchies; they are perceptions shaped by difference and aspiration. In a world of interconnected monads, what appears as superiority may simply reflect unfamiliarity or prestige at a distance. Recognising this turns imitation from a mark of deficiency into a space for the co-production and sharing of knowledge, not replication of the same, but the creative negotiation of difference.

The story of China's science and technology rise is thus more than a national narrative. It is a mirror held to the world, reflecting both the fragility and promise of modern institutions. It compels us to move beyond binaries of imitators versus innovators and to embrace imitation as a shared condition of human creativity.

Whether that creativity is directed towards domination or cooperation remains undecided. But one thing is clear: imitation will remain central. It will shape how societies learn, how technologies evolve, how governance adapts, and how human beings imagine futures together. To attend to imitation, then, is not to look backward, but to see in repetition the seeds of renewal.

What emerges from these chapters is that China's so-called miracle lies not in central planning or technological breakthroughs alone. It lies in the infrastructures that mobilise participation, from software piracy to *shanzhai* electronics to pandemic health codes. These infrastructures enabled the cultivation of a collective self. The challenge now is whether these fragile scaffolds can sustain civic responsibility and ethical imagination, or whether they will ossify into instruments of control. That future, too, will depend on how we govern imitation.

Bibliography

3rd Generation Partnership Project (3GPP). (2001). *Organisational partners.* http://www.3gpp.org

Abrami, R. M., Kirby, W. C., & McFarlan, F. W. (2014). Why China can't innovate. *Harvard Business Review, 92*(3), 107 – 111.

Alford, W. P. (1995). *To steal a book is an elegant offense: Intellectual property law in Chinese civilisation.* Stanford University Press.

Amoore, L. (2013). *The politics of possibility: Risk and security beyond probability.* Duke University Press.

Ardolino, M., Saccani, N., Adrodegari, F., & Perona, M. (2020). A business model framework to characterise digital multisided platforms. *Journal of Open Innovation: Technology, Market, and Complexity, 6*(1), 10. https://doi.org/10.3390/joitmc6010010

Baldwin, C. Y., & von Hippel, E. (2011). Modeling a paradigm shift: From producer innovation to user and open collaborative innovation. *Organization Science, 22*(6), 1399 – 1417. https://doi.org/10.1287/orsc.1100.0618

Barad, K. (2007). *Meeting the universe halfway: Quantum physics and the entanglement of matter and meaning.* Duke University Press.

BBC. (2009, 22 January). Timeline: China milk scandal. *BBC News.* http://news.bbc.co.uk/1/hi/world/asia-pacific/7720404.stm (accessed 15 March 2020)

Beck, U. (1992). *Risk society: Towards a new modernity* (M. Ritter, Trans.). Sage.

Biagioli, M., & Lippman, A. (2020). *Gaming the metrics: New ecologies of academic misconduct.* MIT Press.

Bijker, W. E., Hughes, T. P., & Pinch, T. J. (Eds.). (2012). *The social construction of technological systems: New directions in the sociology and history of technology* (Anniversary ed.). MIT Press.

Borch, C., & Stäheli, U. (Eds.). (2009). *Soziologie der Nachahmung und des Begehrens: Materialien zu Gabriel Tarde.* Suhrkamp.

Breznitz, D., & Murphree, M. (2011). *Run of the red queen: Government, innovation, globalisation, and economic growth in China.* Yale University Press.

Business Software Alliance. (2003). *Eighth annual BSA global software piracy study.* BSA.

Callon, M. (1986). Some elements of a sociology of translation: Domestication of the scallops and the fishermen of St Brieuc Bay. In J. Law (Ed.), *Power, action and belief: A new sociology of knowledge?* (pp. 196 – 233). Routledge.

Castells, M. (2009). *The power of identity: The information age: Economy, society, and culture* (Vol. II, 2nd ed.). Wiley-Blackwell.

Chan, K. W. (2010). The global financial crisis and migrant workers in China: "There is no future as a labourer; returning to the village has no meaning". *International Journal of Urban and Regional Research, 34*(3), 659 – 677. https://doi.org/10.1111/j.1468-2427.2010.00987.x

Chang, H.-J. (2002). *Kicking away the ladder: Development strategy in historical perspective.* Anthem Press.

Chen, M. (2006). The eBay failure in China: Extending Guanxi dynamics beyond dyads. *Academy of Management Proceedings, 2006*(1), E1–E6. https://doi.org/10.5465/ambpp.2006.27162607

China Mobile. (2019). *Annual report 2019.* China Mobile Limited.

Clarke, R. (1988). Information technology and dataveillance. *Communications of the ACM, 31*(5), 498 – 512. https://doi.org/10.1145/42411.42413

https://doi.org/10.1515/9783110757576-016

Cong, W. (2021). From pandemic control to data-driven governance: The case of China's health code. *Frontiers in Political Science*, *3*, 627959.
Cong, Y. (2021). Health codes and the politics of digital compliance in China. *Journal of Contemporary China*, *30*(129), 450 – 465.
Cowan, R. (1992). High technology and the economics of standardisation. In M. Dierkes & U. Hoffmann (Eds.), *New technology at the outset: Social forces in the shaping of technological innovations* (pp. 279 – 300). Campus/Westview.
Creemers, R. (2018). China's social credit system: An evolving practice of control. *Nature Human Behaviour*, *2*(10), 800 – 804.
David, P. A. (1985). Clio and the economics of QWERTY. *American Economic Review*, *75*(2), 332 – 337.
Deleuze, G. (1994). *Difference and repetition* (P. Patton, Trans.). Columbia University Press.
DiMaggio, P. J., & Powell, W. W. (1983). The iron cage revisited: Institutional isomorphism and collective rationality in organisational fields. *American Sociological Review*, *48*(2), 147 – 160.
Dong, X., & Jayakar, K. (2013). The Baidu music settlement: A turning point for copyright reform in China? *Journal of Information Policy*, *3*, 77 – 103. https://doi.org/10.5325/jinfopoli.3.2013.0077
Drahos, P., & Braithwaite, J. (2002). *Information feudalism: Who owns the knowledge economy?* Earthscan.
Egyedi, T. M., & Blind, K. (2008). *The dynamics of standards.* Edward Elgar.
Egyedi, T. M., & Spirco, J. (2011). Standards in transitions: Catalysing infrastructure change. *Futures*, *43*(9), 947 – 960. https://doi.org/10.1016/j.futures.2011.07.002
Elman, B. A. (2005). *On their own terms: Science in China, 1550 – 1900.* Harvard University Press.
Ernst, D. (2011). *Indigenous innovation and globalisation: The challenge for China's standardisation strategy.* UC Institute on Global Conflict and Cooperation; East-West Center.
Ernst, D., & Kim, L. (2002). Global production networks, knowledge diffusion, and local capability formation. *Research Policy*, *31*(8 – 9), 1417 – 1429. https://doi.org/10.1016/S0048-7333(02)00072-0
Evans Data Corp. (2002). *Chinese developer survey.* Evans Data Corporation.
Fairbank, J. K., & Goldman, M. (2006). *China: A new history* (2nd enlarged ed.). Harvard University Press.
Fleck, J. (1993). Configurations: Crystallising contingency. *International Journal of Human Factors in Manufacturing*, *3*(2), 15 – 36.
Foucault, M. (1977). *Discipline and punish: The birth of the prison* (A. Sheridan, Trans.). Allen Lane.
Funk, J. L., & Methe, D. T. (2001). Market- and committee-based mechanisms in the creation and diffusion of global industry standards: The case of mobile communication. *Research Policy*, *30*(4), 589 – 610. https://doi.org/10.1016/S0048-7333(00)00092-6
Gao, X. (2014). A latecomer's strategy to promote a technology standard: The case of Datang and TD-SCDMA. *Research Policy*, *43*(3), 597 – 607. https://doi.org/10.1016/j.respol.2013.10.009
Gibson, J. J. (1979). *The ecological approach to visual perception.* Houghton Mifflin.
Giddens, A. (1991). *Modernity and self-identity: Self and society in the late modern age.* Polity Press.
Guardian, The . (2018, 20 March). China deploys facial recognition to shame jaywalkers. https://www.theguardian.com/cities/2018/mar/20/china-testing-facial-recognition-jaywalkers-shenzhen (accessed 10 April 2020)
Gürkaynak, G., Yilmaz, I., Yeşilaltay, B., & Bengi, B. (2018). Intellectual property law and practice in the blockchain realm. *Computer Law & Security Review*, *34*(4), 847 – 862. https://doi.org/10.1016/j.clsr.2018.05.027

Hangzhou Daily. (2020, 12 February). Health code reapplication channel processes 29,000 cases in eight hours (健康码重新申报通道8小时处理2.9万例). *Hangzhou Daily.* http://hzdaily.hangzhou.com.cn/hzrb/2020/02/12/article_detail_1_20200212A086.html (accessed 20 February 2020)

Hangzhou Municipal Government. (2020, 13 February). Hangzhou Health Code reaches 7 million users in two days (杭州健康码两天突破700万用户). *Hangzhou Municipal Government Official Website.* http://www.hangzhou.gov.cn/art/2020/2/13/art_812262_42378516.html (accessed 20 February 2020)

Haraway, D. (1988). Situated knowledges: The science question in feminism and the privilege of partial perspective. *Feminist Studies*, *14*(3), 575–599.

Harvey, D. (2005). *A brief history of neoliberalism.* Oxford University Press.

Heilmann, S. (2008). From local experiments to national policy: The origins of China's distinctive policy process. *The China Journal*, *59*, 1–30. https://doi.org/10.1086/tcj.59.20066378

Heilmann, S., & Perry, E. J. (Eds.). (2011). *Mao's invisible hand: The political foundations of adaptive governance in China.* Harvard University Asia Centre.

Heller, M. A., & Eisenberg, R. S. (1998). Can patents deter innovation? The anticommons in biomedical research. *Science*, *280*(5364), 698–701.

Hilgartner, S., Prainsack, B., & Hurlbut, J. B. (Eds.). (2017). *Genomic politics: From collective identities to individual rights.* Routledge.

Hong, Y. (2017). *Networking China: The digital transformation of the Chinese economy.* University of Illinois Press.

Hong, Y., & Huang, Y. (2014). The WAPI standard dispute: A perspective from China. *China & World Economy*, *22*(2), 22–39. https://doi.org/10.1111/cwe.12075

Hughes, T. P. (1987). The evolution of large technological systems. In W. E. Bijker, T. P. Hughes, & T. J. Pinch (Eds.), *The social construction of technological systems* (pp. 51–82). MIT Press.

International Development Research Centre, & State Science and Technology Commission of China. (1997). *China's telecommunications infrastructure development.* IDRC.

International Telecommunication Union (ITU). (2000). *IMT-2000 project.* ITU.

Irwin, A., Vedel, J. B., & Vikkelsø, S. (2021). Isomorphic difference: Familiarity and distinctiveness in national research and innovation policies. *Research Policy*, *50*(4), 104220.

iSinoLaw Research Centre. (2001). *Intellectual property.* http://www.isinolaw.com/jsp/ip/main.jsp?LangID=0 (accessed 4 October 2025)

Jacques, M. (2012). *When China rules the world: The end of the Western world and the birth of a new global order* (2nd ed.). Penguin Books.

Jakobs, K. (Ed.). (2014). *Modern trends surrounding information technology standards and standardisation within organisations.* IGI Global.

Kanellos, M. (2002, 5 June). Microsoft gets diplomatic in China. https://www.cnet.com/tech/tech-industry/microsoft-gets-diplomatic-in-china/ (accessed 5 October 2025)

Karippacheril, T., Nikayin, F., de Reuver, M., & Bouwman, H. (2013). Serving the poor: Multisided mobile service platforms, openness, competition, collaboration and the struggle for leadership. *Telecommunications Policy*, *37*(1), 24–34. https://doi.org/10.1016/j.telpol.2012.07.005

Katz, M. L., & Shapiro, C. (1985). Network externalities, competition, and compatibility. *American Economic Review*, *75*(3), 424–440.

Keane, M. (2007). *Created in China: The great new leap forward.* Routledge.

Keane, M., & Zhao, E. J. (2012). Renegades on the frontier of innovation: The *shanzhai* grassroots communities of Shenzhen in China's creative economy. *Eurasian Geography and Economics*, *53*(2), 216–230. https://doi.org/10.2747/1539-7216.53.2.216

Kshetri, N. (2016). Big data's role in expanding access to financial services in China. *International Journal of Information Management*, *36*(3), 297 – 308. https://doi.org/10.1016/j.ijinfomgt.2015.11.014

Kwok, D. W. Y. (1965). *Scientism in Chinese thought, 1900 – 1950.* Yale University Press.

Latour, B. (2005). *Reassembling the social: An introduction to actor-network-theory.* Oxford University Press.

Latour, B. (2010). Tarde's idea of quantification. In M. Candea (Ed.), *The social after Gabriel Tarde: Debates and assessments* (pp. 145 – 163). Routledge.

Law, J. (2004). *After method: Mess in social science research.* Routledge.

Leesti, M., & Pengelly, T. (2002). Institutional issues for developing countries in intellectual property policymaking, administration and enforcement. *Commission on Intellectual Property Rights Study Paper, 9.*

Lewis, O. (2001). China: Protecting the knowledge-based economy and intellectual property rights. *Proceedings of the Harvard Asia Business Conference, IV.*

Liang, F., Das, V., Kostyuk, N., & Hussain, M. M. (2018). Constructing a data-driven society: China's social credit system as a state surveillance infrastructure. *Policy & Internet*, *10*(4), 415 – 453.

Liang, Y. & Shen, W. (2016). Fan economy in the Chinese media and entertainment industry: how feedback from super fans can propel creative industries' revenue. *Global Media and China, 1* (4), 331 – 349.

Lin, L. (2011). Fake it till you make it: A study of the imitation goods industry in China. *Harvard Asia Quarterly*, *13*(3/4), 4 – 11.

Liu, J. (2010). The tough reality of copyright piracy: A case study of the music industry in China. *Cardozo Arts & Entertainment Law Journal*, *27*(62), 621 – 661.

Liu, Q. (1984). 让科学的光芒照亮自己 [Let the light of science illuminate itself]. *Guangming Daily.*

Lu, X. (1918). A madman's diary (狂人日记). *New Youth* (*Xin qingnian* 新青年).

Lundvall, B. A. (2010). *National systems of innovation: Toward a theory of innovation and interactive learning.* Anthem Press.

Lyon, D. (2018). *The culture of surveillance: Watching as a way of life.* Polity Press.

MacKenzie, D., & Wajcman, J. (Eds.). (1999). *The social shaping of technology* (2nd ed.). Open University Press.

Mahbubani, K. (2020). *Has China won? The Chinese challenge to American primacy.* PublicAffairs.

Mao, Z. (1942/1967). *Talks at the Yan'an Forum on Literature and Art* (Foreign Languages Press, Trans.). Foreign Languages Press. (Original work published 1942)

Marketing News. (2002, 22 November). The emergence of Linux in the fore of opportunities and challenges. http://it.sohu.com/14/80/article204508014.shtml (accessed 4 October 2025)

Maskus, K. E. (2000). *Intellectual property rights in the global economy.* Institute for International Economics.

Maskus, K. E., & Penubarti, M. (1995). How trade-related are intellectual property rights? *Journal of International Economics*, *39*(3 – 4), 227 – 248.

McGrath, R. G. (2010). Business models: A discovery driven approach. *Long Range Planning*, *43*, 247 – 261. https://doi.org/10.1016/j.lrp.2009.07.005

Ministry of Finance (MOF), National Development and Reform Commission (NDRC), & Ministry of Information Industry (MII). (2008). *Announcement on deepening the reform of the structure of the telecommunications sector.* Government of China.

Ministry of Industry and Information Technology (MIIT). (2008). *TD-SCDMA implementation plan.* Government of China.

Ministry of Industry and Information Technology (MIIT). (2009). *3G licence issuance announcement.* Government of China.
Ministry of Information Industry (MII). (2003). *Spectrum allocation for TD-SCDMA.* Government of China.
Ministry of Information Industry (MII). (2004). *Statistical report on telecommunications industry.* Government of China.
Ministry of Science and Technology (MOST). (2004). *National medium- and long-term science and technology development plan outline (2006–2020).* Government of China.
Monteiro, E., & Hanseth, O. (1996). Social shaping of information infrastructure: On being specific about the technology. In W. J. Orlikowski, G. Walsham, M. R. Jones, & J. I. DeGross (Eds.), *Information technology and changes in organisational work.* Springer.
Mu, Q., & Lee, K. (2005). Knowledge diffusion, market segmentation and technological catch-up: The case of the telecommunication industry in China. *Research Policy, 34*(6), 759–783. https://doi.org/10.1016/j.respol.2005.02.007
Naughton, B. (2007). *The Chinese economy: Transitions and growth.* MIT Press.
Nelson, R. R., & Winter, S. G. (1982). *An evolutionary theory of economic change.* Belknap Press.
Nolan, P. (2012). *Is China buying the world?* Polity Press.
Ong, A., & Collier, S. J. (Eds.). (2005). *Global assemblages: Technology, politics, and ethics as anthropological problems.* Blackwell.
Oreglia, E. (2013). *From farm to farmville: Circulation, adoption, and use of ICT between urban and rural China* [Doctoral dissertation, University of California, Berkeley]. https://escholarship.org/uc/item/76f677k0
Park, W. G., & Ginarte, J. C. (1997). Intellectual property rights and economic growth. *Contemporary Economic Policy, 15*(3), 51–61.
Peng, M.W. (2013). An institution-based view of IPR protection. *Business Horizons, 56*(2), 135–139. https://doi.org/10.1016/j.bushor.2012.11.006
People's Daily. (1999, 18 December). Microsoft loses suit against Beijing company. *People's Daily.*
People's Daily. (2020, 16 February). National unified health code to be established (国家统一健康码即将建立). *People's Daily.* http://paper.people.com.cn/rmrb/html/2020-02/16/nw.D110000renmrb_20200216_1-04.htm (accessed 20 February 2020)
Perry, E. J. (2008). Chinese conceptions of "rights": From Mencius to Mao, and now. *Perspectives on Politics, 6*(1), 37–50.
Pisano, G. P., & Shih, W. C. (2012). *Producing prosperity: Why America needs a manufacturing renaissance.* Harvard Business Review Press.
Prey, R. (2020). Locating power in platformization: Music streaming playlists and curatorial power. *Social Media + Society, 6*(3), 1–11. https://doi.org/10.1177/2056305120933291
Priest, E. (2014). Copyright extremophiles: Do creative industries thrive or just survive in China's high piracy environment? *Harvard Journal of Law & Technology, 27*(2), 469–541.
Raymond, E. (1998). The cathedral and the bazaar. *First Monday, 3*(3).
Roberts, M.E. (2018). *Censored: Distraction and diversion inside China's Great Firewall.* Princeton University Press.
Rosenberg, N. (1982). *Inside the black box: Technology and economics.* Cambridge University Press.
Russell, A. L. (2014). *Open standards and the digital age: History, ideology, and networks.* Cambridge University Press.
Samuelson, P. (1995). Software compatibility and the law. *Communications of the ACM, 38*(8), 15–22.

Sell, S. K. (2003). *Private power, public law: The globalisation of intellectual property rights.* Cambridge University Press.

Shapiro, C., & Varian, H. R. (1999). *Information rules: A strategic guide to the network economy.* Harvard Business Review Press.

Shen, X. (1988). *The role of science and technology societies in China's science modernisation: The case study of China's Science Society, 1915–1950* [近代中国科学化进程中的"中国科学社", 科学团体个案分析] [MPhil thesis, Chinese Academy of Social Sciences].

Shen, X. (1999). *The Chinese road to high technology: A study of telecommunications switching technology in the economic transition.* Macmillan.

Shen, X. (2005). A dilemma for developing countries in intellectual property strategy? Lessons from a case study of software piracy and Microsoft in China. *Science and Public Policy*, *32*(3), 187–198.

Shen, X. (2005b). Developing country perspectives on software: Intellectual property and open source—A case study of Microsoft and Linux in China. *Journal of IT Standards & Standardization Research*, *3*(1), 21–43.

Shen, X. (2010). Understanding the evolution of rice technology in China: From traditional agriculture to GM rice today. *The Journal of Development Studies*, *46*(6), 1083–1107. https://doi.org/10.1080/00220380903151033

Shen, X. (2015). The contingencies of global imitation—An historical account of Chinese adoption of Western intellectual property regime. In *Proceedings of the 13th International Globelics Conference*, Havana, Cuba.

Shen, X. (2016). Alibaba: The company that made eBay a dwarf. Henry Stewart Talks. http://hstalks.com/main/view_talk.php?t=2990&r=881&c=250 (accessed 15 March 2016)

Shen, X. (2017). How Kelon and Haier innovated to attract the local Chinese market. Henry Stewart Talks. https://hstalks.com/t/3448/how-kelon-and-haier-innovated-to-attract-the-local (accessed 20 June 2017)

Shen, X. (2019). HJD-04: China's indigenous digital switching system and the politics of technological catch-up. *Technology and Culture*, *60*(2), 412–445.

Shen, X. (2019a). Are Baidu, Alibaba and Tencent (BAT) mere imitations of Google, Amazon and Facebook (GAF)? *Medium.* https://medium.com/@xiaobai.shen (accessed 5 October 2025)

Shen, X. (2019b). Building "mass" and "momentum": A latecomer country's passage to large technological systems—the case of China. *Technology Analysis & Strategic Management*, *31*(5), 503–516.

Shen, X. (2019d). A disruptive force or a new dawn for the financial industry? Through the looking-glass of Alibaba's Ant Financial. https://www.research.ed.ac.uk/en/publications/a-disruptive-force-or-a-new-dawn-for-the-financial-industry-throu (accessed 10 October 2024)

Shen, X. (2020). Grass-roots management of Covid-19 in China: Behind the digital health app. *Medium.* https://medium.com/@xiaobai.shen (accessed 5 October 2025)

Shen, X. (2021). 专访丨沈小白:"以人民为中心的数据创新"为什么重要，为什么在中国能够践行 [Interview with Shen Xiaobai: Why is "people-centred data innovation" important, and why can it be practised in China]. 三思派. https://www.163.com/dy/article/G582MN960511D98B.html (accessed 5 October 2025)

Shen, X., & Gao, L. (2025). Ethical AI governance: AI for society and a co-learning approach. *Cultures of Science, Online First.* https://doi.org/10.1177/20966083251336553

Shen, X., & Naughton, B. J. (2013). The power of "a visible hand" to the building of innovation capabilities: A study of China's ICT technologies. *Journal of Science and Technology Policy Management*, *4*(3), 195–214. https://doi.org/10.1108/JSTPM-11-2011-0014

Shen, X., & Williams, R. (2005). A critique of China's utilitarian view of science and technology. *Science, Technology & Society*, *10*(2), 197–223. https://doi.org/10.1177/097172180501000201

Shen, X., & Zhan, F. (2020). *Copyright—A "magic wand"! How did it work in China's digital creative cultural industry?* [Working paper]. University of Edinburgh.

Shen, X., Graham, I., Stewart, J., & Williams, R. (2011). Developing an IT standard in China—What lessons can we learn from this? In *Proceedings of the 7th International Conference on Standardisation and Innovation in Information Technology (SIIT 2011)* (pp. 225–236). IEEE. https://doi.org/10.1109/SIIT.2011.6083618

Shen, X., Graham, I., Stewart, J., & Williams, R. (2013). Standards development as hybridisation. *International Journal of IT Standards & Standardisation Research*, *11*(2), 34–45. https://doi.org/10.4018/jitsr.2013070103

Shen, X., Li, Y., Zheng, S., Liu, Y., & Gerst, M. (2019a). Digital online music in China—A "laboratory" for business experiment. *Technological Forecasting and Social Change*, *139*, 235–249. https://doi.org/10.1016/j.techfore.2018.03.012

Shore, C., & Wright, S. (2000). Coercive accountability: The rise of audit culture in higher education. In M. Strathern (Ed.), *Audit cultures: Anthropological studies in accountability, ethics and the academy* (pp. 57–89). Routledge.

Silverstone, R. (1993). Domesticating the revolution: Information and communication technologies and everyday life. *Aslib Proceedings*, *45*(9), 227–233. https://doi.org/10.1108/eb051356

Smith, C. S. (2000, 7 June). Fearing control by Microsoft, China backs the Linux system. *The New York Times.*

Sørensen, K. H., & Williams, R. (Eds.). (2002). *Shaping technology, guiding policy: Concepts, spaces and tools.* Edward Elgar.

Srnicek, N. (2017). *Platform capitalism.* Polity Press.

Stallman, R. (1999). The GNU operating system and the free software movement. In C. DiBona, S. Ockman, & M. Stone (Eds.), *Open sources: Voices from the open source revolution* (pp. 53–70). O'Reilly.

State Council of the People's Republic of China. (1998). *Institutional reform plan for the State Council.* Government of China.

State Council of the People's Republic of China. (2001). *The 10th Five-Year Plan for national economic and social development (2001–2005).* Government of China.

State Council of the People's Republic of China. (2006). *The 11th Five-Year Plan for national economic and social development (2006–2010).* Government of China.

Steinfeld, E. S. (2010). *Playing our game: Why China's rise doesn't threaten the West.* Oxford University Press.

Stewart, J., Shen, X., Wang, C., & Graham, I. (2011). From 3G to 4G: Standards and the development of mobile broadband in China. *Technology Analysis & Strategic Management*, *23*(7), 773–788. https://doi.org/10.1080/09537325.2011.592284

Stiglitz, J. E. (2000). The contributions of the economics of information to twentieth century economics. *The Quarterly Journal of Economics*, *115*(4), 1441–1478.

Street, J., Zhang, L., Simuniak, M., & Wang, Q. (2015). *Copyright and music policy in China: A literature review* (CREATe Working Paper 2015/06). University of Glasgow. https://www.create.ac.uk/publications/copyright-and-music-policy-in-china/ (accessed 10 May 2015)

Sun, Y. (1924). *The three principles of the people* (三民主义). Shanghai Commercial Press.

Suttmeier, R. P., & Yao, X. (2004). *China's post-WTO technology policy: Standards, software, and the changing nature of techno-nationalism* (NBR Special Report 7). National Bureau of Asian Research.

Tang, D. (2024). *China's "mass-line" music development in the digital age: A study of the online music ecosystem and the diverse values of users, internet platforms, and the state* [Doctoral dissertation, The University of Edinburgh]. University of Edinburgh Research Archive. https://era.ed.ac.uk/handle/1842/41234

Tang, D., & Lyons, R. (2017). An ecosystem lens: Putting China's digital music industry into focus. *Global Media and China*, *1*(4), 350–371. https://doi.org/10.1177/2059436416673623

Tarde, G. (1903). *The laws of imitation* (E. C. Parsons, Trans.). Holt. (Original work published 1890)

Tarde, G. (1999). *Monadology and sociology* (T. Lorenc, Trans.). Univocal. (Original work published 1893)

TD Forum. (2010). *TD-LTE initiative members.* TD Industry Alliance.

TD-SCDMA Industry Alliance (TDIA). (2003). *TD-SCDMA Industry Alliance founding announcement.* TDIA.

Teece, D. J. (1986). Profiting from technological innovation: Implications for integration, collaboration, licensing and public policy. *Research Policy*, *15*(6), 285–305. https://doi.org/10.1016/0048-7333(86)90027-2

Tse, E., Ma, K., & Huang, Y. (2009). *Shan Zhai: A Chinese phenomenon.* Booz & Company.

van Dijck, J. (2014). Datafication, dataism, and dataveillance. *Surveillance & Society*, *12*(2), 197–208. https://doi.org/10.24908/ss.v12i2.4776

van Dijck, J., Poell, T., & de Waal, M. (2018). *The platform society: Public values in a connective world.* Oxford University Press.

Varsity. (2010, November). Shanzhai. *Varsity* (Chinese University of Hong Kong), Issue 117. https://varsity.com.cuhk.edu.hk/varsity/1011/shanzhai.pdf (accessed 15 March 2015)

von Hippel, E. (2005). *Democratizing innovation.* MIT Press.

Wallis, C. (2013). *Technomobility in China: Young migrant women and mobile phones.* NYU Press.

Wang, H. (1991). The fate of "Mr. Science" in China: The concept of science and its application in modern Chinese thought. *Positions*, *3*(1), 1–68.

Wang, H. (2008). *China's new order: Society, politics, and economy in transition.* Harvard University Press.

Wang, S. (2017). How have ISP music players tried to get a slice in the online music industry? *Economic Perspectives*, *195*, 62–65.

Watermeyer, R. (2016). Impact in the REF: Issues and obstacles. *Studies in Higher Education*, *41*(2), 199–214.

Weber, S. (2004). *The success of open source.* Harvard University Press.

Weiss, M. B., & Sirbu, M. (1990). Technological choice in voluntary standards committees: An empirical analysis. *Economics of Innovation and New Technology*, *1*(1–2), 111–133. https://doi.org/10.1080/10438599000000009

Williams, R., & Edge, D. (1996). The social shaping of technology. *Research Policy*, *25*(6), 865–899. https://doi.org/10.1016/0048-7333(96)00885-2

World Health Organization. (2020, 20 April). In our interdependent world no one is safe until everyone is safe. *WHO Director-General's opening remarks at the media briefing on COVID-19.* https://www.who.int/director-general/speeches/detail/who-director-general-s-opening-remarks-at-the-media-briefing-on-covid-19--20-april-2020 (accessed 25 April 2020)

World Trade Organization. (2003). *Understanding the WTO: The agreements—Intellectual property: Protection and enforcement.* WTO.

Wu, J. (1999). 逆风飞飏 [Flying against the wind]. China CITIC Press.

Wynne, B. (1992a). Misunderstood misunderstanding: Social identities and public uptake of science. *Public Understanding of Science*, *1*(3), 281–304.

Wynne, B. (1992b). Uncertainty and environmental learning: Reconceiving science and policy in the preventive paradigm. *Global Environmental Change*, *2*(2), 111–127.

Xia, J. (2011). The third-generation-mobile (3G) policy and deployment in China: Current status, challenges, and prospects. *Telecommunications Policy*, *35*(1), 51–63. https://doi.org/10.1016/j.telpol.2010.11.004

Yan, Y. (2009). *The individualization of Chinese society.* Berg Publishers.

Yang, D. (2003). The development of intellectual property in China. *World Patent Information*, *25*(2), 131–140.

Yang, D. L. (2003). *Remaking the Chinese Leviathan: Market transition and the politics of governance in China.* Stanford University Press.

Yang, R. (2003). Globalisation and higher education development: A critical analysis. *International Review of Education*, *49*(3–4), 269–291.

Young, G. (1980). On the mass line. *Modern China*, *6*(2), 225–240.

Yu, P. K. (2007). Intellectual property, economic development, and the China puzzle. In D. J. Gervais (Ed.), *Intellectual property, trade and development: Strategies to optimise economic development in a TRIPS-plus era* (pp. 173–220). Oxford University Press.

Zeng, J. (2016a). China's date with big data: Will it strengthen or threaten authoritarian rule? *International Affairs*, *92*(6), 1443–1462.

Zeng, J. (2016b). *The Chinese governance model: Flexibility and durability of pragmatic authoritarianism.* Palgrave Macmillan.

Zenglein, M. J., & Holzmann, A. (2019). *Evolving Made in China 2025: China's industrial policy in the quest for global tech leadership* (MERICS Papers on China No. 8). Mercator Institute for China Studies.

Zeschky, M., Widenmayer, B., & Gassmann, O. (2011). Frugal innovation in emerging markets. *Research-Technology Management*, *54*(4), 38–45. https://doi.org/10.5437/08956308X5404007

Zhang, Z. (2002). 劝学篇 [Exhortation to learning]. Huaxia Publishing House. (Original work published 1898)

Zuboff, S. (2019). *The age of surveillance capitalism: The fight for a human future at the new frontier of power.* PublicAffairs.

Index

Note: References following "n" refer footnotes.

https://doi.org/10.1515/9783110757576-017